Longman Exam Guides

BRITISH GOVERNMENT AND POLITICS

David Stephenson

LONGMAN
London and New York

Longman Group UK Limited
Longman House, Burnt Mill, Harlow
Essex CM20 2JE, England
and *Associated Companies throughout the world*.

Published in the United States of America
by Longman Inc., New York

© Longman Group UK Limited 1987

First published 1987

British Library Cataloguing in Publication Data:
Stephenson, David. 1947–
   British government and politics. ——
   (Longman exam guides)
   1. Great Britain —— Politics and
   government —— 1979–
   I. Title
   320.941   JN231

   ISBN 0-582-29681-1

Library of Congress Cataloguing in Publication Data:
Stephenson, David. 1947–
   British government and politics. ——

   (Longman exam guides)
   Includes index.
   1. Great Britain —— Politics and government ——
   Examinations. I. Title. II Series.
   JN125.S74   1987   320.941′076   86–10345

   ISBN 0-582-29681-1

Produced by Longman Singapore Publishers (Pte) Ltd.
Printed in Singapore

Longman Exam Guides
British Government and Politics

Longman Exam Guides

Series editors: **Stuart Wall and David Weigall**

Titles available:

Accountancy: Standards
Bookkeeping and Accounting
British Government and Politics
Business Communication
Business Law
Economics
English as a Foreign Language: Intermediate
                                 Preliminary
English Literature
French
General Principles of Law
Monetary Economics
Office Practice and Secretarial Administration
Pure Mathematics
Quantitative Methods
Secretarial Skills

Forthcoming:

Accountancy: Cost and Management
              Financial
Biology
Business Studies
Chemistry
Commerce
Computer Science
Electronics
Elements of Banking
English as a Foreign Language: Advanced
General Studies
Geography
Mechanics
Modern British History
Physics
Sociology
Taxation

Contents

Editors' Preface

Much has been said in recent years about declining standards and disappointing examination results. While this may be somewhat ex-aggerated, examiners are well aware that the performance of many candidates falls well short of their potential. Longman Exam Guides are written by experienced examiners and teachers, and aim to give you the best possible foundation for examination success. There is no attempt to cut corners. The books encourage thorough study and a full understanding of the concepts involved and should be seen as course companions and study guides to be used throughout the year. Examiners are in no doubt that a structured approach in preparing for and taking examinations can, together with hard work and diligent application, substantially improve performance.

The largely self-contained nature of each chapter gives the book a useful degree of flexibility. After starting with Chapters 1 and 2, all other chapters can be read selectively, in any order appropriate to the stage you have reached in your course. We believe that this book, and the series as a whole, will help you establish a solid platform of basic knowledge and examination technique on which to build.

Stuart Wall and David Weigall

Author's Preface

I should like to thank for their invaluable help colleagues at
Cambridge Seminars, particularly my co-Principal Bruce Lorimer,
and the College Secretary, Jan Hillier.

As ever, my wife Charlotte has been a constant source of
encouragement and help.

Acknowledgements

We are grateful to the following for permission to reproduce copyright material:

Mr. C. James Anderton for an extract from 'Report of Speech by James Anderton' *The Times* 30.11.85; Hamish Hamilton Ltd for extracts from pp 25, 239, 695–6 *The Crossman Diaries* by Richard Crossman, ed. Anthony Howard and an extract from pp 96–7 *The Politics of Consent* by Francis Pym; The Controller of Her Majesty's Stationery Office for extracts from two *House of Commons Papers* and *Cmand. Paper 5460*; author's agents on behalf of Rt. Hon. Michael Heseltine for extracts from his article 'Deliberate Attempt to avoid discussing issues' *The Times* 11.1.86; the Author, Lord Scarman for an extract from his article 'Common Law or Common Market' *The Listener* 31.10.74; Times Newspapers Ltd. for extracts by senior civil servants quoted in the article 'Is tradition of Cabinet Government on the Wane?' by Peter Hennessy *The Times* 16.5.83, extracts by a Tory Back Bencher quoted in the article 'Fellow Tories snub 'Maverick' MP' by Richard Evans *The Times* 28.6.85, extract from 'Report of Parliamentary Answer by Home Secretary' *The Times* 27.11.85, direct quote from article by Peter Evans p 12 *The Times* 27.11.85 and an extract from the article by Anthony Bevins p 2 *The Times* 1.4.85; Weidenfeld and Nicholson Ltd for extracts from pp 259, 261–2 *Downing Street in Perspective* by Marcia Falkender.

and we are grateful to the following Examining Bodies for permission to reproduce past examination questions:

The Associated Examining Board; University of Cambridge Local Examinations Syndicate; Joint Matriculation Board and University of London Schools Examinations Board.

Any answers or hints on answers are the sole responsibility of the author and have not been provided or approved by the above Examination Boards.

The examinations

Politics is an important subject at 'A' level, as part of a wide range of degrees and diplomas, and on a number of professional courses. The purpose of this book is to act as a guide to those preparing for examinations in such courses.

It will be clear that this book concentrates almost exclusively on government and politics in the UK. Chapter 1 outlines the relevance of the topics considered for a range of courses and boards. Chapter 2 presents some hints on techniques to help you prepare for and take the examination itself. Chapters 3–17 each deal with a topic which occurs frequently in government and politics examinations.

It is in no way intended that this book should take the place of a standard textbook. It will be best used as a companion to established texts. The grid in Table 1.1 will give guidance to 'A' level students and those of the ICSA (Institute of Chartered Secretaries and Administrators) on the topics relevant to their particular board or course. The many other students taking a range of degree and diploma courses involving British government and politics should check their individual syllabus. Certainly most of the topics considered here are likely to feature in one guise or another.

It may be helpful at this point to comment briefly on the layout and some of the uses of this book. Its primary purpose is to make students think, and to do so in a manner which will help equip them for the rigours of an examination. It covers a vast field of political behaviour, institutions and problems in a number of short chapters. Students should not expect to obtain all the facts which they may need to handle each topic from the chapter; nor should they expect to find there all of the arguments which they may wish to deploy on any given topic. What each chapter does try to do is to open up, for discussion, the important controversies on a topic, and to suggest ways and techniques for approaching those controversies. Examination questions relate overwhelmingly to controversies rather than to pure

Table 1.1   Topics and courses

Chapter and topic	JMB 'A' level	London 'A' level Paper I	London 'A' level Paper IV	AEB 'A' level Paper I	Cambridge 'A' level Paper I	Cambridge 'A' level Public Affairs Paper I	ICSA Government
3 Cabinet government?	√	√	√	√	√	√	√
4 The policy-makers	√	√	√	√	√	√	√
5 The Whitehall machine	√	√	√	√	√	√	√
6 Parliamentary government: controlling the executive	√	√	√		√	√	√
7 MPs: legislators or lobby-fodder?	√	√	√	√	√	√	
8 Whitehall and County Hall The balance of power	√	√	√	√	√	√	√
9 Representing the people	√	√		√	√	√	
10 Voting	√	√		√	√	√	√
11 Participation in politics	√	√		√	√	√	
12 The redress of grievances	√	√	√	√	√	√	√
13 The expanding executive	√	√	√		√	√	√
14 Public enterprises in crisis	√	√	√		√	√	√
15 Politics and the law	√	√		√	√	√	√
16 The UK and the EEC	√				√	√	
17 Characterisations/Concepts in politics	√	√		√	√	√	√

description of institutions or processes. This can be seen by looking at the section 'Recent examination questions' included in each chapter. Of course the inclusion of recent examination questions is not intended to imply that they are the only ones which appear on that topic, or that they are going to come up in the future. Indeed as the focus of politics changes from year to year, and as new crises and challenges materialise, so the emphasis of an examination changes. Nevertheless, a careful consideration of examination questions set in the recent past will often show the direction in which a particular controversy is moving. If certain common themes are seen in the questions of several examining bodies, covering a number of years, then this will certainly suggest that there are underlying structural problems which the examiners consider to be important and which are not subject to the day-to-day changes of politics. And of course in some topics the questions may remain the same, but the answers will evolve as new material becomes available and as the situation develops.

These remarks are important because they lead on to the question of how the sections on outline answers and tutors' answers should be approached. The object of these sections is *not* to provide model essays. Model essays are out of date a month after they are written. The answers are intended to suggest ways in which information may be organised in order to meet the requirements of a question, and to provide guidance on how to interpret a question. For many questions a wide range of different approaches is possible, only one or two of which can be exploited in the time available. These essays then are to be criticised not copied. It is, of course, always a mistake simply to reproduce an answer which has been learned by rote and which does not quite fit the requirements of the question which is being attempted.

For the most part examination candidates in politics will be confronted with essay questions of a fairly standard type, i.e. four or five to be answered in three hours. One major exception to this is the compulsory set of short answer questions which appears in the London Board 'A'-level Government and Political Studies Paper 1 (as well as Papers 2, 3, and 4). Each of Chapters 3–17 contains an answer to one of these short answer questions. Candidates are often thrown into confusion by these and badly miscalculate their time allocation, which should be six minutes per answer. These questions are in general a test of knowledge rather than of argument: the only way to do well on them is to know the material very well and to set it down as rapidly as possible, with no frills or padding. One final point should be made about the outline answers and tutors' answers: they are written in the light of the political situation at the time of writing this book and not at the time when they were set.

The purpose of the first two sections in each chapter is to bring students as quickly as possible to the point at which they can understand some of the main problems of each topic area, and can formulate arguments in response to them. In many cases the topic will already have been introduced either by use of a textbook or in classes or lectures. The purpose of the first section in each chapter ('Getting started'), is to clear up problems of vocabulary which students frequently find confusing or obscure. It also gives a general factual introduction to a topic where appropriate, and suggests ways in which complex topics may be most helpfully approached. The second section 'Essential Principles' outlines the major controversies in that topic area, and considers the arguments for and against any particular conclusion.

The third section ('Useful applied materials') provides illustrations of points raised in the previous section. It also provides raw material from which students may work up their own arguments. We shall see in the following chapter how important it is that each student of politics should gather together, or have access to, a collection of documents and illustrative material. It is hoped that the 'Useful applied materials' sections in this book may, together with the guidance to further sources in 'A step further' at the end of each chapter, form the nucleus of such a collection.

Chapter 2

Examination techniques

PREPARING FOR THE EXAMINATION

As with most academic subjects, it is helpful to have a basic set of notes which provides something to fall back on during revision periods or during essay writing. This basic set of notes may be derived either from one of a number of standard textbooks, or from class/lecture notes. However, it is both sound examination practice and a most interesting experience to go beyond the textbooks and class notes.

1. Because politics is a subject which is in constant change, a book which is three or four years old will begin to run the risk of being seriously out of date. Institutions may have come and gone, or the political climate may have changed: last year's or even last term's class notes may need to be substantially revised in the light of more recent developments. Examiners increasingly expect students to be up to date and to make accurate reference to political developments within the last few months before the examination. An answer obviously culled from a slightly ageing textbook will stand out as the work of a candidate who has not really entered into the spirit of a politics course.

2. Students will get a lot more enjoyment out of the course if they realise that just one step beyond the basic textbooks there lies a whole host of sources which will bring the subjects to life!

    (a) There are *specialised studies* on political parties, on pressure groups, on elections, on the House of Commons, on the Civil Service, and so on. These sources can be usefully 'plundered' to explain obscure passages in the basic books, to satisfy curiosity on some particular point of detail and to provide additional arguments when essays are being produced.

    (b) There is a growing set of books in which *senior political figures provide us with blow-by-blow accounts of political life*. Harold Wilson's Labour Governments of 1964–70 and 1974–76 have been particularly fruitful in this respect. We have Harold Wilson's own history of the 1964–70 Governments, the account of that period written by George Brown, Deputy leader of the Labour Party and a senior Cabinet minister from 1964 to 1968, and the accounts of Marcia Williams (subsequently Lady Falkender) which cover both of Wilson's periods in power. Indeed for the 1964–70 Governments we have the quite astonishingly useful and absorbing diaries of two Cabinet ministers, Richard Crossman and Barbara Castle, with the added bonus of a second instalment of Mrs Castle's diary for the period 1974–76. Of course all of these sources suffer from the possible criticism that they are by now out of date, and they certainly do not serve as an accurate commentary on the institutions and outlook of Governments in the 1980s. But they *do* reveal a great deal about such important and enduring matters as the pressures on a Cabinet minister's time, and they show us the 'behind the scenes' rivalries and disunity in governments which strive to *appear* on the surface as united as possible. With their different emphases and sometimes in their flat contradictions of each other, such sources remind us that much of our evidence about the nature of politics and the nature of our governmental system is of a subjective nature.

(c) There are the sources of current information. These include the *annual official reports of officers*, such as the Ombudsmen, or the *Sessional Information Digest* produced annually by the Public Information Office of the House of Commons and available free on request. Of particular relevance here are the professionally compiled records of contemporary events, notably *Keesing's Contemporary Archives* (Longman), which are an invaluable source of reference and which may be available in school or college libraries and certainly in the better public libraries.

(d) There are the *newspapers, television and radio*. It is one of the great attractions of this subject that it can be studied while reading a newspaper, looking at a television documentary, or listening to the radio news bulletin. Of course these activities must be undertaken with discrimination and preferably in the context of a sound conceptual framework, into which contemporary events can be placed. It is in the present writer's view a useful tactic to settle into a methodical pattern of reading certain journals and newspapers, and of watching certain television programmes regularly in the hunt for information.

Journals such as *The Economist*, and the so-called 'heavy' (i.e. non-tabloid) daily and Sunday newspapers all make fascinating additions to the stock of knowledge available to a student of politics. In the present book many documentary illustrations of the various chapters have been drawn from one newspaper, *The Times*, not necessarily out of a belief that it is always the best source, but simply to demonstrate the range and the impact of the material that can be derived from a single newspaper. An attempt has also been made to draw most of the illustrations from a single eighteen-month period in order to demonstrate what is possible for those following a conventional politics course at 'A' level or in higher education.

TAKING THE EXAMINATION

A good politics examination essay involves far more than the regurgitation of fact, or the dogmatic presentation of political opinions. A good student will, of course, know a good many facts and is highly likely to have developed opinions of his or her own about the way in which politics works or should work. But in an examination the student's task is quite simply to answer as fully as possible *the question which has been set*. The first step is, of course, to read through the *whole* examination paper, noting carefully the instructions, and identifying the questions to be answered. The second step, is to prepare an outline for answering the question at hand. This will generally involve the following tasks:

- analysis of the question;
- selection of the relevant material;
- arrangement of relevant material.

A question should only be started after you have thought about each of these tasks, and have made a few rough notes to serve as a memory jogger. Let us take each task in turn.

Analysis of the question

Analysis involves breaking something down into its constituent parts, and this will almost certainly require some kind of definition of terms. A definition is much more than finding a synonym for an important word or phrase; it is a careful explanation of the meaning of that word or phrase in the particular context of the question. Remember that many key terms in political debate are capable of being defined in different ways. For example, democracy may be taken to mean the *actual making of political decisions* by the people (however one defines the people), *or* it may mean that the people are able to decide *who shall make such decisions* and *by what process* the decisions are to be made. Again, in order for democracy to exist we may consider that the people should *be able to act free from coercion* and that they should be provided with *sufficient information* or *access to information* to enable them to make informed decisions or choices.

The process of definition, therefore, involves thought and hard work; it should not be restricted to the production of some rather simple and hackneyed catch-phrase such as 'government by the people' as a definition for democracy. The reason for this is that definition of terms is not simply a ritual demanded by examiners. It is actually a way of structuring the essay. It stands to reason that it is rather difficult to discuss a topic coherently until you know what it means. If a candidate makes a simple assumption about the meaning of a word like democracy then that limits the number of points which can be made in the essay. But once a candidate has established that there are *several* possible elements which may go to make up the concept of democracy, or indeed any other complex political notion, the number of points which can be made in the essay begins to increase.

It is worth remembering, too, that analysis of the question will often involve paying close attention to words which do not at first sight appear to be technical. Let us suppose that you have to deal with a question which asks for a discussion of the advantages of the present electoral system in use in the UK. The whole essay is clarified, and indeed a structure begins to suggest itself once we ask the question: advantages to whom? Governments which are placed in power having obtained only a minority of the vote, will presumably see advantages in the *present* system in so far as it tends to produce firm majorities. Conservative and Labour politicians will presumably see far more party advantage in the present system than will their counterparts in the Liberal and Social Democratic Parties. Some voters may be impressed and indeed relieved by the simplicity of the present system. Others may be disturbed by the fact that the views of many of the electorate are not being adequately reflected by it.

Selection of materials

One simple point cannot be stressed too much, namely that the purpose of an examination answer must be to respond to *the question which the examiner has set*. The question will deal with one or two particular aspects of a general topic. Assuming that you have worked hard during the course, and have put in a strenuous burst of revision before the examination, there is naturally a temptation to throw into the answer lots of information and lots of discussion points which you have proudly amassed and which deal with the general topic to which the question relates. But this is a temptation which must be resisted. Each point, each piece of information, must be subjected to the simple test: is the inclusion of this helping to formulate the answer to the question? If it is not relevant to the question set, then it must be rejected and abandoned. If it is not clear how it is helping to answer the question set, then it must be reconsidered. Material should *not* be included in an answer simply in the hope that in some mysterious fashion it may be of some use. This brings us to the third task.

Arrangement of material

It is the purpose of an examination essay to score points. Typically this takes the form of arranging material so as to make points for and against a proposition. Questions which include phrases such as 'How far?' 'To what extent?' 'To what degree?' are signalling that a for and against discussion is going to be appropriate. This is also usually the case with questions which take the form of quotations followed by some such formula as discuss or examine this statement. At the risk of stating the obvious, writing an examination essay is not quite the same as writing a book. Candidates do not have the time to develop ideas with great subtlety. As a general rule each paragraph should contain a major point, with illustrations to support that point. The layout of paragraphs will probably be determined by two factors: firstly, the need to discuss the key terms introduced and defined at the start of the essay, and secondly, the need to assess the merits and demerits of some institution or process. It is here that you will reap the benefit of having thought through the points to be made and having jotted them down in some logical order. A clear well-organised essay will create a much more favourable impression than will one which has the same material, but which presents that material in a haphazard sequence.

Conclusions are something of a problem. They should not be included simply to announce to the examiner that the candidate has now nearly finished and is winding the essay down. They should either make a point or they should be omitted. If all the points have already been covered then there is very little purpose served by simply repeating them. On the other hand, a conclusion may be of great value if, for example, it serves as an assessment, setting down the student's preferences as between the various arguments which have been advanced in the body of the essay.

SOURCES

The purpose of this section is to discuss a few books and other sources which may prove to be of particular help during a politics course. It is not proposed to attempt a survey of general textbooks. Many students will have a general textbook prescribed by a teacher or lecturer. If this is not the case then it is worth trying to look briefly through two or three different textbooks before buying one, in order to establish which one has the most accessible style. There is also something to be said for choosing a recently published or revised textbook. The date of publication can generally be found immediately after the title-page of a book, and the key dates to look out for are those of publication, revision or new edition: a new impression does not enhance the value of the book as it is simply a fresh printing of the old text.

For students who want to go a little beyond the basic textbooks, a number of very useful *collections* of essays and short studies are available. Notable examples of these are: *British Politics in Perspective* (ed. J. N. Borthwick and R. E. Spence, Leicester University Press 1984); *Political Issues in Britain Today* (ed. Bill Jones, Manchester University Press 1985); and *Developments in British Politics*, 2nd edn (ed. H. Drucker and others, Macmillan 1984).

Two books which may perhaps be labelled as textbooks, though they are very superior examples of the breed, are John Greenwood and David Wilson, *Public Administration in Britain*, Allen and Unwin 1984) and Dennis Kavanagh, *British Politics, Continuities and Change* (Oxford University Press 1985). The first of these is relevant to rather more than half the chapters in the present book and it contrives to make the study of administrative structures and processes, often regarded as somewhat dry, into a most exciting experience.

Finally, all students should be aware that R. K. Mosley has produced, since the late 1960s, an annual *British Government and*

Politics Survey which picks up many of the important themes and developments of the previous twelve months and sets them out in a style which is both clear and entertaining. Copies, which are well within student budgets, may be obtained from K. and N. Mosley, at 51 Austin Avenue, Lilliput, Poole, BH14 8HD.

In addition to these sources, in the section 'A step further' at the end of each chapter, the reader is guided to documents, chapters of books, etc. which can deepen his or her insight into that topic area.

Chapter 3

Cabinet government?

GETTING STARTED

The Cabinet is generally reckoned to be the principal institution of executive government. Consisting of around twenty senior government ministers, and chaired by the Prime Minister, the Cabinet meets at regular intervals to discuss, decide upon, and co-ordinate government policy. It is backed up by the Cabinet office, a team of senior civil servants led by the Secretary to the Cabinet. Cabinet decisions, recorded in its minutes, act as orders to the various departments of government, establishing the policies to be pursued.

The characteristics, procedures, and functions of the Cabinet are not, in the main, defined by statutes, but by *conventions*, i.e. constitutional rules which are regarded as binding but which do not have the sanction of strict law. Examples of these conventions are:

(a) The Prime Minister appoints the members of the Cabinet and dismisses them;
(b) Certain ministers, such as the Chancellor of the Exchequer, the Home Secretary, the Foreign Secretary, and the Lord Chancellor, must be included in the Cabinet. (The Prime Minister, of course, in practice appoints to these and all other ministerial posts);
(c) The proceedings of the Cabinet are secret;
(d) All Cabinet ministers are collectively responsible for Cabinet decisions. In other words they must give public support to any Cabinet decision which is announced as government policy, and must not dissociate themselves from any such decision. If they fail to observe these rules, then they may be required to resign. This convention of collective responsibility now extends to the whole ministerial team, including those, about 100 strong, who are below Cabinet rank.

In the past generation there has been a great deal of urgent discussion on whether the Cabinet is truly the central decision-making body of British government, or whether it has simply become a kind of supervisory rubber stamp, registering the decrees of the Prime Minister, and swamped by a powerful network of back-room Cabinet committees.

RELATIONSHIP BETWEEN PRIME MINISTER AND CABINET

The Prime Minister does indeed have significant control over the Cabinet, although there are limitations to most aspects of that control. Here are some of the factors which govern the relationship between the Prime Minister and the Cabinet:

(a) The Prime Minister has power of appointment and dismissal. Nevertheless, in making appointments to ministries which command a seat in the Cabinet the Prime Minister must bear in mind that a minister's task is a heavy one: he has to direct the efforts of the civil servants inside his department, and must defend its policies inside and outside Parliament. The Prime Minister would be unwise to appoint mere 'yes-men', whose inadequacies would soon be revealed, and would reflect badly on him. Nor can the Prime Minister safely exclude from the Cabinet senior members of his party known to be the leaders or representatives of important factions within it.

(b) The Prime Minister can reshuffle the Cabinet – by moving members from one ministry to another. Thus a troublesome minister, or one who threatens to become a rival, can be moved to a 'difficult' ministry, which will absorb the new minister's energies, or will perhaps damage his political reputation. Yet *too many* reshuffles may unsettle ministers in general, reduce their efficiency, and may create an impression of uncertainty and instability which will damage the Government in the eyes of the electorate.

(c) The Prime Minister draws up the agenda of Cabinet meetings, and can, in theory, omit issues for discussion from an agenda – though it is unlikely that an obviously urgent or crucial matter can be excluded without causing serious unrest in the Cabinet.

(d) The Prime Minister can influence the minutes of the Cabinet. This can be done in collusion with the Cabinet Secretary, who compiles the minutes, and who is also the chief official adviser to the Prime Minister. It may be suggested that resorting to this kind of manoeuvre is rather a sign of weakness than of strength on the part of the Prime Minister.

(e) The Prime Minister decides *how* decisions will be reached in Cabinet. He may decide to take a vote (i.e. to 'count heads') or simply to sum up what he considers to be 'the sense of the meeting'.

(f) The Prime Minister appoints the members, and the chairmen of Cabinet committees. These are a more than usually secret sector of central government: most of them are not officially acknowledged to exist. But in practice Cabinet committees deal with a wide range of governmental topics, and their decisions are normally accepted by the Cabinet, or are treated as having the force of a full Cabinet decision. It is usually claimed that the committees pose no threat to Cabinet government; in fact quite the reverse, by reducing the workload which the Cabinet has to carry, the committees aid the Cabinet in performing its tasks of major decision-making and policy co-ordination.

(g) Having no departmental responsibilities the Prime Minister has a better grasp of overall policy than do other members of the Cabinet, and is the only minister in touch with all Cabinet committees. This situation is reflected in the fact that the Prime Minister is regularly expected to defend the entire range of government policies.

Such a state of affairs has its drawbacks: the demands on the Prime Minister's attention are so wide-ranging that there may be insufficient time to devote to the personal control of any one area of policy.

There is therefore a case for suggesting that the Cabinet has ceased to be a vital decision-making body, and has become one of the 'dignified' elements in the Constitution. Those who hold this view argue that the purpose of the Cabinet is no longer to wield power or to make a serious contribution to administration, but merely to confer dignity and authority upon the decision-making system. It is also argued that a seat in the Cabinet is still prized by politicians mainly for the prestige it confers upon them, and for the departmental responsibilities that ministerial office usually conveys, rather than for any expectation of serious involvement in collective decision-making.

It should be stressed that the debate on the Cabinet is really one about the *potential* powers of the Prime Minister to control or override Cabinet, and the *potential* powers of the Cabinet to resist such treatment. How far such potential is exploited depends on the personalities and stamina of those involved, and on the political circumstances. Cabinet as a body may well need to be more assertive when confronted by a Prime Minister who is weak or ill, or whose record of achievement if poor.

USEFUL APPLIED MATERIALS

For recent Cabinets much information is provided from time to time by the reports of investigative journalists, often based on the 'leaks', calculated or inadvertent, of Cabinet ministers or civil servants. The following notes and extracts contain some examples of such leaks and diaries.

CABINET APPOINTMENTS

In September 1966, Prime Minister Harold Wilson reshuffled his Cabinet. Richard Crossman was moved from the Ministry of Housing and Local Government to become Lord President of the Council and Leader of the House of Commons. 'It looks as though he has selected me for this key job as the only person who hasn't political ambitions against him . . . Harold . . . was enormously exhilarated, and openly claiming that he had now got his friends about him.' (*The Crossman Diaries*, p. 239)

THE CABINET AGENDA

In the spring of 1975, a referendum was due to be held on Britain's membership of the EEC. The Government recommendation to the voters was in favour of staying in the Community, though some ministers were deeply opposed. On this occasion, ministers were allowed to campaign against the official Cabinet line. Barbara Castle, then a member of the Cabinet, records how Harold Wilson handled this situation.

'Harold has effectively de-natured Cabinet. Whether he is just trying to clear the decks for the referendum, or whether it is a deliberate ploy to take any kind of control out of the hands of the anti-marketeers, I don't know. All I know is that Cabinet agendas have never been thinner and this morning's was a record: not a single item of business, apart from next week's parliamentary business and foreign affairs.' (*The Castle Diaries, 1974–76*, 14 June 1975, pp. 376–7)

THE CABINET MINUTES

In December 1974, the Cabinet was discussing ways of limiting top salaries in the public service. It was agreed that Harold Wilson should see Lord Boyle, Chairman of the Top Salaries Review Body, to work out an announcement on 'staging' such salaries. Barbara Castle records the sequel:

'I asked, "What does staging mean? That next year's increase is merely postponed till 1976, when these people catch up with time and a half?" John Hunt (Secretary to the Cabinet) passed me a note saying that staging meant that the postponed increase was lost for ever. . . .' (*The Castle Diaries, 1974–76*, 14 Dec. 1974, pp. 251–2)

'. . . I was appalled to read the Minutes of Thursday's Cabinet. Gone is all the talk of "staging" in the sense that John Hunt had put it to me: instead, it read that we had agreed that part of the increases had merely been "deferred." One of the hazards of Cabinet government is that one is at the mercy of the Minutes, which often come out very differently from what one remembered. Yet it is almost impossible to get them altered afterwards, particularly if the PM has a vested interest in the official version.' (op. cit., 14 Dec. 1974, pp. 251–2)

CABINET COMMITTEES

In March of 1970 Richard Crossman recorded a minute which Harold Wilson had circulated on procedure in Cabinet committees:

'. . . it is clearly understood that Cabinet Committees operate by a devolution of authority from the Cabinet itself, and their procedure therefore follows the Cabinet's own procedure, particularly in the sense that it is the Chairman's responsibility at the end of a discussion to specify clearly the decision which has been reached, and that he does so, not by counting heads, but by establishing the general consensus of view around the table. . . . If the Cabinet system is to function effectively, appeals to Cabinet must clearly be infrequent. Chairmen of Committees must clearly be free to exercise their discretion in deciding whether to advise me to allow them. . . .' (*The Crossman Diaries*, 17 Mar. 1970, pp. 695–6)

More recently, revelations about Cabinet committees in the press have given a picture of the nature and number of these bodies, and how they may be used by the Prime Minister. During the James Callaghan premiership, an article by Bruce Page on 'The secret constitution' in the *New Statesman* (21.7.78) revealed the existence of over twenty standing committees, including the Energy Committee, chaired by Eric Varley, the Industry Secretary, rather than Tony Benn, the Energy Secretary. Another article, by Peter Hennessy, on Whitehall's real powerhouse, in *The Times* (30.4.84) suggests that Margaret Thatcher's Cabinet is backed up by some 25 standing committees and over 100 *ad hoc* groups.

PRIME MINISTERIAL STYLES

Comments by (anonymous) senior civil servants on Prime Ministerial style were reported by Peter Hennessy in an article 'Is the tradition of Cabinet government on the wane?' in *The Times* (16.5.83).

'I think Ted [Heath] dominated to a greater extent than the others, including Mrs Thatcher. Ministers were frightened of him . . .'

'Ted did not really believe in Cabinet government. He was never happy in Cabinet . . .'

'Harold [Wilson] worked very hard at Cabinet government. He saw the Cabinet and the Cabinet committee system as a crucial element in retaining the balance. Harold counted heads. He also expected everyone to have a view.'

It is difficult to make general statements as to the relationship of a Prime Minister to Cabinet. For instance Hennessy comments that as many as twenty-six Cabinet meetings were called in autumn 1976 to discuss the negotiating of an International Monetary Fund loan, representing 'the high water mark of Cabinet government in recent times'. On the other hand, economic strategy was subsequently planned by a small group of ministers and officials, described by Callaghan as his 'economic seminar'.

THE GROWING ARMOURY OF THE PRIME MINISTER

The Prime Minister is served by: a *Press Office*; a *Private Office* (a team of civil servants who deal with correspondence, the Prime Minister's engagements, and so on); and a *Political Office* (a team of political aides providing advice on party and policy matters).

In 1974 Harold Wilson also created a *Policy Unit*, to provide an independent source of policy advice and research. In 1983 the *Efficiency Unit*, which scrutinises the management and working of the Civil Service machine, was made directly answerable to the Prime Minister.

COLLECTIVE RESPONSIBILITY

The convention of collective Cabinet responsibility (as outlined above) is both wider and often weaker than may at first be assumed. It extends to all members of the Government, not only to those of Cabinet rank. Indeed it even applies to the parliamentary private secretaries of ministers, who are appointed by the ministers themselves and *not* by the Prime Minister.

In rare circumstances the convention may be waived in favour of an 'agreement to differ'. This was the case in 1975 over the EEC referendum (see the section on the Cabinet agenda), when members of the Government were permitted to speak against membership of the Community *outside Parliament*, but were required not to voice their opposition when speaking from the dispatch-box in the House of Commons. One anti-Market minister, Eric Heffer, who ignored this request was dismissed from his post by the Prime Minister. We have in this instance both an acknowledgement that a rigid application of the doctrine of collective responsibility would create intolerable strains within the Government, and a demonstration that the doctrine as redefined would have to be respected.

One further illustration of the often flexible interpretation of the doctrine is provided by the incident of February 1979 in which Tony Benn, Secretary of State for Energy, and a member of the Cabinet, voted in the National Executive Committee of the Labour Party *against* a cabinet decision to sell Harrier aircraft to the People's Republic of China. He nevertheless retained his post. The point being that at that time the Labour Government had no majority in the House of Commons, and faced the imminent possibility of being forced into a General Election. Prime Minister Callaghan was probably unwilling to risk the sort of internal strife which would ensue if he dismissed Mr Benn, then the head of a powerful left-wing faction in the Labour Party.

THE CONDUCT OF CABINET GOVERNMENT UNDER MARGARET THATCHER: EVIDENCE FROM THE WESTLAND AFFAIR

From an early point in the Thatcher administrations there had been persistent rumours that the Prime Minister was conducting Cabinet business in a somewhat autocratic fashion. But with the development of the Westland crisis in late 1985 and early 1986, a crisis which culminated in the resignation of Defence Secretary Michael Heseltine, there came unprecedented allegations about the manner in which Cabinet business was approached. Stated briefly, the crisis, up to the resignation of Michael Heseltine, developed as follows.

Westland, a helicopter manufacturer fell into severe financial difficulties in mid-1985. Sir John Cuckney was installed as chairman of the company and began to look for possible rescuers of the firm. By the autumn of 1985 it was clear that there were two possibilities: (a) a basically American rescue bid headed by the helicopter firm of Sikorsky; (b) a European consortium bid in which British Aerospace and GEC were prominent. By late November Cuckney was pressing for the Sikorsky option to be taken up and was followed in this by the Westland Board. By December it was clear that a clash was developing within the Government between the Trade and Industry Secretary, Leon Brittan, and the Defence Secretary, Michael Heseltine, with Brittan favouring the Sikorsky deal and Heseltine backing the European consortium (though it seems that originally the Government had supported the European option). Publicly the Prime Minister stated that the matter was one for Westland's shareholders, but Heseltine began to form the opinion that the Prime Minister was in fact manoeuvring against the European consortium, together with Trade and Industry Secretary Brittan. Heseltine came to feel that attempts to assert the doctrine of collective Cabinet responsibility behind a neutral stance were simply attempts to gag him; on 9 January 1986, in the midst of a Cabinet meeting, Heseltine walked out and subsequently announced his resignation from the Government. Heseltine's resignation statement was unprecedentedly frank about the conduct of Cabinet and portions of it are given below.

'There were three ministerial meetings chaired by the Prime Minister at the beginning of December, two of them ad hoc groups on December 4th and 5th and finally a discussion in the ministerial sub-committee on economic strategy on December 9th.

'The Prime Minister attempted at all three meetings to remove the recommendation of the National Armaments Directors [made in late November 1985, that in future European defence needs within the main helicopter classes should be met solely by helicopters designed and built in Europe] and thus leave the way clear for the Sikorsky deal.

'The ad hoc meetings were both ill tempered attempts to overcome the refusal of some colleagues to thus close off the European option.

'The Prime Minister failing to secure that preference, called a meeting of the sub-committee on Economic Strategy on Monday December 9th. I proposed delay until the following Friday to give the Europeans time to come forward with a proper proposal. If they failed, I said that I would back Sikorsky.

'Virtually every colleague who attended the enlarged meeting and thus came fresh to the arguments, supported me despite the fact that Sir John Cuckney had been invited to put his views to the meeting.

'Time was limited and, as I have said, I was given to the following Friday to come up with such a proposal.

'The Prime Minister clearly stated on that Monday that Ministers would meet again to consider the result on Friday at 3.00 p.m. after the Stock Exchange had closed.

'There would thus be a further opportunity for colleagues to consider the outcome and to inform the Board of their views if they wished. I was content. There was time. There would be further collective discussions.

'The Cabinet office subsequently began arrangements for that meeting and a number of Whitehall departments were contacted about the availability of their Minister.

'These arrangements were, however, cancelled on the instructions of the Prime Minister. Having lost three times, there was to be no question of risking a fourth discussion.

'As a result the meeting on December 9th represents the only occasion on which there was a collective discussion of the issues involved, as opposed simply to the question of their public handling by the government. By December 13th I produced proposals for ministerial agreements.

'A complementary offer by the companies concerned to participate in the reconstruction of Westland was also made that day. They were not addressed collectively, but I circulated them to colleagues.

'Following the decision not to proceed with the meeting on December 13th, I sought on a number of occasions to have the issues properly addressed.

'The first attempt had been made at the Cabinet on Thursday, December 12th. The Prime Minister refused to allow a discussion in Cabinet that day. I insisted that the Cabinet Secretary should record my protest in the Cabinet Minutes.

'When the minutes were circulated there was no reference to any discussion about Westland and consequently no record of my protest.

'Before the next Cabinet meeting I complained to the Secretary of the Cabinet. He explained that the item had been omitted from the Minutes as the result of an error and he subsequently circulated an addendum in the form of a brief note of the discussion. Such an error and correction was unprecedented in my experience.

'The Minutes, as finally issued, still did not record my protest and I have since informed the Secretary of the Cabinet that I am still not content with the way in which this discussion was recorded. . . .

'At the Cabinet discussion on December 19th there was again no attempt to address these fundamental issues.

'It was laid down that it was the policy of the government that it was for Westland to decide what was the best course to follow in the best interest of the company and its employees; that no minister was entitled to lobby in favour of one proposal rather than another; and that major issues of defence procurement were for collective decision. Information about the implications of defence procurement for Westland's workload should be made equally available to both groups as well as to Westland. . . . [On 20 December the European consortium put forward a rescue package to Westland.]

'I wrote on December 23rd to my colleagues setting out my views on the implications of both offers and their comparative merits and asking that the government should exercise its proper responsibility on so important a matter of defence industrial policy.

'I explicitly recognised that the holiday period was a difficult time for such a judgement. But before the directors came out with a final recommendation last Sunday, it would still have been possible for the government to meet and to re-state the preferences so clearly expressed at the outset. My request for a meeting was refused by the Prime Minister. . . .

'The government, in its official position, has sought to suggest that it has adopted an even-handed approach between the viable offers. In practice throughout, the attempt has been made to remove any obstacles to the offer by Sikorsky/Fiat, even to the extent of changing existing government policy.

'Although, as I explained earlier, at the outset there was a clear recognition of the attractions of involvement by British Aerospace, I understand that last night the Secretary of State for Trade and Industry, in the presence of another minister in his department and his officials, told Sir Raymond Lygo of British Aerospace that the role which British Aerospace were taking in the European consortium was against the national interest and that British Aerospace should withdraw.

'So much for the wish of the sponsoring department to leave the matter to the shareholders on the basis of the most attractive choice available to them.

'Finally, we come to today's Cabinet. It was suggested that any questions in connection with the competing offers for Westland should be referred by all ministers to the Cabinet office to be handled by them in the first instance.

'To have done so would have been to imply doubt and delay in any and every part of the assurances I had publicly given on behalf of my ministry and of my European colleagues. Such a procedure would have allowed the advocates of the Sikorsky proposals to make mayhem over what is now the superior British/European offer.

'While I agreed that all new policy issues should be referred to the Cabinet office I refused to abandon or qualify in any way assurances I have given or my right as the responsible minister to answer questions on defence procurement issues in line with policies my colleagues have not contradicted.

'The Prime Minister properly summed up the view of Cabinet that all answers should be referred for collective clearance. I could not accept that constraint in the critical few days before the Westland shareholders decide. I had no choice but to accept or to resign. I left the Cabinet.'

Many of the allegations made by Mr Heseltine were, perhaps predictably, instantly repudiated by Downing Street sources. It is quite likely that evidence, and consequently fresh arguments, on what actually happened in the course of the Westland affair will still be coming to light for several years. Obviously, in the light of the issues discussed in this chapter, we need to take note of the evident importance of Cabinet committees in the affair, of the allegations of apparent manipulation of the Cabinet minutes, of the Prime Minister's ability to control the Cabinet agenda, and of the attempts to assert a particularly vigorous form of collective Cabinet responsibility. The latter involved the vetting of ministerial statements by the Cabinet Office, even though Heseltine alleged that collective decisions had not really been made. It may be suggested that some of the tensions between the Defence Secretary and the Prime Minister arose, at least in part, because of the very high degree of flexibility which is part of the Cabinet system. The Cabinet minutes, for example, remain a mysterious compilation: as long as there is no publicly stated rule as to their purpose then disagreements over their content will always occur. An aggrieved minister, such as Michael Heseltine was, is hardly likely to take kindly to the suggestion that the minutes are there simply to *record decisions made* on items which featured on the agenda of the Cabinet.

The full text of the important resignation statement by Michael Heseltine is to be found in *The Times* (10.1.86), p. 2.

As the crisis triggered off by Michael Heseltine's resignation developed, there were immediate repercussions for the composition and style of government. Leon Brittan, one of the Cabinet ministers most closely associated with the Prime Minister and regarded by many as the 'courtier', was forced to resign and rumours began to circulate that the conduct of Cabinet business had changed. The number of Cabinet papers was alleged to have increased and the Prime Minister was said to have stepped back from her normally highly directive style of conducting Cabinet so that Cabinet discussions seemed to have taken on a new importance. When the Government announced in early February 1986 that it was withdrawing some of its plans to sell off parts of British Leyland to American companies, this was widely reported as the outcome of Cabinet resistance to the idea.

RECENT EXAMINATION QUESTIONS	A variety of essay and short answer questions are now presented, and you will find it useful to spend ten minutes or so preparing an outline answer to each question, before turning to the 'Outline answers' for questions **2**, **4**, **12**, and the 'Tutor's answer' for question **8** which follows.
Question 1.	'Better to have an outright presidential system than continue with the myth of Cabinet government.' Discuss. (London, Gov't and Pol. Stud., June 1980)
Question 2.	What are the main factors which militate against Prime Ministerial government in Britain? (London, Gov't and Pol. Stud., Jan. 1981)

Question 3.

What sorts of pressures bear on Cabinet when it tries to make public policy? Give examples from various sectors of policy.

(London, Gov't and Pol. Stud., June 1981)

Question 4.

'The Cabinet is essentially a political not an administrative agency.' Discuss.

(London, Gov't and Pol. Stud., Jan. 1982)

Question 5.

Do the weaknesses of Cabinet government now outweigh its strengths?

(London, Gov't and Pol. Stud., June 1982)

Question 6.

By what means and to what extent does the Prime Minister control the activities of his Cabinet colleagues?

(Cambridge, EPA, Summer 1979)

Question 7.

'Collective responsibility is in fact a series of dictatorships by departmental Ministers.' Discuss.

(Cambridge, Politics, Summer 1980)

Question 8.

Describe the principal changes in the organisation and operation of the Cabinet system since 1945.

(Cambridge, Politics, Summer 1981)

Question 9.

'Prime Ministers have assumed almost dictatorial powers and the process cannot be reversed'. Discuss.

(Cambridge, EPA, Summer 1983)

Question 10.

What factors are likely to influence a Prime Minister in his choice of members of his Cabinet?

(Cambridge, Public Affairs, Summer 1984)

Question 11.

What are the constraints on the power of the Cabinet?

(London, Gov't and Pol. Stud., short answer question Jan. 1980)

Question 12.

What is Cabinet government?

(London, Gov't and Pol. Stud., short answer question June 1980)

Question 13.

What are the main sources of a Prime Minister's power over his or her government colleagues and what are the main limitations on this power?

(JMB, Brit. Govt and Pol., June 1982)

OUTLINE ANSWERS

Question 2.

What are the main factors which militate against Prime Ministerial government in Britain?

Answer

[This is a straightforward question, though candidates who have thought about the material only in terms of demonstrating how far we have gone *towards* Prime Ministerial government may be disconcerted to find the topic stood on its head in this way.]

The Prime Minister is the chairman and the directing force of the Cabinet, and has more media coverage than any other minister. Nevertheless, the Prime Minister cannot govern alone or against the wishes of a majority of political colleagues.

- The Prime Minister has to keep the confidence of the party, e.g. Macmillan's 'massacre of ministers' (seven Cabinet ministers sacked at once) in 1962 weakened party loyalty to him. Within a year he had resigned.
- Parties are coalitions, and have to be managed: the different factions must be given a voice. The Prime Minister cannot therefore simply appoint personal supporters to office.
- The Prime Minister has not got the administrative support to govern without reference to colleagues. Even having the Political Unit, the Policy Unit, and the Private Office, still leaves the Prime Minister without the administrative support enjoyed by, say, departmental ministers or by a chief executive such as the President of the United States. This means that the Prime Minister is heavily dependent on advice *received* from departmental ministers and from civil servants.
- Perhaps the Prime Minister has *too* many tasks – being part diplomat, part parliamentarian, and part party manager; Mrs Thatcher herself chairs at least ten Cabinet committees. The Dutch writer Hans Daalder sums it up: 'the sheer burden of office prevents any Prime Minister from intervening at all closely except in the most urgent matters. If he can make his will prevail in any matter he chooses, he can only do so by leaving most things alone.'
- The Prime Minister's chances of dominating the Cabinet and the Whitehall machine depend on a combination of a strong personality and favourable political circumstances. This combination is rarely achieved. For instance, in 1981 Margaret Thatcher's Government was at a very low ebb in the public opinion polls, so that the Prime Minister's position was weak. She had therefore to agree that in future the budget would be settled only *after extensive Cabinet discussions* rather than by the Chancellor and Prime Minister alone, as had long been the custom.

Q. 4.

'The Cabinet is essentially a political not an administrative agency.' Discuss.

Answer

The distinction between politics and administration is often blurred. But basically politics = the resolution of conflict, while administration = the *implementation of policy* decided on *as a result of* that resolution, or the *accumulation of data* on which policy may subsequently be based.

Cabinet is clearly a *political* agency, resolving conflict:

- It is *the* principal forum in which government departments struggle against each other for resources (mainly money).
- It is *a* principal forum in which different factions of the Government party contend for influence over the decision-making process.
- Membership of, and success in, Cabinet is a crucial factor in a politician's attempts to establish himself as a contender for party leadership.
- In the same way the Prime Minister is able to make or break potential successors by promoting or demoting them within the Cabinet, or by excluding them from it.

Cabinet does perform some *administrative* functions:

- It is an executive body, sending orders to the government departments. (Note here the potential Prime Ministerial influence over the Cabinet minutes.) But the *practical* work of policy implementation is carried out by the departments themselves, i.e. by the civil servants who dominate administration, and who often 'interpret' policy to suit their own views.
- It does little in the way of accumulating data on which policy may be decided. Cabinet ministers are dependent largely on their civil servants, who carry out research and who collect and present the resulting data. Much of the discussion of such data is in any case handled in Cabinet committees.

We do not *have* to accept the view that Cabinet has become simply a 'dignified' element of the system of government to agree that its administrative functions have virtually disappeared as the work of administration has become more extensive and more complex.

SHORT ANSWER

Q. 12. 'What is Cabinet government?'

Answer The Cabinet is ultimately responsible for all major governmental decisions. The Cabinet itself frequently does not make the decisions: this process takes place in Cabinet committees or on the Prime Minister's initiative, but the policies are issued in the name of the Cabinet. Decisions are not issued in the name of individual ministers, but instead the doctrine of collective Cabinet responsibility ensures that the whole Cabinet is held to be the decision-making body. The record of Cabinet decisions (the minutes) serves as orders to the various government departments to carry out policy.

Q. 8.
Describe the principal changes in the organisation and operation of the Cabinet system since 1945.

Answer
Many commentators, most particularly the late Richard Crossman, have suggested that the post-war period has seen the virtual extinction of Cabinet government, with power passing upwards to the Prime Minister and downwards to the Cabinet committees. In reality, there have been few consistent developments in the operation of the Cabinet system in these years.

In its task of discussing and planning government policy, the Cabinet has been supplemented by some other bodies. The Central Policy Review Staff (CPRS), was created in 1970 by Edward Heath, and was designed to supply the Cabinet with material and policy analysis which might improve the quality of the decision-making. The CPRS was, however, wound up by Margaret Thatcher in 1983.

Harold Wilson created the No. 10 Policy Unit, in 1974, designed to give the Prime Minister advice on policy issues. This has perhaps strengthened the capacity of Prime Ministers to argue a case through Cabinet. Some Prime Ministers have also discussed policy with informal groups, such as Harold Wilson's 'kitchen cabinet' grouped around Marcia Williams, his personal and private secretary. Margaret Thatcher is reported to have a liking for using small *ad hoc* groups of advisers consisting of ministers, civil servants, and staff of the Policy Unit. These groups may have usurped some Cabinet functions.

There have been interesting developments in the field of Cabinet committees. The number of these committees has actually declined since the 1945–51 Labour Government. The then Prime Minister Clement Attlee employed a total of 466 Cabinet committees. More recently, James Callaghan (1976–79) used 190, and Margaret Thatcher, in the period 1979–85, has used less than 150 such committees. Indeed, it is reported that Mrs Thatcher intended to scrap Cabinet committees altogether, but was reluctantly compelled to accept their usefulness. Because the committees are an even more than usually secret area of the Cabinet system, we cannot be sure of current procedure in them, though the Crossman school of commentators point to the decision of Harold Wilson in 1967 that appeals to the full Cabinet by a minister serving on a committee would only be allowed if the chairman of the committee gave his consent. It should not be forgotten, however, that powerful Cabinet committees have a history which goes back beyond 1945. The 1944 Education Act, for example, was actually planned in a committee, and did not go before the full Cabinet.

The Cabinet is also, of course, a policy co-ordinating body, designed to harmonise the whole range of government policy. Some of this co-ordinating role has been periodically eroded since 1945. In 1951 Churchill created a group of 'overlords', ministers who co-ordinated the work of two or more ministries or spheres of government. This experiment met with opposition and was ended in 1953. Since then, however, several super-departments have been set up, each covering the work of several former ministries. By 1968, the separate ministries of National Insurance, of Pensions, and Health, had, together with the National Assistance Board, all come together in the Department of Health and Social Security. Again, by 1970, the Department of the Environment was made up of the former ministries of Housing and Local Government, Land and Natural Resources, Public Buildings and Works and Transport. These are the sort of departments described by Harold Wilson as 'great federal central planning ministries'. They inevitably resulted in a transfer of co-ordination down from the Cabinet to the internal working of the super-departments. But the trend has not been all one way: in 1976 the Department of Transport was once again split off from the Department of the Environment; and by the end of 1974 the huge Trade and Industry Department had fragmented into four separate departments, Trade, Industry, Energy and Prices, and Consumer Protection. In 1983 Trade and Industry were once more welded into a single department. The degree of co-ordination expected from the Cabinet has therefore fluctuated considerably.

Similar fluctuations have marked the relations of Prime Ministers with their Cabinets: Harold Wilson was reported to be attentive to the views of Cabinet members, and on occasion to settle issues by 'counting heads'; Edward Heath and Margaret Thatcher have both gained reputations for being more autocratic.

Even where the constitutional conventions regarding the Cabinet have remained fairly stable, there have been exceptions which may represent the beginning of a trend or which may simply be aberrations. Thus collective Cabinet responsibility has been fairly consistently upheld, at least in periods of majority government. But it was suspended in 1975 and in 1978, on the respective issues of the EEC referendum and the European Assembly Elections Bill. Inconsistency of practice seems to have marked developments in the Cabinet system since 1945: this is perhaps to be expected in an area of government which is virtually untouched by statutory definition, but simply develops according to political circumstances.

A STEP FURTHER

Great secrecy surrounds the working of the Cabinet: its official papers are not made public for at least thirty years. But some of the gaps in our knowledge may be filled by the published diaries and memoirs of Cabinet ministers. These are most plentiful in the case of Labour Governments; Conservative politicians have proved more reticent or discreet. We are very well informed on Cabinet politics in Harold Wilson's Government of 1964–70 and 1974–76. For the first period we have Richard Crossman's *Diaries*, published in three volumes as *The Diaries of a Cabinet Minister*, and in a condensed version as *The*

Crossman Diaries (ed. A. Howard, Methuen 1979). The serious student should not stop at the extracts given earlier, but should read the diaries at length: they are fascinating. For both Wilson premierships we have *The Castle Diaries 1964–70* and *The Castle Diaries 1974–76* (Weidenfeld aud Nicolson 1980/1984) by another senior Cabinet Minister, Barbara Castle. See also Harold Wilson's account of *The Labour Governments, 1964–70* (M. Joseph 1971), and his study of *The Governance of Britain* (Sphere Books 1977). A useful defence of the idea of Cabinet government is provided by yet another Cabinet minister of the Wilson era, Patrick Gordon Walker, in *The Cabinet* (Fontana 1972).

Perhaps the most important recent piece of work to appear on the Cabinet is a book by Peter Hennessy who left *The Times* to become Senior Research Fellow at the Policy Studies Institute. In *The Quality of Cabinet Government in Britain*, (Policy Studies, Vol. 6, Part 2, 1985) Hennessy argues that departmental ministers have become overloaded and now have to combine several political and administrative functions, with the result that Cabinet has become a much less meaningful institution. Under Mrs Thatcher, he claims, the number of Cabinet papers has dropped to one of its lowest levels ever, and the Thatcher technique for dealing with ministers is to talk to them individually after asking them to present a paper to her rather than to the Cabinet. Also worth consulting are Anthony King, *The British Prime Minister* (Macmillan 1985) and M. Rush, *The Cabinet and Policy Formation* (Longman 1984).

Chapter 4

The policy-makers

GETTING STARTED

Whatever the precise balance of power at any one time between the Prime Minister and the Cabinet it is clear that they do not have an exclusive hold over the policy-making process. When a Bill is introduced into Parliament by a minister it is usually the product of a lengthy and complex process of policy formation. It is the object of this chapter to examine some of the sources which may have been responsible for the development of a piece of legislation. These might include:

1. The political party from which the Government is drawn.
2. The major pressure groups.
3. The media, possibly reflecting a wave of public opinion.
4. The Civil Service, in other words the administrators themselves.
5. Academics and experts in a specific field.

It is quite impossible to formulate *general rules* concerning the quantity and the quality of the inputs to policy which derive from these sources, or indeed from any others which may be involved. Nevertheless, it will help us understand the process of policy-making if we subject some of these sources to closer examination.

ESSENTIAL PRINCIPLES

POLITICAL PARTY

The political party from which the Government is drawn may exert pressure on its leadership in a variety of ways.

Annual conference

First, and perhaps most obvious, there is the *annual conference* of the party. This provides the leadership with the opportunity to sense the mood of the party in the constituencies, to listen to the demands of the important factions within the party and, by listening to delegates, to try to form some impression of the strength of public opinion on any given issue. The role of the conference varies from party to party. For example, according to the constitution of the Labour Party, the conference is its supreme policy-making body, whereas in the Conservative Party there still survives something of the attitude revealed by Balfour when he remarked that he would just as soon take advice from his valet as from the Conservative Conference. In practice a party conference cannot bind a government to act upon its demands, for the Cabinet can always fall back on the argument that it is privy to confidential information, which makes the adoption of any given policy unwise or impossible. Although the party leadership must pay careful attention to feelings within the party, it may perhaps reflect that a conference tends to be attended by activists and that party activists tend to be more extreme in their views than the bulk of the voters of the party. It may therefore be electorally quite safe to ignore even the most strident demands of a party conference.

Associations

The annual conference represents an occasion when ideas circulating within the party can emerge in a particularly public form. There are, of course, other means by which party members may exert more long-term pressure on their leadership to adopt particular policies. The larger parties contain *associations* whose aim is to promote particular policies, such as the Conservative Monday Club consisting of right-wing radicals, or the Labour Tribune Group, operating to the left of the party. Organisations like Labour's Fabian Society or the Conservative Bow Group are also important as a source of ideas, which are frequently expressed in intellectually rigorous pamphlets. Such associations can hardly be said to have great popular appeal and they do not generally seek to mobilise mass opinion behind their views, but they are influential within the upper strata of their respective parties.

Research departments

Full-time party workers and researchers may also be influential, with the larger parties maintaining official research departments. One of their aims is usually to establish a substantial data base, which can be used to fuel the arguments which go to make up the party platform.

PRESSURE GROUPS

In the case of *pressure groups* there are again many avenues by which they may get involved in the process of policy formation. It is unlikely that any real influence on policy formation can be exercised by a pressure group which is in *fundamental opposition* to the aims of a government: there can be no real dialogue, for example, between the Campaign for Nuclear Disarmament (CND) and a government committed to accepting the deployment of Cruise missiles in the United Kingdom. In these circumstances the best hope for a pressure group is to attempt to mobilise public opinion in the expectation that this may affect the result of the next General Election. In the process they may succeed in securing the adherence to their aims of the opposition parties in Parliament. But circumstances in which a pressure group and a government are in constant and fundamental conflict are relatively rare.

For instance, even trade unions affiliated to the Labour Party, though probably unsympathetic to the aims of a Conservative Government, will have an interest in co-operating on such matters as legislation to improve industrial safety. Co-operation of this sort is facilitated by the existence of such institutions as the National Economic Development Council (NEDC) which provides a forum for discussion between the Government, employers, trade unions and relevant experts and academics. The exchanges of information which take place during meetings of the NEDC are valuable to all of the parties concerned and certainly help augment the stock of ideas from which Government policy is formed. The NEDC is paralleled by a large range of advisory committees, which operate under the auspices of government departments and on which experts and members of relevant pressure groups may meet to offer ideas to the Government.

In discussing the role of pressure groups and policy-making we should note the important controversy over whether Britain displays *corporative* or *pluralist* characteristics. In a system marked by *corporatism* a relationship develops between the Government and major pressure groups such as employers and trade unions in which *all* share in making major decisions about policy. This means that such groups are incorporated into the process of decision-making, and having been incorporated they help in the implementation of any policy which is agreed upon. In a *pluralist* system, on the other hand, groups table demands, but do not normally regard themselves as the makers of governmental policy and consequently are *not* prepared to take any share of responsibility for such policy. They see themselves in other words as external to the process of policy formation and to the process of policy implementation.

In practice Britain seems to represent a basically pluralist system in which tendencies towards corporatism sometimes emerge quite strongly. Of the recent Prime Ministers, Edward Heath is alleged to have been attracted by corporatist notions, particularly in the later stages of his government; Harold Wilson and James Callaghan frequently emphasised their governments' consultations with institutions such as the Confederation of British Industry (CBI) and the Trades Union Congress (TUC). On the other hand it has become quite conventional to see the Thatcher administration as one which is firmly opposed to the principle and practice of corporatism.

MEDIA

In the post-war period the media themselves have come to act as a kind of pressure group, sometimes pushing particular causes before the Government and sometimes affecting the general tone of political debate. This is a process known as 'agenda-setting', and one former minister, Lord Boyle, suggested in the early 1970s that Cabinets increasingly tended to be preoccupied with the agenda presented by the media.

CIVIL SERVICE

Yet another major element in the process of policy formation is that provided by the civil servants themselves. Much has been written on the powers of civil servants *vis-à-vis* their ministers, and more will be said on this topic in the following chapter. For the moment it is sufficient to note that each government department becomes the repository of accumulated wisdom. This produces what is known as the 'continuing policy' of the department. Essentially this is a set of policy options which past experience has shown to be both feasible and desirable, and which may or may not coincide with the objectives of an incoming Government or an incoming minister. The politicians may have formulated their policies in ignorance of some of the administrative facts known to the civil servants: consequently they may do well to take account of the latters' suggestions.

Finally, it is worth recalling that in addition to these domestic contributions to the evolution of government policy, the demands and susceptibilities of Britain's trading partners, of her military allies and of international financial bodies are also likely to have a significant effect on the policies pursued by a British Cabinet.

USEFUL APPLIED MATERIALS

THE ROLE OF PRESSURE GROUPS

In the extract below, Dr G. Alderman – an academic who has made a special study of pressure groups – discusses the contribution which they make to the democratic process:

'Far more people in this country are involved in the re-ordering of society through their involvement in pressure groups than through their involvement in political parties or in putting a cross on the ballot paper once every five years. Pressure groups are a way of involving more people in the running of the country and that is very important as an ingredient in the social cement of this country. People will not accept laws simply because Parliament passed them. They will accept laws because they believe that they have had some input into the framing of them.'   (In Malcolm Davis, *Politics of Pressure*, pp. 43–4).

Lobbying for the arts: an ambiguous case

In 1985 a book published in conjunction with the BBC television series *Politics of Pressure* included under the general chapter heading of 'Artful lobbying' a section on lobbying for the arts. This clearly demonstrated the connections that exist between the world of the visual and performing arts and that of politics. It went on to suggest that the arts world had effectively adapted its image to suit the economic and political climate of the 1980s, shifting the basis of its demands for State subsidies from the *need* to support a valuable cultural medium to the *possible economic benefit* which might derive from the arts as a tourist attraction and as an agency of wealth creation.

The following example from the series usefully illustrates how difficult it often is in practice to assess the effectiveness of pressure-group activity. In November of 1985 it was announced that the government grant to the Arts Council had risen by £30.6 million to a total of £135.6 million for the coming financial year. At first this announcement seemed like a qualified victory for the arts lobby which, of course, promptly denounced the grant as insufficient in the light of its claim for a grant of £161 million for the year. On the other hand the story soon began to circulate that the Minister for the Arts, Richard Luce, had in fact been severely hampered in his attempt to wrest *more money* from the Treasury by the virulent criticism of the Government made earlier in the year by some members of the arts lobby. It was reported that there was not a lot of sympathy around for the Arts in the Cabinet at that time, a fact blamed on the attitudes of some prominent members of the arts lobby. It is therefore difficult to know quite what to make of this particular case. Was the vigorous arts lobby responsible for a substantial increase in grant over the *provisional* figure of £122 million which had already been set, or did the lobby make life unduly difficult for an assiduous minister in Cabinet? (Malcolm Davis, op. cit., pp.141–7)

From pressure group proposal to Private Member's Bill to Government policy.

In the summer of 1983 David Tench, the Legal Adviser to the Consumers' Association, drafted a House Buyer's Bill which he hoped would be accepted by a back-bench MP as a Private Member's measure. The Bill was eventually taken up by Austin Mitchell (as explained on p. 76–7), although in reality it had been drawn up with a view to its being taken on board by the Government. David Tench explains the process:

'Here was a new Government with a new intake of new boys all zealously accepting competition as the key to political philosophy. So we, as it were, dressed up the reform of the House Transfer System as being a *matter of competition*. We actually believe that as well, but it's a question of emphasis and of highlighting it. Now if we had a Labour Government in power I think our approach would be totally different. It would have essentially been a matter of *protecting the citizen*, giving better rights, a better deal to the ordinary individual by virtue of consumer protection. . . . The Government was minded to do something. The Bill had announced rather half-baked proposals about reforming the House Transfer System . . . in the expectation that the Bill would be lost. But when the Bill was passed at its second reading the Government attitude changed very markedly . . . we spent about two months negotiating with the Government about what they might do to take on the main issues raised by the Bill. Finally, in the following February, a Government policy was hammered out and the Government came forward with very positive and exciting proposals. This was a big issue that couldn't really go through as a Private Member's Bill [the House Buyer's Bill was withdrawn on 15 February 1984] but it demonstrated the value of a Private Member's Bill by raising a major issue and getting it in front of the public and in front of Parliament.' (Malcolm Davis, op. cit., pp. 73, 80; *HC Sessional Information Digest 1983–84*, p. 25)

Policy formulation in consultation with pressure groups

Harold Wilson, Prime Minister in the 1964–70 Labour Governments, describes a stage in the development of the 1967 Prices and Incomes Bill: 'During the period of severe restraint which followed the ending of the total wages freeze in December 1966, we had been engaged in discussions with the TUC and the CBI about the criteria which should govern prices and incomes decisions from the middle of the year.'   (Harold Wilson *The Labour Government 1964–70,* p. 534)

AN ATTEMPT AT CORPORATISM

In the late summer of 1972 Edward Heath, then Conservative Prime Minister, launched an attempt to secure the co-operation in economic policy-making of both the employers and the TUC. His Employment Secretary, Robert Carr, commented that 'we really did bring the Trade Union movement and employers into . . . the guts of macro-economic policy and we really did open the books . . . to look at the national income figures, the expected growth in national income over the coming year . . . to get common agreement that that was the most growth we could expect and how best to distribute it.' Jack Jones, then General Secretary of the Transport and General Workers Union, comments that Heath was 'prepared to be patient and listen to our point of view and our arguments, and within his limits as a Conservative Prime Minister I think he did try to respond'.   (Philip Whitehead, *The Writing on the Wall*, Michael Joseph in association with Channel 4 Television Co Ltd, p. 87)

THE NEC, THE TUC AND A LABOUR GOVERNMENT

The following extract, from Barbara Castle's *Diaries*, illustrates the pressures which may be brought to bear on a Labour Government, on the one hand by the Labour Party's National Executive committee (NEC), which is elected annually at the Party Conference, and on the other by the TUC, which supports the Labour Party financially to the tune of some 80 per cent of its expenses, and which urges policy upon the party by means of a liaison committee. Barbara Castle describes Cabinet proceedings in 1974. The government was at the time under pressure from the NEC over its attitude to the problem of Chile where, in September 1973, the socialist President Allende had been murdered and his government ousted by a military coup.

'Jim [Callaghan] of course, could not let the Chile question pass. Mildly he said that yesterday's proceedings at the NEC had been "unusual" with some members of the NEC behaving as though they were not members of the government. . . . When Wedgie [Anthony Wedgewood Benn] said earnestly "the question is whether Cabinet is prepared to receive representations for a review of its decision", Jim replied that he had expressed his willingness to take the views of the NEC into account "on matters not yet decided". . . . At last we turned to the main item of business: Mike's [Michael Foot's] Bill to replace the Industrial Relations Act. He apologised for raising the matter yet again, but this time he is in trouble over the clause providing machinery for independent review. His previously modified formula has apparently not done the trick with the TUC. In his memo he says that to persist with the clause could cause a "grave breach" with the unions, and he therefore wanted to postpone the matter until the second Bill. That was in any case the more logical place for it and he thought the TUC had good grounds for their objections because they say this matter should have been settled at the liaison committee.' (*The Castle Diaries, 1974–76*, 25 Apr. 1974, pp. 89–90).

RECENT EXAMINATION QUESTIONS

A number of examination questions are outlined below. You can usefully spend ten minutes or so planning an answer to each question. Outline answers are provided in the next sections to questions **6**, **8**, and **10** and a full tutor's answer to question **3**.

Question 1.

Do private individuals or groups of individuals have any chance of influencing projected legislation in Great Britain?
(Cambridge, Public Affairs, Nov. 1985)

Question 2.

Is the Government of Britain a tripartite relationship between industry, the unions and Whitehall?
(London, Govt and Pol. Stud., Paper 1, June 1982)

Question 3.

'Government by agreement with pressure groups is now an essential feature of British government.' Discuss.
(London, Govt and Pol. Stud., Paper 1, Jan. 1983)

Question 4.

Assess with examples the relative ability of (a) interest groups, (b) promotional groups to influence the formulation and legislation of public Bills.
(AEB, Govt and Pol., Paper 1, June 1982)

Question 5.

Assess the relative effect of the annual party conference on the policies of (a) Labour in opposition, (b) Labour in government.
(AEB, Govt and Pol., Paper 1, Nov. 1982)

Question 6.

Assess the effect of the annual party conference on the policy-making of Conservative and Labour Governments since 1945.
(AEB, Govt and Pol., Paper 1, June 1984)

Question 7.

'Most policy initiatives do not originate in Whitehall and Westminster.' Discuss.
(London, Govt and Pol. Stud., Paper 1, June 1985)

Question 8.

What are the main types of pressure group?
(London, Govt and Pol. Stud., Paper 1, short answer question, June 1982)

Question 9.
In what ways are trade unionists and industrialists involved in government?
(London, Govt and Pol. Stud., Paper 1, short answer question, June 1983)

Question 10.
Is there any evidence that direct action like strikes, demonstrations or riots, can influence policy-making?
(Cambridge, Govt and Pol., Paper 1, June 1984)

Question 11.
It has been said that Britain's ruling élites are remarkably closely knit. Explain and discuss this statement.
(JMB, Brit. Govt and Pol., June 1981)

OUTLINE ANSWERS

Q.10.
Is there any evidence that direct action like strikes, demonstrations or riots can influence policy-making?

Answer
There are three major ways in which direct action may have an influence.
(a)   the action may convince the Government of the urgency of the cause; it may adapt its policies in order to benefit those who are taking the action;
(b)   the Government may not respond but opposition parties may take up the cause with a view to implementing a sympathetic policy when they come into power;
(c)   the Government may respond adversely.

Governments do not in general like to be seen to have their hands forced. But see the visit of Environment Secretary Michael Heseltine to the Liverpool district of Toxteth after the riots in 1981. Heseltine was prompted by the disorders to pump money into the city in an attempt to alleviate some of its social problems. Similarly the Brixton riots of 1981 provoked Home Secretary Whitelaw to set up the investigation by Lord Scarman whose report certainly affected some aspects of policy formation, e.g. the establishment of the Police Complaints Authority in the Police and Criminal Evidence Act of 1984. Lord Scarman's other recommendations for action to tackle inner-city problems have not met with such a clear response. Other examples show governments *abandoning* policy in the face of direct action, e.g. the abandonment of the 'Sunningdale' machinery for Northern Ireland (a power-sharing executive, a new Ulster Assembly, a Council of Ireland), as a result of the Protestant strike of May 1974.
The renewed vitality of CND in the 1980s seems to have had an effect on policy. It has *not* converted the Conservative Government, but has arguably pushed the Labour Party into a virtually unilateralist stance.

Governmental backlash is fairly common. The tough Conservative trade-union legislation of the 1980s (1982 Employment Act, 1984 Trade

Union Act) together with the Government's confrontational approach to the miners' strike of 1984–85, can be interpreted as a reaction against the troubles which *previous* governments had experienced in the 1970s in dealing with trade unions and trade-union agitation. Civil disturbances have also prompted the Government to extend police powers.

It is often very difficult to establish the effectiveness of direct action in influencing policy-making as it is only *one* of the means by which policy changes are advocated. Direct action may coincide with pressure exerted in the same direction within Parliament or with more covert bargaining.

Q.6.

Assess the relative effects of the annual party conference on the policies of (a) Labour in opposition, (b) Labour in government.

Answer (a)

The party conference is technically a kind of sovereign body within the Labour Party. It has the power to establish policy and to elect the NEC of the party which is then charged with ensuring that conference decisions are implemented. When Labour is in opposition one of its major tasks is to hold its party activists together, and consequently the party leadership tends to take considerable notice of conference decisions. When in opposition the Labour Party tends also to engage in internal ideological and organisational conflict: the annual party conference represents a focal point in this process when symbolic victories are won and defeats suffered. In recent years conference has vividly displayed the grass-roots advance within the Labour Party of radical forces. These have gained important votes at conference for constitutional rule changes within the party, e.g. the mandatory reselection of MPs before every election and the new electoral college procedure by which the party leader is selected. Even in opposition it is still possible for the party leadership to reject conference decisions, since the party constitution states that a resolution only becomes automatic party policy when carried by a two-thirds majority.

(b)

Once in government, the Labour Party has inevitably to face a constitutional conflict between its *own constitution*, giving ultimate control over policy to the conference, and the *national constitutional convention* that it is the Cabinet which decides governmental policy. Harold Wilson claimed in 1976 that 'a Prime Minister and the Cabinet cannot be instructed by the National Executive Committee or by the Conference'. In fact his Governments, particularly those of 1964–70, ignored conference resolutions on many issues. Once in power the Labour leadership has to adjust its responses to changing circumstances and must often do so quickly and without reference either to the conference or to the NEC as the guardian of conference policy. On many matters of foreign policy and budgetary policy the conference will simply be called upon to endorse what a Labour Government has already done rather than to give its approval to a proposed course of action. As Clement Atlee said, when the King invites you to form a government you don't say that you cannot reply for forty-eight hours.

SHORT ANSWER

Q.8.

What are the main types of pressure group?

Answer

First, there are pressure groups which are referred to as *interest* or *sectional* or *protective* groups, and which generally seek to protect and advance the interests of a *specific occupational group* such as miners or company directors. The membership of the group is generally limited to those whom it seeks to protect. Second, there are the *promotional* or *cause* groups. These seek to promote a *specific cause* which is *not* to the immediate advantage of members on the pressure group. In this category come groups such as Shelter, the Child Poverty Action Group, or Friends of the Earth.

A TUTOR'S ANSWER

Q.3.

'Government by agreement with pressure groups is now an essential feature of British government.' Discuss.

Answer

This statement is perhaps more obviously true of recent Labour Governments than it is of recent Conservative ones. An illustration of this occurred in 1969, when Harold Wilson's Labour Government attempted to introduce an industrial relations policy based on legislation. The policy was outlined in the White Paper *In Place of Strife*, and immediately met severe opposition from the trade-union movement. In consequence the Labour Government was forced to abandon the attempt. During the subsequent Wilson Government of 1974–76, Government and trade unions *did* come to an agreement on industrial relations policy. This was known as the Social Contract, in which the trade-union leaders agreed to attempt to moderate wage increases and wage demands in return for a package of governmental social and economic policies.

It could of course be argued that arrangements such as the Social Contract do not really constitute government by agreement, but instead represent an agreement *not to govern*. The suggestion here is that such arrangements involve the renunciation by a Labour Government of policies which might antagonise the trade-union movement, which after all provides Labour with many of its voters and some 80 per cent of its finances. Nevertheless the later 1960s and much of the 1970s could reasonably be described as a period of *corporatism*, in which major pressure groups such as the CBI and the TUC were involved with, or incorporated into the Government decision-making process. This was true of both Labour and

Conservative Governments, being particularly evident in the period 1972–73 of Edward Heath's Conservative Government.

When, during the 1960s and 1970s, there were occasions during which relations between Government and pressure groups did break down, as after the Conservative Industrial Relations Act of 1971, during the conflict with the National Union of Mineworkers (NUM) in 1973–74 and in the so-called winter of discontent of 1978–79, then the Government in question suffered in public esteem and ultimately at the polls. Nor was the TUC the only industrial pressure group able to resist government policies during this period; for example in 1977 the CBI was able successfully to head off moves towards the appointment of worker directors through trade unions as had been suggested by the Bullock Commission. Evidence of the later 1960s and most of the 1970s suggests that while the major pressure groups were unable to force their own programmes upon governments except in rare cases, they were able to conduct successful opposition to government policy if it displeased them. It therefore became essential for governments to attempt at least to secure pressure-group agreement if their policies were to stand a chance of being implemented successfully. Governments of this period clearly valued the contribution to policy-making of pressure groups, especially in controversial areas. The very structure of government reflected the importance of their role, as in pressure-group membership of the advisory councils and of the committees attached to government departments, the primary example being that of the NEDC.

The whole situation seems, however, to have changed dramatically with the arrival in power of Margaret Thatcher's Conservative administration in 1979. One commentator on the first Thatcher administration has referred to the 'end of corporatism'. In the field of labour relations, for example, the Government's policy has been to impose legislation *against* the wishes of the trade unions, as in the case of the 1982 Employment Act or the 1984 Trade Union Act. The Government has pressed on with such legislation regardless of a raising of the political temperature. For example the government ignored the trade unions' withdrawal from the NEDC in 1984 in protest at the Government's banning of union membership at GCHQ, Cheltenham. Complaints have also been heard from the CBI that its opinions are not sought by the Thatcher administration. Less powerful organisations received similar treatment. The National Retailers Association, which had had regular meetings with Labour ministers over prices policy, was told when it attempted to meet Geoffrey Howe, the Conservative Chancellor after 1979, that he was too busy to see them. All this certainly suggests that in contrast to the received wisdom of the late 1960s and 1970s government *can* be carried on without the agreement of major pressure groups. Whether it can be carried on *satisfactorily* is of course quite another matter.

A STEP FURTHER

If we are to gain further insight into the complexities of policy-making, it will be necessary to look carefully at the Cabinet ministers' and Prime Ministers' diaries and recollections mentioned in the previous chapter. It will also be worth looking at Malcolm Davies, *Politics of Pressure* (BBC 1985), Hugo Young and Anne Sloman, *No Minister* (BBC 1982), and *But, Chancellor* (BBC 1984), for examples of the sort of pressures which are often brought to bear upon governments and politicians. One survey of 'those who really run Britain today' which is certainly entertaining and absorbing is provided by Anthony Sampson, *The Changing Anatomy of Britain* (Coronet Books 1983).

For those who want to take their examination of policy-making much further a crucial book is J. J. Richardson and A. G. Jordan, *Governing Under Pressure* (Basil Blackwell, 1985). One of the key themes of this book is that the boundaries between the Government and groups are becoming less clear as the result of a wide range of interactions and transfers of personnel, e.g. secondments from pressure groups and from industry to the Civil Service, movement of civil servants on retirement to industry, and indeed movements of civil servants into industry during their working life in order to secure a better pay or career structure. (Politicians also, of course, conform to this pattern.) As a result 'we see policies being made and administered between a myriad of interconnecting, interpenetrating organisations' and this is labelled by Richardson and Jordan 'the policy community'. The reservation that one has about this book is that its edition date of 1985 simply reflects a change of publisher for the volume. The 1985 'edition' is unchanged from the original first edition of 1979. The book is therefore an excellent analysis of policy-making in the pre-Thatcher era. We may or may not agree with Richardson and Jordan that Britain is a post-parliamentary democracy in the sense that Parliament is no longer the focal point of the policy-formation process. What is more certain is the suggestion that it is the so-called policy community which is now under pressure as a result of several years of 'conviction government'.

Chapter 5

The Whitehall machine

There can be few institutions of British political and governmental life so regularly assailed by politicians of all parties as the Civil Service, particularly its senior ranks. As we shall see, this general attitude is reflected in examination questions. The Civil Service has been defined as that body of men and women who work directly for ministers held to account in Parliament. It has been attacked on the following grounds:

(a) Its upper ranks are too powerful: they dominate or at the very least manipulate the ministers who are supposed to direct their efforts.

(b) The Service, particularly its upper ranks, is too narrowly recruited: consequently it displays the unpleasant characteristics of an élite.

(c) The Service is dominated by generalists whose outlook leads to the cult of the amateur and to incompetent administration.

(d) The Service is too large and is in consequence cumbersome and far too costly.

In this chapter we shall examine and then illustrate some of the main arguments surrounding these accusations. It may be suggested at the outset that senior civil servants perhaps cannot win: if they display great competence then they will almost inevitably appear sinister or condescending to their political 'masters'; if they do not then they will be attacked by reformers as mere amateurs who are playing at the serious task of administration.

ESSENTIAL PRINCIPLES

CRITICISMS OF THE CIVIL SERVICE

Excessive power

It is perhaps inevitable that the senior Civil Service should be accused of being too powerful. Civil servants are permanent: they are not replaced when political administration changes; they do not follow their minister from department to department when Cabinet reshuffles take place. Consequently they gather much expertise and become the repositories of considerable departmental wisdom over the course of the years. Thus a permanent secretary is likely to have far more awareness of the problems confronting his department and of the feasibility of suggested lines of policy than a minister in a newly arrived government. The information previously available to the new minister is likely to have been far more scanty, based on gossip, on the informed newspapers, and on his party research department. Some sections of a new government's manifesto may have been designed more for their appeal to the voters than for their administrative sense. In this context it is all too easy to understand the reported comment of one former senior civil servant that it takes an incoming government eighteen months to realise that its manifesto is unworkable: and that it is the task of a permanent secretary to reduce that period of time to six months.

Perhaps the really crucial element in the relationship between senior civil servants and ministers is that of *personality*. There can be no doubt that a really determined government minister can force his views upon his senior administrators and will have things done in his way. Richard Crossman, a Labour minister during the 1960s, whose *Diaries* contain one of the frankest accounts of a minister/civil servant relationship, refers many times to the strong-mindedness necessary in a minister if he is to resist the advice which is constantly proferred to him by his department.

Narrow base of recruitment

Britain's generally less than impressive record among the industrialised powers over the course of the last forty years has certainly inclined many politicians to blame poor performance on the obstruction and amateurishness of the senior civil servants. These are traditionally held to be a clique of former public-school boys educated at Oxford or Cambridge, and in arts rather than science or social science subjects. This is the sort of argument which appears frequently in the report on the Civil Service drawn up by the House of Commons' Expenditure Committee (the so-called 'English Committee') in 1976. This report prompted a Civil Service Committee of Inquiry, the Allen Committee, to examine the *recruitment patterns* to the crucial grade of administration trainee from which most of the future high fliers of the Civil Service will be drawn. The complex findings of the Allen Committee on the nature of administration trainee recruitment suggested, at least to the committee's satisfaction, that the notion of prejudice in favour of Oxbridge, public schools and arts graduates was a myth. It was conceded that Oxford and Cambridge between them put forward a disproportionately high percentage of candidates for the administration trainee selection procedure. It was, however, argued that the nature of the Oxbridge educational system made the products of the two ancient universities more suitable for the purposes of higher administration.

Lack of specialists

The classic statement that the senior levels of the Civil Service are dominated by the cult of the amateur or by the generalist is to be found in the opening section of the Fulton Report of 1968:

'. . . the ideal administrator is still too often seen as the gifted layman who, moving frequently from job to job within the service, can take a practical view of any problem irrespective of its subject matter, in the light of his knowledge and experience of the Government machine. The cult is obsolete in all levels and in all parts of the Service.' (Report of the Committee, 1966–68, Cmnd 3638, section 15.)

The Fulton Committee consequently called for greater efforts to be made to recruit *specialists* with relevant training to government departments. It called also for an *improved career structure* within the Service for such specialists, and for the creation of a Civil Service College to provide *more effective in-service training.* Even though steps have been taken to implement all these recommendations, few regard the outcome as being conspicuously successful in any of these areas. However, it is perhaps fair to say that a reluctance to place technical specialists in positions of overall administrative responsibility is hardly confined to the Civil Service: it exists also throughout British industry. It may thus be thought to reflect a widely held British attitude towards the leadership of large organisations.

Excessive bureaucracy

Finally, let us consider the question of the organisation and the allegedly over-inflated size of the Civil Service: here it is perhaps worth while stressing that the *reforms* of one generation often turn out to be the *problems* facing the next. A case in point was the creation, as a result of the Fulton Report in 1968, of a Civil Service Department whose job was to take over the function of pay and management of the Service from a section of the Treasury. Growing suspicions developed in the late 1970s that the Civil Service Department and the Treasury were now simply duplicating each others functions, since the Treasury was the ultimate source of cash and, consequently, influence. The Thatcher Government struck at the Civil Service Department as part of its economy measures and abolished it in 1981. Indeed the Thatcher Government has firmly dispelled the notion that the Civil Service is an unstoppable bureaucratic monster. At least this appears to be so from the data available: the Civil Service statistics for 1985 revealed that the total numbers of civil servants had shrunk since 1979 by some 133,000 (to under 600,000) as a result of swinging government cuts. These cuts, however, have had their major impact in the *industrial sector* of Civil Service employment rather than in the field of *administration.* It seems to many as though the capacity of the bureaucrats to defend themselves against attack has remained substantially undiminished.

LOYALTIES OF THE CIVIL SERVICE

Perhaps it is the pressure exerted upon the Civil Service machine in recent years that has led some civil servants to consider seriously, and sometimes quite dangerously, where their true loyalties lie. That is to say, the question has arisen as to whether a civil servant's loyalty is to the *Government* of the day, to the *State*, or more vaguely, to the *public*. Certainly some civil servants have concluded that they have a public duty which may involve an element of disloyalty to the Government of the day. This disloyalty is generally manifested in leaks of important information to Members of Parliament or to the media. In the five years following Mrs Thatcher's arrival in power in 1979 there were more than twenty major leaks, most of which were either attributed to civil servants or suspected as having been the result of the work of civil servants.

Perhaps the most spectacular such case was the leaking of Ministry of Defence (MOD) documents relating to the sinking of the Argentinian cruiser *General Belgrano,* by a senior official of the MOD, Mr Clive Ponting, to a Member of Parliament, Mr Tam Dalyell. Ponting was subsequently put on trial for a breach of the Official Secrets Act. His defence was that Section 2 of the Act allows that someone may legitimately pass information to 'a person to whom it is in the interests of the State his duty to communicate'. Now the definition of 'the interests of the State' has proved particularly difficult to establish. Previous judicial opinion was unclear on this point, ranging from Lord Reid's view that 'the State is not an easy word, it does not mean the government or the executive. Perhaps the country or the realm are as good synonyms as one can find', to Lord Devlin's definition of the State as 'the organs of government of a national community'. The judge in the Ponting case directed that the phrase 'the interests of the State' had to be regarded as synonymous with the policies of the Government of the day. This direction, if it had been followed, would have led to Clive Ponting being found guilty. The jury however, seemed not to follow the judge's direction since Ponting was acquitted. The whole case illustrates the sort of difficulties which may face civil servants, particularly senior civil servants, in handling material which may be politically extremely contentious. The Ponting case has reinforced calls, including some made by senior civil servants themselves, for the upper levels of administration to be staffed not by permanent civil servants, but by *political appointees* who would be removed and replaced with a change of government.

USEFUL APPLIED MATERIALS

AN ACCUSATION OF CIVIL SERVICE BIAS

In 1977 the House of Commons Expenditure Committee published a report (named the 'English Report' after its chairman, Michael English), into developments in the Civil Service. The committee in fact split into majority and minority factions, each issuing its own comments. From the *minority* there came a stinging attack on political bias in the Civil Service, including for example, the allegation that civil servants had obstructed both the radical aspects of Edward Heath's Conservative programme in the early 1970s and the more socialist policies of Harold Wilson's 1974 Government. It went on as follows:

'Civil Servants at the Department of Industry have been culpable of frustrating interventionist industrial policies . . . in this case political bias may have played a part. The result is that instead of an industrial strategy we have a series of industrial problems. The Department of Trade contains Civil Servants who are steeped in 19th century Board of Trade attitudes. Civil Servants are also known to be hostile to any meaningful form of industrial democracy although it is Labour Party policy. The Home Office, the graveyard of free thinking since the days of Lord Sidmouth early in the 19th century, is stuffed with reactionaries ruthlessly pursuing their own reactionary policies. Some Foreign Office officials interpret being a good European as being synonymous with selling out British interests. The Vichy mentality which undoubtedly exists in some parts of our Foreign Office establishment does not, to the best of our knowledge and belief, reflect the views of Her Majesty's Ministers'. 'English Report', HC 535, p. xxx, in Geoffrey K. Fry, *The Changing Civil Service*, p. 20)

CIVIL SERVICE ATTITUDES

Marcia Williams, who was created Baroness Falkender in 1974, was personal and political secretary to Harold Wilson during the 1964–70 Labour Governments and again during the 1974–76 Government. In that capacity she was very much involved in the workings of central government. In the extract below she discusses what she sees as the political leanings of the senior ranks of the Civil Service.

'Despite the scrutiny to which it has been subjected over the last ten years the Civil Service has changed little either in the way it organises itself or in the way it selects those who staff the administrative grades. These, the powerful élite, still come mainly from the same backgrounds – the public schools and Oxbridge, from the south of England rather than the north.

'Nor have the greater proportion of reforms recommended by the Fulton Inquiry of 1969 yet been carried out. The one major change that did come about – the removal of the Civil Service from the aegis of the Treasury to a separate independent existence in its own department responsible for itself – has been reversed. Control over the Service has passed back to the Treasury, the most powerful department in Whitehall with the exception of the Foreign Office.

'Few would suggest that the Civil Service is neutral. The questions posed by the Fulton Inquiry ten years ago still remain. When Labour took over in 1964, I remarked then (and again in 1970) that the Civil Service administrative grades were in the main pro-Conservative.

'I believe I was wrong for the right reasons. How could they be anything else? They came from backgrounds and families that were usually Conservative. They moved in the circles where Conservative politicians moved and Conservative politics were the order of the day. Their politics and inclination tailored them for service with a Conservative, rather than a Labour Government. By 1964 thirteen continuous years had been spent in servicing Conservative administrations. The violent change was traumatic for them much as they had tried to prepare themselves for the incoming Socialists, and despite the isolated individuals – some distinguished ones in the Treasury – who welcomed Wilson's victory.

'Despite the failure to reform the Service it is now obvious that it has changed. As the methods of selection have remained the same this alteration is not so much due to any greater objectivity on the part of the selectors as to the changes in society that have occurred as a result of reforming Governments (both Labour and Conservative) over the last 30 years.

'My guess is that those who now staff the administrative class of the Civil Service are more likely to be potential SDP and Alliance supporters. The switches in policy between left and right, especially since 1964, have deeply affected attitudes in the Civil Service. This, together with changes in society since the war (and particularly since the 1960s) has produced Civil Servants from a different sort of background that is, in its turn, politically tuned in to the changing political scene – a background which in my view produces people more likely to be interested in the new Alliance parties than the old regimes.'   (Marcia Falkender, *Downing Street in Perspective*, Weidenfeld and Nicholson, 1983, pp. 261–2)

ALLEGED POLITICISATION OF THE SENIOR CIVIL SERVICE

The early 1980s saw persistent rumours to the effect that the Prime Minister, Margaret Thatcher, was attempting to remodel the senior Civil Service along 'political' lines by appointing to top posts those who were known to favour her policies. Here the Secretary to the Cabinet, Sir Robert Armstrong, speaking at the Centenary Conference of the Chartered Institute of Public Finance and Accountancy denies that such political choices were being made. 'She wants, as I want, to have the best person for the job. I can vouch for the fact that she does not seek to ascertain the political views or sympathies of any of those that are recommended to her. Nor do I.'   (*The Times*, 19.6.85, p. 2)

A MINISTER CONFRONTS THE CIVIL SERVICE

This is an extract from the first of Richard Crossman's diary entries. It is dated 22 October 1964 when he had been Minister of Housing for some five days:

'Already I realise the tremendous effort it requires not to be taken over by the Civil Service. My Minister's Room is like a padded cell and in certain ways I am like a person who is suddenly certified a lunatic and put safely into this great vast room, cut off from real life and surrounded by male and female trained nurses and attendants. When I'm in a good mood they occasionally allow an ordinary human being to come and visit me but they make sure that I behave right and the other person behaves right and they know how to handle me. Of course, they don't behave quite like nurses because the Civil Service is profoundly deferential – "Yes Minister", "No Minister", "If you wish it Minister" – and combined with this there is a constant preoccupation that the Minister does what is correct. . . . It is also profoundly true that one has only to do absolutely nothing whatsoever in order to be floated forward on the stream. I have forgotten what day it was when I turned to my Private Secretary, George Mosley, and said "Now you must teach me how to handle all this correspondence" and he sat opposite me with his owlish eyes and said to me "Well Minister, you see there are three ways of handling it, a letter can either be answered by you personally in your own handwriting, or we can draft a personal reply for you to sign, or if the letter is not worth your answering personally we can draft an official answer". "What's an official answer?" I asked. "Well it says the Minister has received your letter and then the department replies. Anyway we'll draft all three variants" said Mr Mosley "and if you just tell us which you want." "How do I do that?" I asked. "Well you put all your 'in tray' into your 'out tray'" he said, "and if you put it in without a mark on it then we deal with it and you need never see it again." I think I've recorded that literally. I only need to transfer everything that's in my "in tray" to my "out tray" without a single mark on it to ensure that it will be dealt with. All my private office is concerned with is to see that the routine runs on, that the Minister's life is conducted in the right way.' (*The Crossman Diaries*, p. 25)

THE POWER OF THE PERMANENT SECRETARIES

Here former Labour minister Tony Benn offers a jaundiced view of the political role of senior civil servants:

'I think that the Civil Service by being professional has a great deal to offer. On the other hand their power is too great. I think that when Permanent Secretaries sit down together they're supposed to call themselves Cabinet O. O standing for official. They do think that they are the ultimate Government of the country and that Ministers may come and go, but in them resides the ultimate responsibility. I believe they think that although they recognise that Cabinets may not always uphold their view, so the problem of getting democratic control of the accumulation of power that is vested in the permanent state machine is a formidable one.' (Hugo Young and Ann Sloman, *No, Minister: An Inquiry into the Civil Service*, pp. 94–5)

CONFLICTING VIEWS OF A CIVIL SERVANT'S DUTY

In late 1979 a senior civil servant, Richard Wilding, produced an article entitled 'The professional ethic of the administrator' in which he argued that 'it is absolutely necessary to pursue today's policy with energy; it is almost equally necessary, in order to survive, to withhold from it the last ounce of commitment . . . and to invest that commitment in our particular institution, the civil service itself, with all its manifest imperfections.'

In 1985, as a consequence of the unease which had become particularly visible at the time of the Ponting case, the head of the Home Civil Service, Sir Robert Armstrong, issued a 'note of guidance on the duties and responsibilities of civil servants in relation to ministers'. In this document Sir Robert argued that

'civil servants are servants of the Crown. For all practical purposes the Crown in this context means and is represented by the government of the day. . . . [the Civil Service has] no constitutional personality or responsibility separate from the duly elected government of the day. . . . When, having been given all the relevant information and advice, the minister has taken a decision, it is the duty of civil servants loyally to carry out that decision with precisely the same energy and good will, whether they agree with it or not.'   Quoted in Richard Norton-Taylor, *The Ponting Affair*, pp. 113–15)

RECENT EXAMINATION QUESTIONS

Spend ten minutes or so planning an answer to each of the following questions. Outline answers for questions **4**, **6**, and **8** and a full tutor's answer for question **7** are provided in the next sections.

Question 1.

Why does the Left of the Labour Party regard the higher Civil Service with great suspicion?
(London, Govt and Pol. Stud., Paper 1, Jan. 1985)

Question 2.

(a) Assess the extent to which civil servants may exercise political power. (b) What are the major limitations on such power?
(AEB, Govt and Pol., Paper 1, June 1985)

Question 3.

'The British Civil Service was generally thought to be subordinate to political parties.' Is this still the case?
(London, Govt and Pol. Stud., Paper 1, June 1985)

Question 4.

Are senior civil servants too powerful or are they too pliable?
(London, Govt and Pol. Stud., June 1984)

Question 5.

'Ministers need not only the traditional forms of advice, but political advice as well; this the Civil Service is not equipped to provide.' Discuss.
(Cambridge, Pub. Aff., June 1983)

Question 6.

'The function of the State change but the Civil Service has shown itself incapable of parallel adaptation.' Do you agree?
(Cambridge, Econ. and Pub. Aff., June 1981)

Question 7.	'The British Civil Service is now the most powerful pressure group in Britain.' Discuss.
	(London, Govt and Pol. Stud., Paper 1, June 1983)
Question 8.	What restrictions are there on the freedom of British civil servants?
	(London, Govt and Pol. Stud., Paper 1, short answer question, Jan. 1983)
Question 9.	What is meant by saying that civil servants should be generalists?
	(London, Govt and Pol. Stud., Paper 1, short answer question, June 1984)
Question 10.	How important is it that senior civil servants should be politically impartial?
	(Cambridge, Pub. Aff., Nov. 1984)
Question 11.	What restrictions are there on the freedom of British civil servants?
	(London, Govt and Pol. Stud., Paper 1, short answer question, Jan. 1983)

OUTLINE ANSWERS

Q.4.

Are senior civil servants too powerful or are they too pliable?

Answer

The two propositions are not necessarily mutually exclusive. Some senior civil servants may be powerful; others may be pliable. It is perhaps the very quality of 'pliability', i.e. of being able to work with *different Governments* and to pursue *different lines of policy* from one year to the next, which gives to senior civil servants that fund of expertise which makes them such powerful advisers.

The charge that the Civil Service has excessive power is well known and most frequently comes from left-wing politicians. Such a charge can take a number of forms:

(a) Civil servants frustrate the intentions of ministers; they fail to co-operate fully in the implementation of policies with which they do not agree; they manipulate the flow of information on which ministers have to base decisions; they sometimes hold back information on which ministers may wish to base decisions; sometimes they effectively make decisions without the minister's knowledge.

(b) The bulk of the work of a ministry is in any case never seen by the minister, as it would be practically impossible for him to supervise everything that a huge government department does. Ministers are not sufficiently well equipped with political advisers to control anything more than, say, 1 per cent of the work of their departments.

(c) Civil servants are considerable repositories of information and experience and as such are often personally intimidating. It is easy for ministers to be overcome by the environment and the personalities of their departments and to become their servants rather than their masters.

These are all by now fairly conventional criticisms. None of them can be proved or refuted absolutely. The fact is that government policies *do* change from government to government and even from minister to minister. Where criticisms of Civil Service power and obstructionism have been most detailed, as in the cases of Richard Crossman and Tony Benn (see above, pp. 44–5), the counter-charge has been levelled that these accusations say more about the incapacities of the ministers themselves than about the conspiratorial activities of their civil servants. It is perhaps inevitable that radicals, whether on the left like Tony Benn and Brian Sedgemore or on the Thatcherite Right, should be highly suspicious of a Civil Service which, as Marcia Falkender has argued, is perhaps naturally inclined to adopt a centrist 'SDP-ish' stance.

This brings us to the *pliability* of senior civil servants. The fact is they know that today they may have to implement right-wing policies and tomorrow left-wing policies. The whole ethic of the Civil Service is to do as the Government bids; but the knowledge that one's work may be undone in a fairly short time may lead to rather less than total commitment in the implementation of policy. The Civil Service is indeed pliable: it knows that it must be so. But this means that civil servants, particularly senior civil servants, cannot be committed to the policies of any one government. Indeed it would be dangerous for them to become so committed because they would perhaps lose the capacity to go smoothly into reverse gear. This has led to the demand that senior Civil Service posts should become political, that is to say, they should be filled by political appointees rather than by career civil servants. Political appointees would have no tendency to pliability; their tenure of office would depend on whole-hearted enthusiasm for a specific government's policy.

Whether we consider civil servants too pliable depends on what model of politics we prefer to adopt. If we believe that success in politics is based on the *successful search for consensus*, a Civil Service which is neither fanatically left wing nor right wing is a powerful instrument in obtaining such consensus. If, on the other hand, we believe that success in politics is based on *whole-hearted conviction*, and that moderation is a euphemism for feeble compromise, then we must suspect that our senior civil servants are indeed too pliable.

Q.6.	'The functions of the State change but the Civil Service has shown itself incapable of parallel adaptation.' Do you agree?
Answer	The functions of the State have indeed changed and changed dramatically, particularly since the Second World War. The State has become a Welfare State; it has taken charge of large areas of industry

by means of nationalisation, and seeks to manipulate other parts of commerce and industry by fiscal means. During the period of these developments from the mid-1940s to the late 1970s there have been many claims that the Civil Service has not kept itself up to date with the demands which are made upon it.

A graphic statement of these complaints is the *Fulton Report* in the late 1960s which:

(a) accused the Civil Service of being dominated by the cult of the *generalist* and of not giving enough prominence to specialists in every area of government;

(b) criticised the *rigid class structure* of the Service as a cause of inflexibility and too much compartmentalisation;

(c) criticised senior civil servants for their *lack of management skills*, and their *isolation* from the outside world, both as regards their background (public school and Oxbridge arts dominated) and their attitudes;

(d) criticised the poor level of *personnel management* practised in the service.

In response, reforms in the Civil Service have been attempted though their success rate has been variable. Examples include the following:

(a) The creation of a *Civil Service Department* as recommended by Fulton to break away from the old cautious Treasury domination of the Service and to develop a coherent central management strategy. This never achieved much success: the new department never really broke away from the Treasury; its key personnel were often drawn from the Treasury and had the sort of generalist backgrounds which Fulton had so disliked. The Treasury's continuing financial control over the workings of government departments meant that the new department was never able really to supplant the Treasury as the controlling force in the Civil Service. The new department was disbanded in 1981 and many of its functions were returned to the Treasury.

(b) There has been considerable simplification of the *class structure*, but only at the very senior ranks has a so-called open structure been introduced. Below that level the generalists in the administration group are still separate from the specialists who are organised in their own groups or classes. Effectively, this still keeps the specialists away from the topmost jobs.

(c) The *Civil Service College* was established at Sunningdale to provide more up-to-date training for the Service, though the college has had much less impact than was anticipated by the Fulton reformers. It has not developed its research functions and there have been criticisms that it mounts too many courses which are too short and aimed at too low a level in the Service.

(d) A new *administration trainee scheme* was introduced, partly designed to facilitate promotion of middle-ranking executive officers into the higher ranks of the Service. Even so the very great majority of successful administration trainee applicants have still come from outside, with a continuing bias in favour of humanities graduates from Oxford and Cambridge. The Fulton recommendation that the candidates' degrees should have some direct relevance to his or her future Civil Service work has actually been rejected. All of this certainly suggests that the cult of the generalist is still thriving within the senior Civil Service.

The notion that an expanded role for the State requires a more sophisticated initial training on the part of administrators, with greater prominence being given to specialists and to financial, economic, and scientific disciplines, seems not yet to have taken root.

SHORT ANSWER

Q.8.

What restrictions are there on the freedom of British civil servants?

Answer

Some, mostly in the industrial grades, are not subject to any restrictions. About half can take part in both local and national political activities with the permission of their department, with the caveat that they must not stand as MPs or MEPs, or act in a way embarrassing to their minister. Around a quarter, in the upper ranks, *are* highly restricted as regards involvement in political activities: they cannot engage in *national* political activities and can engage in *local* political activities only with their department's permission. They cannot speak or write in public about matters of *national* political controversy. It is the Thatcher Government's policy that civil servants at GCHQ, Cheltenham, should not even belong to a trade union.

A TUTOR'S ANSWER

Q.7.

'The British Civil Service is now the most powerful pressure group in Britain.' Discuss.

Answer

Civil servants, or rather senior civil servants, certainly have plentiful, perhaps unique, opportunities to exert pressure upon governments, since they are themselves part of government. They in effect constitute the machinery which implements policy and which gathers the information upon which policy is based.

Senior civil servants have experience of administration which generally far outweighs that of their departmental ministers. This can result in the sort of power complex which is expressed in the comment attributed to one former mandarin, that 'it takes an incoming government 18 months to realise that its manifesto is unworkable: it is the job of the Permanent Secretary to reduce that period of time to six months'. Senior civil servants can also largely control the flow of departmental information to ministers. In policy formation it is often the case that knowledge is power, so that by withholding or transmitting information the senior civil servants may materially affect a minister's decisions. Senior civil servants undoubtedly have their own ideas as to what is feasible and what is desirable in the area of policy-making, and it would be unrealistic to expect them not to try to promote those ideas and to sway the minister's judgement.

What is much more difficult to prove, however, is the allegation that the Civil Service, or at least the senior ranks of the Service, act in some concerted fashion, i.e. as a kind of pressure group. Senior civil servants have often undergone similar formative experiences: there is a tendency for them to be drawn from Oxbridge graduates, and their progress through the administration has undoubtedly established common values and a certain *esprit de corps*. Nor is it impossible to imagine ways in which these shared attitudes may be refined and co-ordinated. The permanent secretaries of the various departments, for example, meet regularly in what Joe Haines has described as a third Cabinet operating behind the full Cabinet and the Shadow Cabinet (Joe Haines, *The Politics of Power*, Jonathan Cape 1977). Civil servants from several departments may be involved in servicing a particular Cabinet committee: Richard Crossman was shocked to discover that Cabinet committees were paralleled by official committees which provide them with information and whose work, so he thought, might easily 'pre-cook' the issue before the Cabinet committee (The Crossman Diaries, p. 92).

Some commentators have discerned the pervasive and conservative influence of the Treasury throughout the upper ranks of the Service. We have indeed to enquire to what purpose any Civil Service network might be put! Here the most frequent answer, and one given by radical governments, whether of the Left or the Right, is that the object of the senior civil servants is too often to stifle novelty and to safeguard the established ways of doing things. But this hardly rings true: many senior civil servants have suggested that they *prefer* to serve a minister with strong views and the ability to push those views through Cabinet. The Civil Service does not appreciate drift and uncertainty. And if we simply look at the record of governments in recent years we see at once that administrations are not the same: they have distinct characteristics of their own. For example, Ted Heath's industrial relations legislation of the early 1970s was repealed by Labour in the mid-1970s; again Labour's creation of the National Enterprise Board was reduced almost to nothing by the incoming Thatcher Government, whose policy of privatisation was in its turn a complete novelty in the context of the politics of the previous decades.

There are few signs in all this of the pervasive pressure exercised by a conspiratorial and powerful Civil Service. It is indeed the Thatcher Government whose record provides the clearest indications that we should not regard the Civil Service as an all-powerful pressure group. It is the upper ranks of the Service who have in fact felt pressurised by the Government's demands for evidence of commitment to current policy on the bureaucrats' part. This has led even the First Division Association (the 'trade union' of the higher

Civil Service) to suggest that the upper ranks of the Service should be politicised, that is, should be made subject to political appointment. Persistent rumours that the Prime Minister herself has insisted that only those likely to sympathise with her policies should be promoted to the rank of permanent secretary may or may not be true, but they do indicate quite clearly the atmosphere and the distribution of power.

Finally, the civil servants have been unable to stave off severe cuts in their own numbers: over 130,000 Civil Service jobs have been lost since Mrs Thatcher came into office. We seem therefore to see more pressure being exerted on, than by, the Civil Service. In any case, recent events might suggest that we should no longer see the Civil Service as a group with a *common* identity and objectives. Individual civil servants have allegedly transgressed against the Civil Service code by leaking controversial information to MPs and to the media, and various departments have been locked in struggle with each other and against the Treasury in a competition for diminishing resources.

A STEP FURTHER

Both the Fulton Report and the so-called 'English Report' (11th Report from the Expenditure Committee; The Civil Service) are now rapidly passing into history. Both are adequately summarised in secondary sources such as Geoffrey K. Fry. *The Changing Civil Service* (G. Allen and Unwin 1985). Anyone with a serious interest in Whitehall should look at the reports from the House of Commons Treasury and Civil Service Committee available (though not cheaply) from HMSO. These and other important reports are usually summarised in the serious press. Two important and richly informative glimpses inside the machine are provided by books by Hugo Young and Anne Sloman, *No Minister: an Inquiry into the civil Service*, (BBC 1982) and *But Chancellor: an Inquiry into the Treasury*, (BBC 1984). What happens when the machine breaks down can be read in Richard Norton-Taylor, *The Ponting Affair* (Cecil Woolf 1985).

Chapter 6

Parliamentary government: controlling the Executive

GETTING STARTED

The phrase 'parliamentary government' does not mean that Parliament actually governs. Rather it suggests that:

(a) the Government is based on Parliament in that the politicians who make up the Government are drawn from the Members of the Commons or the Lords;

(b) the Government is responsible or answerable to Parliament for its actions;

(c) the Government must subject its policy proposals to examination and debate by Parliament and must rely on Parliament to approve and pass those proposals.

In the present chapter we are concerned mainly with the second and third of these aspects of parliamentary government.

ESSENTIAL PRINCIPLES

EXECUTIVE ACCOUNTABILITY

There are three ways in which the system of *executive accountability* operates.

- Firstly, the Government has a legislative programme, that is, a number of topics on which it wants to issue laws. The items in this legislative programme must, however, be submitted to Parliament in the form of Bills, which Parliament then has the opportunity to discuss both in *principle*, that is during the Second Reading debate, and in *detail* in Standing Committee or the Report stage. Though it is rare for a Government Bill to be rejected outright it is possible that it may be substantially amended as it progresses through the Commons and the Lords.

- Secondly, the Government's policies are subjected to discussion and criticism in regular debates. In the House of Commons there are, for example, *annual* debates on the Queen's Speech, when policy for the coming session is outlined, and on the Budget. There are also twenty *Opposition days* when the Opposition may select the subject of debate, and each day there are *adjournment debates* in the last half-hour of business when the work of individual government departments may be probed.
- Thirdly, the Government is subjected to regular investigation by *individual Members of Parliament* and by *special investigative committees*, i.e. the select committees.

Individual Members

One of the prime opportunities for individual MPs to examine government policies is *Question Time*. This takes place on four days per week, for one hour on each day, during which questions may be put forward for either oral or written answer by the relevant minister. There are a number of reasons why the value of Question Time as a vehicle for the *serious* probing of government activities is often in doubt.

(a) Because of the large numbers of Members wishing to put forward questions for oral answer, very little cross-questioning is allowed. Therefore a Minister may be asked one or two embarrassing questions, but there is little likelihood that he will be further pressed on any one particular point. A sequence of questions for written answer may develop into a long-running correspondence between an MP and a minister, but this gives ministers time to organise their material and their thoughts and to deflect the most seriously embarrassing questions.
(b) Questions for oral answer may be 'planted' by supporters of the minister, thereby giving him the opportunity to make a statement, or perhaps crowding out questions likely to be more hostile.
(c) The *rota system* by which each Question Time tends to be dominated by a single minister (the ministers take it in turns to face the House) also poses problems, for it means that ministers are only infrequently available to answer questions orally.
(d) Assiduous or perhaps obsessive questioners among the Members of Parliament may dominate Question Time, crowding others out.

Select Committees

This leaves the *select committee system* as perhaps the most potent method by which Parliament can scrutinise the activities of the executive. Some select committees are venerable institutions, e.g. the Public Accounts Committee of the House of Commons was set up in the mid-nineteenth century, but most date from a major reorganisation in 1979 when a series of committees was established, each committee shadowing a particular government department. The power of the select committees appears on the surface to be quite formidable:

(a) they may *compel* production of documents and witnesses, including ministers and senior civil servants;

(b) they may issue *reports* and therefore seriously embarrass government departments.

Nevertheless, there are serious drawbacks to their effectiveness. First, the committees have very little research back-up and are, therefore, in a sense dependent on the willingness to co-operate of the departments they are investigating. Second, the committees conventionally refrain from investigating matters in which their probing might prejudice national security, however defined. Third, if, as is quite frequently the case, the investigations of a committee become entangled with party political considerations, there is a tendency for the committee to become divided along party lines and this perhaps tends to diminish the effectiveness of its report.

There are indeed several ways in which the investigation of select committees can be somewhat blunted. In contrast to the backup provided by the National Audit Office for the Public Accounts Committee, the newer 'departmental' select committees have very few research assistants available to them. This has led one Member of Parliament to comment that working on the Public Accounts Committee is like working for a professional body, while working on the departmental committees is like working for a pressure group. Again, many civil servants who appear before select committees to give evidence are not as forthcoming as some MPs may wish. In 1980, almost immediately after the creation of the departmental committees, an assistant secretary in the Civil Service Department, Edward Osmotherly, drew up the so-called *Osmotherly memorandum*. This lists in some sixty paragraphs the issues and areas in which civil servants should *not* allow themselves to be drawn out by a committee. The main areas for reticence being the *advice* which civil servants have given to ministers, matters which may be described as *in the field of public controversy*, the precise *administrative level* at which decisions have been taken, and *interdepartmental discussions*.

Despite these problems, and despite occasionally casting envious glances across the Atlantic to the much more powerful Congressional committee system of the United States, the select committees *are* beginning to chalk up some impressive achievements. These have occurred both by way of useful reports and by way of victories in occasional constitutional skirmishes with ministers who are unwilling to co-operate. Altogether, the committees are a valuable sign that there is still vitality in the House of Commons.

House of Lords

One particularly interesting aspect of parliamentary surveillance over the activities of government is the role of the *House of Lords*. This has become much more important since the 1983 elections which gave the Government such a large majority in the House of Commons. Even if embarrassed by back-bench rebellion, by disasters at Question Time, or by the close attentions of a select committee, the Government can usually rely on its whips to summon up enough support to push through legislation with comfortable majorities in the House of Commons. This has *not*, however, been the case in the House of Lords. Even if there is a Conservative majority in the Upper House, many of the Conservatives in question are of an 'old-fashioned' variety who have shown themselves disturbed by the Thatcher Government's willingness to tamper with established structures and practices. For example, in mid-1984 the Government was defeated in the Lords during the Committee stage of the so-called *Paving Bill*. This was the Bill proposing the *abolition of elections* due in 1985 to the Greater London Council (GLC) and the Metropolitan County Councils, paving the way for the total abolition of all those councils in 1986. The Lords clearly suspected that the measure was of dubious constitutional legitimacy, since at that stage *no Bill had been passed through Parliament* for the actual abolition of the councils themselves. Eventually a compromise was reached by which the Lords agreed to the scrapping of the elections on condition that the councils should remain in existence and that their members should remain in office *until* the Abolition Bill was passed and came into effect. This is just one of the many instances in which the House of Lords have harried the Government over the last few years, forcing the Government to justify its proposals at greater length and with greater clarity than was necessary in the Commons. In the same way the probings of *House of Lords select committees* have often been telling and frequently uncomfortable for the executive. It is arguable that the principal task of *Parliament* is progressively becoming one of investigation and critical debate of the proposals and the work of the *executive branch*. Such circumstances would seem to reinforce the case for Parliament retaining a rather more leisured chamber, in which a high proportion of the active Members have been appointed as a result of their long and eminent public service, thereby gaining expertise in various branches of the national life.

USEFUL APPLIED MATERIALS

QUESTION TIME

During the 1983–84 session of the House of Commons 13,386 questions were put down for oral answer by ministers, and 9,435 oral replies were made. Since this number includes replies to supplementaries from Members other than the original questioner, the figure for questions which were *actually answered by ministers* orally is estimated at just over 3,000. This gives some indication of the pressure on Question Time itself in that only one in four questions put down for oral answers will actually receive such a response. In addition 36,798 *written replies* were issued by ministers, reflecting the barrage of questions put down for written answer and with which government departments have to deal. (*HC Sessional Information Digest 1983–84*, Dec. 1984, p. 1)

Marcia Falkender (previously Marcia Williams) in her book *Downing Street in Perspective* discusses the impact upon Prime Ministers of Prime Minister's Question Time in the House of Commons.

'All in all the two fifteen-minute periods between 3.15 p.m. and 3.30 p.m. every Tuesday and Thursday when the House is sitting are dreaded by most Prime Ministers. The cut and thrust of debate is one thing; being responsible for the sole handling of some questions to which the 'wrong' answer may produce embarrassment, humiliation, triumph for the opposition or a major internal party row, or a field day for the press is enough to strain the nerves of the coolest performer.

'Harold Macmillan himself confessed that he used to feel physically sick before Prime Minister's question time; and towards the end of his last term of office Harold Wilson confessed to steadying his nerves with a small glass of brandy.' (p. 259)

THE SELECT COMMITTEE FLEX THEIR MUSCLES

In the course of 1984 and 1985 House of Commons select committees scored a number of notable victories over reluctant government ministers. In July 1984 Norman Tebbitt, Secretary of State for Trade and Industry, ordered Graham Day, the Chairman of British Shipbuilders, not to hand over reports about the nationalised industry's future to the House of Commons Select Committee on Trade and Industry. But the committee insisted on seeing the reports and eventually Mr Tebbitt had reluctantly to give way and permit them to be handed over. Again in April 1985 the House of Commons Select Committee on Public Accounts successfully insisted that Michael Heseltine, Secretary of State for Defence, should hand over to the Comptroller and Auditor-General, Sir Gordon Downey, four reports prepared for the Secretary of State by a private adviser. These reports involved the future of the royal dockyards, the equipping of the armed forces, warship procurement, and defence stockholding. (*The Times*, 18.4.85; 26.4.85)

PARTY DIVISIONS ON SELECT COMMITTEES

In June 1985 the House of Commons Select Committee on Employment, under the chairmanship of the Labour MP, Ronald Leighton, issued a report which recommended that miners who had been dismissed from their jobs during the 1984–85 pits dispute and who had not subsequently been reinstated should have their cases reviewed. The report was passed by the committee only because John Gorst, a Conservative MP, sided with Labour Members in order to guarantee its acceptance. The other Conservatives on the committee were furious: 'our confidence in the Chair is pretty thin and a lot of fences are going to have to be repaired. The final report was the culmination of two months of bitter acrimony.' One leading Conservative on the committee said of Mr Gorst: 'we will treat and consider him as if he were an Independent or minority party member on the Committee. We have spent two years trying to work with him but it is an impossibility.' (*The Times*, 28.6.85 p. 4)

In July 1985 the House of Commons Select Committee on Foreign Affairs issued its report on the sinking of the Argentinian cruiser *General Belgrano* during the Falklands War. The committee manifested a clear political split, with the four Labour members issuing their own minority report on the crucial question of whether government ministers had withheld important information about the sinking from the House of Commons. The *majority* committee report was cautiously critical, suggesting that the House had remained for too long in ignorance of information which MPs were entitled to request. It further concluded that it would have been preferable if ministers had attempted a more comprehensive statement on the sinking, but that reluctance to provide such information was a result of excessive caution rather than a desire to mislead the House. On the Government claim that the sinking of the *Belgrano* was authorised for legitimate *military* reasons and not for *political* ones, the majority committee report concluded that the House had not been misled. The *minority* Labour report, however, went much further. On the question of a political motive for the sinking of the *Belgrano*, namely an attempt to bring to nothing the Peruvian peace initiatives, the minority report stated that

'in our view the possibility of a link between the Peruvian peace initiatives and the sinking of the *Belgrano* is still an open question. The Government's suppression of evidence and giving of false evidence throughout the whole of this affair make it risky to base a firm conclusion on what they have said and that is one reason why we recommend a further enquiry.' (*The Times* (25.7.85), p. 5)

RECENT EXAMINATION QUESTIONS	It will be helpful if you spend ten minutes or so planning an answer to each question. Outline answers to questions **7**, **9** and **10** and a full Tutor's answer to question **1** are provided in the following sections.
Question 1.	What is the function of Question Time in the House of Commons? How successful is it? (Cambridge, Pub. Aff., Nov. 1985)
Question 2.	(a) In what ways are ministers held accountable to Parliament? (b) How may a back-bench MP effectively call a minister to account on a particular issue? (AEB, Govt and Pol., Nov. 1983)
Question 3.	(a) Outline the methods used by Parliament to scrutinise the Executive. (b) Assess the effectiveness of these methods. (AEB, Govt and Pol., Paper 1, June 1983)
Question 4.	What evidence is there to support the view that select committees are the most effective parliamentary method of holding the Executive accountable? (AEB, Govt and Pol., Paper 1, Nov. 1985)

Question 5.	How have the development and work of parliamentary select committees influenced the relations between Parliament and the executive? (Cambridge, Pol. and Govt, Paper 1, June 1981)
Question 6.	To what extent have back-benchers managed to regain control over the activities of government and administration in recent years? (Cambridge, Pol. and Govt, Paper 1, June 1984)
Question 7.	Should MPs be generalists or specialists? Does the answer have implications for parliamentary government? (London, Govt and Pol. Stud., Paper 1, Jan. 1983)
Question 8.	How does parliamentary government differ from any other form of representative government? (London, Govt and Pol. Stud., Paper 1, short answer question, June 1985)
Question 9.	Define the word 'control' in the phrase 'parliamentary control of Government'. (London, Govt and Pol. Stud., Paper 1, short answer question, Jan. 1981)
Question 10.	The function of Parliament is not to govern the country but to control the Government. How far have recent changes in the committee system of the House of Commons enhanced Parliament's capacity to perform this function? (JMB, Brit. Govt and Pol., June 1982)

OUTLINE ANSWERS

Q.7.

Should MPs be generalists or specialists? Does the answer have implications for parliamentary government?

Answer

The answer to the first part of this question is inextricably bound up with the answer to the second part, because whether we require MPs to be generalists or specialists will depend very largely on the precise type of parliamentary government which we require. There are several elements involved in parliamentary government:

(a) Government is drawn from Parliament.
(b) Government needs to have its legislative proposals processed and legitimised by Parliament.
(c) The operation of government is open to parliamentary scrutiny and the Government is accountable to Parliament.

In the light of these elements we can see that there are some advantages to each of the possible roles of MPs, i.e. as generalists and as specialists.

1. The *generalist* is better able to play an active part in debates which range over the whole spectrum of government policy. He is able to deal fairly competently with a wide range of problems faced by his constituents, and to raise a diversity of issues at Question Time. He can help in his party's policy-formation process by serving on any one of a number of party committees. He is a useful Member of Parliament in that he is able to take part in a wide range of standing and select committees. He has a broad sympathy for political issues.

   These are the sort of defences which are brought forward in support of the predominantly generalist role which MPs occupy today. Such a role is well adapted to a style of parliamentary government in which Parliament takes its legislative function seriously, attempts wide-ranging debates, and attempts to scrutinise the operation of government. But there are those who argue that the effectiveness of Parliament as investigative body, scrutiniser of government legislation, and debating body would be greatly enhanced if back-bench MPs were to specialise much more than they do.

2. If MPs were to *specialise* in certain areas of policy or in certain types of problems, then their effectiveness as members of standing and select committees would probably increase. A detailed working knowledge of specific areas of government would give MPs greater authority in discussion on matters involving legislation or administration. With a diversity of specialisms throughout Parliament, there would always be a small number of MPs able to contribute more effectively to any given debate.

   The effect of greater specialisation would probably be to shift many of the balances which currently exist between the different roles of Parliament. For instance, the specialists would be most at home in committees, and this might shift much of the emphasis *away* from the floor of the House of Commons. Debate would cease to be so important if most of the work were actually being done by highly specialised MPs in committee. Then MPs might lose much of their capacity to deal with the problems of their constituents in that many of these problems would be in areas with which they were no longer familiar. There would thus be an increased tendency for MPs to hand over such work to other bodies, for example the Parliamentary Commissioner for Administration. It might also become more difficult to staff those committees which did not coincide with the interests of a large number of specialist MPs. As a result the range of investigative and scrutinising functions of Parliament might diminish.

SHORT ANSWER

Define the word 'control' in the phrase 'parliamentary control of government'.

Answer

Control involves Parliament ensuring that the Government's suggestions and firm recommendations for policy are made public. This could take the form of publishing Green and White Papers, Bills and statutory instruments. Control also involves ensuring that such suggestions and recommendations are subjected to critical debate and that once policy is outlined and implemented that ministers are made answerable to Parliament for that policy, particularly at Question Time. Control also involves Parliament in scrutinising the processes of government, and in publishing the reports on that scrutiny. Ultimately control may involve the rejection by Parliament of the Government's proposals and the censuring of its conduct of administration.

Q.10.	The function of Parliament is not to govern the country but to control the Government. How far have recent changes in the committee system of the House of Commons enhanced Parliament's capacity to perform this function?

Answer	(a) The major development in select committees in recent years has been the inauguration of the so-called 'departmental' select committees in 1979, i.e. committees which investigate the affairs of a single department.
	(b) This development of departmental committees has enabled greater attention to be focused on the work of individual ministries. As a result any given area of administration is more consistently subject to investigation than was previously the case.
	(c) The new departmental system has encouraged greater specialisation among committee members and consequently perhaps greater sharpness and perceptiveness during committee investigations. This has helped committees to become more widely known and in particular to receive much greater media attention in recent years than was hitherto the case.
	(d) Some of the old select committees which disappeared in 1979 are nevertheless sorely missed, for example the Select Committee on Nationalised Industries. While the sponsoring department of each public corporation is now under separate investigation, there is no committee which has a *regular overview* of the whole field of nationalised industries. This is seen by many to be a defect of the present system. The Thatcher Government's process of privatisation has however narrowed the range of industries covered by the public corporations.
	(e) The new committees have been subject to a number of restrictions on their effectiveness. When an issue under investigation is especially contentious and of a potentially party political nature, the committees have tended to split along party lines. This perhaps detracts from the effectiveness of their reports. Cases in point include the reports of the Employment Committee on the treatment of suspended miners following the 1984–85 miners strike and of the Foreign Affairs Committee on

the sinking during the Falklands War of the Argentinian cruiser the *General Belgrano*. When the new select committees approach the more contentious matters it is perhaps inevitable that they should begin to appear as extensions of the floor of the House.

(f) There are still several areas of investigation which are effectively closed to the select committees. For example, matters relating to security are by convention avoided by the select committees. Select committee investigation may also be impeded by a lack of access to information. The Ponting case starkly revealed how the Foreign Affairs Committee had been denied access to a good many documents of importance during its investigation of the sinking of the *General Belgrano*.

(g) In the final analysis there are obvious limits to the control which can be achieved by committees which, in party political matters, tend to split along party lines, are denied access to potentially important material, and have to report to a House of Commons which is subject to the whip system.

A TUTOR'S ANSWER

Q.1.

What is the function of Question Time in the House of Commons? How successful is it?

Answer

There are many possible functions for Question Time. At its simplest it is an opportunity for back-benchers to gather information from ministers, sometimes of a straightforward factual nature. It could, however, be argued that the provision of factual information is not properly a function of Question Time itself (i.e. the period of a little under an hour allocated to questions each day from Monday to Thursday). Questions which merely seek factual information could be submitted in the form of questions for written rather than oral answer.

If we assume that the essence of Question Time is the opportunity for MPs to ask oral questions, and within limits to follow them up, then we can see that its principal function is political; it represents an opportunity for MPs to call ministers to account. In this respect Question Time does not appear to be a wholly successful exercise: MPs are *not* allowed to cross-examine ministers at length, as this would cut down the time available for other questions. Each MP who does ask a question *is* allowed to put in a supplementary or follow-up question, but the content of this will often have been guessed by the minister or by his civil servants, who will have been allocated the task of going over likely areas for questions in advance. The Speaker may also allow one or two additional questions, but these opportunities for questioning the minister tend to be presented to opposition front-bench spokesmen or, in the case of Prime Minister's Question Time, to the Leader of the Opposition. They often become the occasion for predictable party political statements rather than authentic questions. Question Time is therefore a highly ritualised form of verbal combat.

The rota system, by which departmental ministers take it in turns to receive questions, also means that MPs' opportunities to put ministers under pressure are restricted. It is very unusual for the minister who is head of the rota on a specific day to exhaust *all* of the questions directed at him, and it follows that each day is in practice devoted to questions for a *single* department. It will usually be some weeks before that department is at the top of the rota once more. Questions which have not been answered orally on the department's allotted day and which came up for answer between days on which the department is on top of the rota, will be given a written reply. Thus the opportunity for supplementaries and for further probing is removed. Only about one-third of the questions which are actually put down for oral reply receive one. The rest get a written answer.

There are many other possible functions of Question Time. For example, it is an opportunity for ministers to answer 'planted' questions, i.e. questions which enable them to make a statement. It is an opportunity for back-bench MPs to get themselves noticed: there are a few persistent questioners who seem more interested in getting into Hansard or in proving a point about their work-rate to their constituency party than in the quest for knowledge! Question time as it operates at present seems to be an uneasy compromise. It allows MPs to question ministers, but not *too* probingly. Governments with heavy legislative programmes are often hard pressed for parliamentary time. Members of such governments, together with those back-benchers frustrated by the constraints of Question Time, might be prepared to see it abolished. Many government ministers, and in particular Prime Ministers, have claimed to find Question Time a considerable ordeal, though for them it may have appeared more of a test of *political* style and wit than a serious examination of government policies. We should remember that although Question Time is probably the most celebrated of the means by which the Executive is called to account, it is not, since the introduction of a wide range of select committees, the only or even the most impressive means. Perhaps its principal function is as a symbolic affirmation, constantly repeated, of the *principle* of the accountability of government to Parliament.

A STEP FURTHER

The media are becoming increasingly conscious of Parliament's efforts to control the Executive. Consequently reports by parliamentary select committees and reports of clashes at Question Time are becoming quite common in the more serious newspapers and periodicals. Obviously it is better to read Hansard, the record of events in the Commons, and to read the actual text of select committee reports, but these are not easily available outside the very biggest public libraries and college libraries. The works by Walkland and Ryle and Philip Norton referred to at the end of the following chapter are useful for the topic of parliamentary government. By far the best single source is represented by the Radio 4 programmes 'Today in Parliament' and 'Yesterday in Parliament', which are broadcast in the late evening and early morning respectively when Parliament is sitting.

For some specialist studies see D. Englefield, *Commons Select Committees: Catalysts for Progress*? (Longman 1984), and *Parliament in the 1980s*, ed. Philip Norton, (Basil Blackwell 1985) especially the chapters by the editor on back-bench independence in the 1980s, and that by Stephen J. Downs, on the development of the select committees.

Chapter 7

MPs: legislators or lobby-fodder?

GETTING STARTED	It will be helpful to clarify some of the basic terminology of House of Commons procedures and institutions before we examine the role of the MP.
1. Committees	Members of Parliament will normally be involved in at least two sorts of Commons committee. *Standing committees* consider legislation once it has passed its Second Reading stage. Members of standing committees are appointed by the *Committee of Selection*. The Committee of Selection ensures that the parties are represented in proportion to their strength in the House and tries to ensure that the backgrounds and interests of the Members appointed are appropriate to the piece of legislation under consideration. *Select committees* divide into two main categories: those which scrutinise the *work of government* and those which deal with the *domestic arrangements of the House* such as catering and the library.
2. Bills	These fall into several categories, the most common of which is the Government-sponsored *Public Bill*. A *Private Bill* is introduced on behalf of some specific group or area such as a local authority. A *Private Member's Bill* should not be confused with a Private Bill for it is in fact a Public Bill which is introduced by a back-bencher rather than by a member of the Government.
3. Whips	A whip refers either to a member of a party who has the responsibility for maintaining discipline within the parliamentary party or to the instructions to attend debates (and by implication to vote) which the whips' office of each party issues to its MPs. The instructions are underlined once, twice or three times in an ascending scale of urgency.

ESSENTIAL PRINCIPLES

PRESSURES ON A MEMBER OF PARLIAMENT

The House of Commons presents a puzzling spectacle. Some of the country's most able and ambitious men and women struggle, sometimes for years, to gain admission to it as Members of Parliament. Yet, it is frequently reviled by academic observers as a place of little consequence in the process of government – a place in which legislation is not made but simply rubber-stamped by groups of subservient MPs. Perhaps we should start this examination of the Members of Parliament by pointing out that the pressures on them are indeed enormous.

Party pressures

First, there are *party pressures*. Once elected, a Member of Parliament becomes subject to the party whip-system. Members who defy the whips occasionally may simply escape with firm lectures on the need to toe the line. More persistent defiance may result in the withdrawal of the whip, in which case the MP is deprived of all party assistance. In extreme cases, the MP may be expelled from the parliamentary party. Pressure from the whips' office is, however, only part of the story.

Constituency pressures

Second, there are *constituency pressures* which the MP must take into account, particularly those from his constituency party. These pressures have in recent years become especially acute for MPs on the Labour side of the House since they now have to face mandatory reselection as candidates before every election. Many Labour MPs have found it difficult, and some impossible, to secure adoption as the candidate in the constituency which they have served for years. As well as ensuring that they are well regarded by their *constituency parties*, MPs also have the task of ensuring that their *constituents* think well of them. Even if they do not intend to seek re-election themselves they have the task of maintaining their party's interest in the constituency, and consequently they must attempt at all times to square the needs and aspirations of important sections of their electorate with the requirements of the party leadership.

Party advancement pressures

Third, there are *party advancement pressures* for the MP who has ambitions to climb the ladder into Government. The MP who comes into this category will also have to ensure that his electoral base is secure. Yet at the same time he will have to tread the parliamentary tightrope of appearing basically loyal and constructive while being just outspoken enough to bring himself to the attention of the party leaders, suggesting that he is more than a 'yes man'.

Occupational pressures

Fourth, there are *occupational pressures*. Most MPs are subject to more than party, constituency and party advancement pressures. Some still refuse to see membership of the sovereign body of the kingdom as a full-time occupation, and retain jobs around which they fit their parliamentary work. The justification for this is generally that it prevents them from leading too cloistered a life in Westminster and keeps them in touch with the real world. Again, many MPs (in 1985 at least 140) become parliamentary consultants to commercial organisations or to professional and pressure groups. In return for a retainer, which very often runs into many thousands of pounds per year, the MP will undertake to keep his organisation informed of parliamentary developments which may affect it. The growth of business consultancies in particular has been condemned by one Labour MP as parliamentary political prostitution.

FUNCTIONS OF THE MP

The party leadership, the constituency party, constituents, and outside sponsoring organisations all, therefore, compete for the MP's time and attention and loyalty. Most MPs must also fit a domestic life into this complex of relationships and pressures. Perhaps these often competing demands would be less stressful if the MP's basic task was simple, but it is not. He is expected to perform many functions; he is a *channel of complaint against authority* when acting on behalf of his constituents, sometimes raising matters in the House, sometimes passing complaints on to the Parliamentary Commissioner for Administration, and sometimes attempting to deal informally with the subject-matter of complaints, often through contacts with ministers. He is a Member of a House which *debates government policy* and the great issues of the day, which *passes legislation*, or at least goes through the various motions of passing legislation, and which *investigates the way in which government is conducted*.

In addition, all back-bench MPs can expect to find themselves periodically selected to *serve on the standing committees*: but as in practice the whip system applies in standing committees there is little opportunity to achieve amendments of which the Government does not approve. Also, because standing committees are broken up and their Members returned to the general pool of MPs after the consideration of a single Bill, there is little opportunity for MPs to build up a particular specialisation in any one form of legislation. The MP will generally take part in the investigative function of the House by way of *membership of a select committee* and by way of *addressing questions to ministers at Question Time*. Both of these topics have been examined in the previous chapter.

Debates are, of course, carried out, if they are of any significance, under the watchful eye of the whips and it has been well said that speeches of Gladstonian power or Disraeli-like wit may fail to move a single vote. On the other hand, rebellions are no longer unknown: small numbers of MPs quite regularly vote against the wishes of their party whips and can do so in relative safety if they have the backing of their constituency parties. A concomitant of this is that governments no longer fail if they are defeated on even quite major issues: both the 1974–79 Labour Government and the 1979–83 Conservative Government suffered defeat on budget motions but did not resign in consequence. Even the 1983 Conservative Government, with a huge majority in Parliament over all other parties, faced a

Conservative back-bench revolt of such dimensions that the proposal by the Education Secretary, Sir Keith Joseph, to increase parental contributions to student grants was radically revised and scaled down.

What other opportunity does the MP have to make some sort of an impact upon the life of the Commons? He may try to *legislate* by means of a *Private Member's Bill*, but these are generally squeezed into the recesses of the parliamentary timetable. Statistically the chance of a Private Member's Bill getting through *all* its stages and receiving Royal Assent is very limited. Many of those that do, have been covertly taken up and helped along by the Government. In addition the MP may bring forward a *Private Member's Motion* for debate. But once again these are very strictly limited. He may raise an issue relating to the work of a *specific department* during the *adjournment debate*, but this by definition takes place only in the last half-hour of business, and consequently the opportunities for a probing discussion or indeed for being heard by many other MPs are very limited.

Perhaps the real problem for MPs is not that they have no powers, but that they try to exercise *too many* responsibilities, generally with inadequate backing. For most, a secretary, a temporary research assistant, and access to the House of Commons Library and the research resources of their party is all the back-up they can expect. Not that there is very much danger that the House of Commons will lose its allure. An institution with centuries of achievement behind it will continue to be attractive. Because the road to government office lies through the House of Commons it will continue to call the able and the ambitious.

USEFUL APPLIED MATERIALS

ASPECTS OF A BACK-BENCHER'S PARLIAMENTARY TIMETABLE

The following documents (pp. 69–74) give some idea of the *parliamentary* calls upon the time and attention of one MP (in this case, a Conservative back-bencher), during the course of one week. First come two pages of notices from the *party whip*, requesting, and in some case requiring, the MP's attendance at divisions. Then come two pages of notices of *party* (i.e. not parliamentary) *committees*, and finally come some *all-party notices of meetings*, *events*, etc. of general interest. These materials omit references to the work of standing and select committees which further add to the pressures on an MP.

The House will meet at

On MONDAY, 25th November, 1985, at 2.30 p.m. for Energy Questions.

Agriculture Bill: 2nd Reading, Money and Ways and Means Resolutions.
                    (Money Resolution EXEMPTED BUSINESS for 45 minutes)

Motion relating to the Education (Mandatory Awards) Regulations.
                    (EXEMPTED BUSINESS for 1½ hours)

Divisions will take place, and your attendance at 9.30 p.m. for 10.00 p.m.

and until the business is concluded is essential unless you have registered

a firm pair or a bisque.

        NOTE: A Motion to suspend the ten o'clock rule for the Ways
              and Means Resolution will be moved at 10.00 p.m.

On TUESDAY, 26th November, at 2.30 p.m. for Defence Questions.

Debate on a Government Motion to approve the agreement between the Government
of the United Kingdom of Great Britain and Northern Ireland and the
Government of the Republic of Ireland, November 1985 (Cmnd.9657) (1st day)

Debate on a Government Motion to take note of European Community Document
No. 11118/83 as amended by 10681/84, a proposal for a directive on parental
leave and leave for family reasons and the explanatory memorandum of the
Department of Employment dated 12th January 1984 and 18th January 1985.
                    (EXEMPTED BUSINESS for 1½ hours)

Divisions will take place, and your attendance at 9.30 p.m. for 10.00 p.m.

and until the business is concluded is essential unless you have registered

a firm pair or a bisque.

On WEDNESDAY, 27th November, at 2.30 p.m. for Trade and Industry Questions.

Conclusion of the debate on a Government Motion to approve the Agreement
between the Government of the United Kingdom of Great Britain and Northern
Ireland and the Government of the Republic of Ireland, November 1985
(Cmnd. 9657)

Important divisions will take place, and your attendance at 9.30 p.m. for

10.00 p.m. is essential.

Northern Ireland (Loans) Bill: 2nd Reading and Money Resolution.
                    (Money Resolution EXEMPTED BUSINESS for 45 minutes)

Divisions will take place, and your continued attendance until the business

is concluded is essential, unless you have registered a firm pair or a bisque.

        NOTE: A Motion to suspend the ten o'clock
                rule will be moved at 10.00 p.m.

                                    PLEASE TURN OVER

69

On <u>THURSDAY, 28th November</u>, at 2.30 p.m. for Treasury Questions.

Housing (Scotland) Bill: 2nd Reading and Money Resolution.
                    (Money Resolution EXEMPTED BUSINESS for 45 minutes)

Divisions will take place, and your attendance at 9.30 p.m. for 10.00 p.m.
━━━
and until the Money Resolution is obtained is essential unless you have
━━━
registered a firm pair or a bisque.
━━━━━━━━━━━━━━━━━━━━━━━━━━━━━━━━━━━━

On <u>FRIDAY, 29th November</u>, at 9.30 a.m.

PRIVATE MEMBERS' MOTIONS

1. Dr. N. Godman - Child Abuse
2. Mr. Andrew Rowe - The County of Kent
3. Rt. Hon. Terence Higgins - Transport Safety

Your attendance is requested.

....

On <u>Monday, 2nd December</u>, at 2.30 p.m. for Transport Questions.

Dockyard Services Bill: 2nd Reading and Money Resolution.
                    (Money Resolution EXEMPTED BUSINESS for 45 minutes)

There will be a 2-line whip at 9.30 p.m. for 10.00 p.m.
━━

21. 11. 85   JOHN WAKEHAM

<u>NOTE</u>:

BALLOT FOR PRIVATE MEMBERS' MOTIONS

After Questions on Wednesday, 27th and Thursday, 28th November, the Ballot
will be taken for Private Members' Motions to be debated on Friday, 13th
and Monday, 16th December.

Members are reminded that arrangements of Party Committees and
the proceedings which take place in these Committees are secret.

MONDAY, 25th NOVEMBER

5 p.m. Room 18   WEST COUNTRY MEMBERS   (Mr. Tony Speller)
Election of a Chairman, 2 Vice-Chairmen (Avon/Somerset
ELECTION   and Devon/Cornwall) and Secretary.
Meeting at 5.15 p.m. The Chief Executive and members of the
South West Water Authority will attend. Members are invited
to dine as guests of the SWWA in the Harcourt Room. Names to
Tony Speller.

5.15 p.m. Room 9   LEGAL   (Mr. David Ashby)
Election of Officers.   (Mr. Humfrey Malins)
ELECTION   Please note that on 2nd Dec. the Lord Chancellor
will attend.

5.30 p.m. Room 13   ARTS AND HERITAGE   (Dr. John Blackburn)
Mr. Colin Tweedy, Director of the Association (Mr. Alan Howarth)
for Business Sponsorship of the Arts, will attend.

6 p.m. Room 12   HOME AFFAIRS   (Mr. John Wheeler)
Election of Officers.   (Mr. Teddy Taylor)
ELECTION

TUESDAY, 26th NOVEMBER

NO MEETING   SHIPPING AND SHIPBUILDING SUB-CTTEE   (Mr. Jonathan Sayeed)
Election of Officers on Tuesday, 3rd December.
Nominations to Mr. Austen's Office by noon on Monday, 2nd December.

4.15 p.m. Room 10   FOREIGN AND COMMONWEALTH AFFAIRS   (Mr. Andrew MacKay)
Sir Anthony Parsons, former Ambassador to the UN, will speak on
his perception of HMG foreign policy over the last six years and
give his thoughts for the future.

4.30 p.m. Room 11   HEALTH AND SOCIAL SERVICES   (Mr. Roy Galley)
ELECTION   Election of Officers.   (Mr. Tony Favell)

4.45 p.m. Room 14   AGRICULTURE, FISHERIES AND FOOD   (Mr. Edward Leigh)
ELECTION   Election of Officers.   (Mr. Robert Jackson)
Nominations to Mr. Austen's Office by noon on Monday, 25th November.
Mr. Denis Chamberlain, former editor of Farmers' Weekly, will attend.

5 p.m. Room 6   TRADE AND INDUSTRY   (Mr. Richard Hickmet)
ELECTION   Election of Officers.   (Mr. Bowen Wells)
Sir Lawrie Barratt, Chairman and Chief Executive, Barratt Developments plc
will discuss Inner City Problems and ways of stimulating home ownership.

5 p.m. Room 19   MEDIA   (Mr. Roger Gale)
Election of Officers on Tuesday, 3rd December.
Nominations to Mr. Austen's Office by noon on Monday, 2nd December.

5 p.m. Room 18   NORTH WEST MEMBERS   (Mr. Alistair Burt)
ELECTION   Election of Officers.
Nominations to Mr. Austen's Office by noon on Monday, 25th November.
Discussion on the future of Manchester Airport.

5.30 p.m. Room 16   URBAN AND NEW TOWN AFFAIRS   (Mr. David Gilroy Bevan)
    (Mr. Warren Hawksley)

6 p.m. Room 9   AVIATION
Election of a Joint Secretary.   (Mr. Gerald Howarth)
ELECTION   Nominations to Mr. Austen's Office by noon on Monday, 25th November.

Sir Norman Payne, Chairman, British Airports Authority, will attend.

6 p.m. Room 14   FINANCE   (Mr. A. Beaumont-Dark)
ELECTION   Election of Officers.   (Mr. Tim Yeo)

6 p.m. Room W4   WELSH MEMBERS   (Mr. Gwilym Jones)
Representatives of Community Service Volunteers,
Wales, will attend.

(PLEASE TURN OVER)

COMMITTEES (Continued)

WEDNESDAY, 27th NOVEMBER

4.15 p.m. Room 10	**DEFENCE** (Dr. Keith Hampson)
ELECTION	Election of a Vice-Chairman. (Mr. Tony Marlow)
	Nominations to Mr. Austen's Office by <u>noon on Tuesday, 26th Nov.</u>

5 p.m. Room 17   SCOTTISH CONSERVATIVE AND UNIONIST MEMBERS   (Mr. Albert McQuarrie)
  ELECTION   Election of Officers.
                     Nominations to Mr. Austen's Office by <u>noon on Tuesday, 26th Nov.</u>
                     The Chairman of the CBI in Scotland will attend.

5 p.m. Room 5   EUROPEAN AFFAIRS   (Mr. John Taylor)
                     Sir Henry Plumb, MEP, will attend. Strasbourg Report.

5 p.m. Room 9   EDUCATION   (Mr. Gerald Bowden)
                                                  (Mr. Peter Bruinvels)

5.30 p.m. Room 11   GREATER LONDON MEMBERS   (Mr. Martin Stevens)
  ELECTION   Election of Officers.
                     Nominations to Mr. Austen's Office by <u>noon on Tuesday, 26th Nov.</u>

                     <u>Rt. Hon. Kenneth Baker will attend.</u>

5.30 p.m. Room 12   CONSTITUTIONAL AFFAIRS   (Mr. Jerry Hayes)
                     Col. Professor G.I.A.D.Draper will speak on ' The security of
                     the State and a possible legal solution.'

6 p.m. Room 9   SMALLER BUSINESSES   (Mr. Henry Bellingham)
                     Policy discussion.

6 p.m. Room 7   TOURISM SUB-CTTEE   (Mr. John Butterfill)
                     Mr. Clive Derby CBE, Chief Executive of the   (Mr. Roger Gale)
                     British Hotels, Restaurants, and Caterers' Assoc. will attend.
                     (9 a.m.- 2.30 p.m. Tour of Heathrow Airport by Cttee followed by
                       lunch with BA's Chief Executive, Colin Marshall.)

6.15 p.m. Room 10   PARTY ORGANISATION   (Mr. Phillip Oppenheim)
  ELECTION   Election of Officers.   (Mr. Tony Favell)
                     Nominations to Mr. Austen's Office by <u>noon on Tuesday, 26th Nov.</u>

THURSDAY, 28th NOVEMBER

4 p.m. Room 7   EMPLOYMENT   (Mrs. V. Bottomley)
                                               (Mr. Robert Jones)

4.15 p.m. Room 5   ENERGY   (Mr. Michael Portillo)
                     Election of a Vice-Chairman and a Joint Secretary.
  ELECTION   Nominations to Mr. Austen's Office by <u>noon on Wednesday, 27th Nov.</u>

                     The British Wind Energy Association will give a presentation.

4.15 p.m. Room 16   JOINT MEETING   (Mr. Michael Brown)
                     NORTHERN IRELAND   (Mr. Henry Bellingham)
                     TRADE AND INDUSTRY   (Mr. Richard Hickmet)
                     Mr. John Parker, Chairman of Harland and   (Mr. Bowen Wells)
                     Wolff plc, Shipbuilders and Engineers, will attend,
                     with a delegation of management and unions.

4.15 p.m. Room 18   TRANSPORT   (Mr. Conal Gregory)
                     <u>Rt. Hon. Nicholas Ridley will attend.</u>   (Mr. Gary Waller)

5 p.m. Room 6   ENVIRONMENT   (Mr. Chris Chope)
                                              (Mr. Tim Wood)

6 p.m. Room 14   CONSERVATIVE AND UNIONIST MEMBERS   (Sir John Osborn)
                                                (Dame Jill Knight)

<u>PARTY NOTICE</u>

<u>BRIEFS.</u> Briefing will be available in the Whips' Office on Agriculture Bill; Student Grant (25th
       EEC Directive on Parental Leave (26th); Housing (Scotland) (28th); and Northern
       Ireland (Anglo-Irish Agreement) (NI (85)5) already published.

21.11.85

ALL PARTY NOTICES

MONDAY, 25th NOVEMBER

4.45 p.m. Room 8	ANGLO-IRISH PARLIAMENTARY GROUP H.E. The Irish Ambassador, Mr. Noel Dorr, will attend.	(Mr.M.Mates) (Mr.P.Duffy)
5.30 p.m. Room W4	BRITISH-TAIWAN PARLIAMENTARY GROUP A.G.M. and Election of Officers.	(Sir P.Wall) (Mr.L.Abse)
6 p.m. Room W4	BRITISH-SOUTH AFRICAN PARLIAMENTARY GROUP A.G.M. and Election of Officers followed by a report from Mr. Jerry Wiggin, MP and others on their recent visit to S.A.	(Mr.J.Carlisle)

TUESDAY, 26th NOVEMBER

4.30 p.m. Room W4	BRITISH-ISRAEL PARLIAMENTARY GROUP A.G.M. and Election of Officers. Mr. Moshe Raviv, Minister Plenipotentiary, Israeli Embassy, will speak.	(Mr.M.Latham) (Mr.R.C.Brown)
5 p.m. Dining Room B	ALL PARTY FOOD AND HEALTH FORUM Speaker, Prof. Geoffrey Rose, Prof. of Epidemiology University of London on "Food Policy, the next five years".	(Mr.M.Morris) (Lord Ennals)
5 p.m. Jubilee Room	BRITISH-AMERICAN PARLIAMENTARY GROUP A Report back by those Members who visited the U.S. in September. Drinks will be served.	(Sir G.Johnson Smith) (Mr.E.Deakins)
5 p.m. Room 17	PARLIAMENTARY FOOTBALL GROUP A.G.M. and Election of Officers.	(Mr.P.Bottomley) (Mr.K.Barron)
5.30 p.m. Room 20	ALL PARTY DISABLEMENT GROUP Speakers on Human Fertilisation and Embryology Research.	(Mr.J.Hannam) (Rt.Hon.J.Ashley)
6 p.m. Room W1	PARLIAMENTARY GROUP ON POPULATION AND DEVELOPMENT A.G.M.	(Mr.S.Dorrell) (Mr.E.Deakins)
7 p.m. Room 5	ALL PARTY GROUP ON NON-PROFIT MAKING CLUBS A.G.M. and Election of Officers. Nominations to Lord Brooks by 6 p.m. on Monday, 25th November.	(Mr.G.Knight)

WEDNESDAY, 27th NOVEMBER

1.30 p.m. Room W2	INTERMEDIATE FRENCH CLASS	(Mr.R.Galley)
5 p.m. Jubilee Room	PARLIAMENTARY MINERALS GROUP "Tax Relief on Mining Capital Allowances" speaker Alan E. Willingdale, Group Tax Manager, B.P. Company, plc.	(Mr.T.Skeet) (Rt.Hon.A.Williams)
5.30 p.m. Room 6	ALL PARTY GROUP FOR THE CHEMICAL INDUSTRY "Additives in Food".	(Dr.M.Clark) (Mr.T.Garrett)
6 p.m. Room 21	ALL PARTY RACING AND BLOODSTOCK INDUSTRIES COMMITTEE Election of Officers. The Senior Steward, Deputy Senior Steward and the Secretary of the Jockey Club will attend.	(Hon.C.Morrison)

THURSDAY, 28th NOVEMBER

1.30 p.m. Room W1	GERMAN LANGUAGE CLASS	(Mr.P.Rost)
3.30 p.m. Room 11	ALL PARTY GROUP ON RACE RELATIONS Leading experts on Sickle Cell Disease will speak.	(Mr.G.Lawler) (Miss C.Short)
3.45 p.m. Room W1	ALL PARTY TRUSTEE SAVINGS BANK GROUP A.G.M.	(Mr.E.Cockeram)
4 p.m. Room W5	ADVANCED FRENCH LANGUAGE CLASS Newcomers and occasional attenders welcome.	(Lord Moyne) (Mr.D.Anderson)
4.30 p.m. Room 19	ALL PARTY GROUP FOR PENSIONERS JOINT MEETING WITH PARLIAMENTARY PANEL FOR PERSONAL SOCIAL SERVICES	(Mr.J.Hannam) (Mr.A.Rowe) (Mr.A.Bowden)

MASS LOBBY   WEDNESDAY, 27th NOVEMBER at 2.30 p.m. about 1,500 members of the
Association of University Teachers.

EXHIBITION   By British Conference and Exhibition Centres Export Council in the Upper Waiting
Hall on   25th November at 6.30 p.m.   Opening by Rt. Hon. Lord Young of Graffham,
Secretary of State for Employment.   (Mr.I.Grist)

PLEASE TURN OVER

OKEHAMPTON BY-PASS EXHIBITION

An Exhibition and reception sponsored by the Department of Transport setting
out the background to the legislation on the building of the Okehampton By-Pass is being
held on Tuesday, 26th November between 5 p.m. and 7 p.m. at the Department of Transport,
2 Marsham Street, London SW1.   A Minister will be present to assist Members' queries, and
interested M.P.s and Peers should arrive at the South Tower, Entrance 2 where they will be
directed to the First Floor.

CHURCH SERVICE

The Moderator of the General Assembly of the Church of Scotland, the Rt. Rev. Dr. David
M. B. A. Smith MA. BD, will conduct a service for Scottish Parliamentarians in the Crypt
Chapel on Tuesday, 26th November at 11 a.m.   The lesson will be read by the Secretary of
State for Scotland, the Rt. Hon. George Younger, TD. DL. M.P.   All welcome.

MEMORIAL SERVICE LORD BAKER

A Memorial Service for the late Lord Baker will be held in Great St. Mary's Church,
Cambridge, on Saturday, 30th November at 2.30 p.m.

BRITISH GROUP I.P.U.

A delegation comprising of four Members will visit the Somali Democratic Republic from
Monday, 20 th January to Monday, 27th January 1986.   Members wishing to apply for this
delegation are requested to notify the Secretary, British Group, IPU IN WRITING NOT LATER
THAN 12 NOON on TUESDAY, 3rd DECEMBER 1985.   Successful applicants will be notified
after Mr. Speaker's selection on Tuesday, 10th December and a briefing will be offered on
Wednesday, 18th December at 12.30 p.m. in the IPU Room, Westminster Hall.

DEFENCE VISIT

A visit to the Falklands for M.P.s and Peers, the programme will include civil and
military components.   Depart 9th December and return early on 18th December.
Names please as soon as possible to Hon. Archie Hamilton, M.P.

INDO-BRITISH PARLIAMENTARY GROUP

The High Commissioner for India, Dr. Alexander, has invited members of the Indo-British
Parliamentary Group for a curry lunch at the Indian High Commission, India House, Aldwych,
London WC2, at 12.30 for 1 p.m. on Wednesday, 18th December.   If you wish to attend please
contact Mr. Toby Jessel, M.P. joint Secretary.   NEW MEMBERS WELCOME.

HISTORY OF PARLIAMENT TRUST

The five completed books on the History of Parliament are
available to M.P.s at the following concessionary rate (70% of normal prices):
1509 - 1558 £85.   1558 - 1603 £85.   1660 - 1690 £85.   1715 - 1754 £35.   1754 - 1790 £58.
Further particulars from the Chairman Mr. Robert Rhodes James, M.P.

ADJOURNMENTS

MONDAY, 25th NOVEMBER	Mr.P.Thurnham.	Government policy towards the adoption of handicapped children.
TUESDAY, 26th NOVEMBER	Mr.M.Madden.	Bradford rail services.
WEDNESDAY, 27th NOVEMBER	Mr.G.Gardiner.	The capital programme for voluntary aided schools - St Bede's school, Redhill.
THURSDAY, 28th NOVEMBER	Mr.D.Campbell-Savours.	The future of Matthew Brown following the Monopolies and Mergers Commission Enquiry.
FRIDAY, 29th NOVEMBER	Sir J.Ridsdale.	Health services in North East Essex.
MONDAY, 2nd DECEMBER	Mr.A.Kirkwood.	Future development of the Forestry Industry in South East Scotland.

21.11.85

A ROYAL COMMISSION EVALUATES THE ROLE OF THE BACK-BENCHER

The most important survey of British government in modern times was the report of the Kilbrandon Commission on the Constitution which appeared in 1973. The following extract, taken from the majority report, deals with the powers and perceived weaknesses of MPs.

'Members of Parliament appear to be regarded on the whole to be sympathetic to the views of ordinary people, and as effective champions of constituents in difficulty. But it is widely thought that the present system does not provide them with sufficient useful work or give them any great satisfaction. Many people are under the impression that Members' main function in Parliament is to vote for their party. According to this view the rigidity of party discipline has brought the back-bench member more and more under the control of the party Whips, turning debate into what one eminent parliamentarian has described as a ritual dance. It is said that Members are frustrated by their inability to influence the making of policy, and that as a result they tend to seek greater opportunities to interfere with and criticise government. It is suggested that they should have a more constructive role, so that they would not merely act as an irritant to government departments, but would advise the administration in the formative stage of policy making. Members of Parliament have themselves complained that at present practically everyone is consulted at this stage except them, and that they are brought in only to be presented with decisions already formulated in draft legislation.

The majority of respondents in the attitude survey – 55 per cent – thought that Members do not have enough power and influence over the decisions that are made; and judging by our other evidence the support for this view among informed observers is even greater. There is a feeling that the Member of Parliament has become devalued as the people's representative, and that he ought to be given the status and facilities accorded to his opposite numbers in countries such as the United States. The resources of government departments have far outstretched those available to him. The business of government has become bigger and more expert, and he has been left behind. He is said to have insufficient information and opportunity to exercise any substantial influence over the policy decisions of the executive.

The contrary view is that Members of Parliament do still have considerable power, and that at best the complaints are exaggerated. It is easy to see how the exaggeration can arise. The fact that so few Members appear willing to question the party line in public, much less vote against it, lends support to the notion that they are merely acting under party orders, and have little influence on the government as individuals. It is not generally appreciated that the influence of Members is largely brought to bear in committees and party meetings operating *off* the floor of the House, usually without publicity, and that important Parliamentary votes are often preceded by much pressing and canvassing of individual opinions. Behind the scenes the Member of Parliament is still someone to be reckoned with. Although government policies and draft legislation may be prepared without his participation, they are decided in the light of what Members generally can be expected to support; and their views are sometimes sought in the preparatory stages of legislation through the medium of debates on reports of independent committees or government green or white papers.

'Although critics often refer to the small amount of influence exercised by the ordinary Member, it seems to us that the real complaint is that the kind of influence which he exercises is increasingly inappropriate for government on the modern scale. Changes in his role are under way, but his influence is still regarded as largely negative. His strongest power is one of obstruction and criticism, and it can be exercised only in relation to what is put before him or comes to his notice. In an age of experts and new management techniques, some Members at least would like the opportunity to be more professional, and to have more direct influence over the many decisions which affect their constituents. They are not content to await their chance as Ministers, but want to be able to participate in government in a more constructive way as backbench members. In this the weight of general opinion seems to be on their side.' (*The Royal Commission on the Constitution, 1969–73*, Cmnd. 5460 1973, Sections 297–300)

(Of course some of the criticisms which are listed in this section of the Kilbrandon Report have been met in part by the institution of the system of 'departmental' select committees in 1979.)

GOVERNMENT BILLS AND PRIVATE MEMBERS' BILLS

During the 1983–84 session of Parliament the following numbers of Bills were introduced into the House of Commons. There were 60 *government Bills*, all of which successfully passed through the Commons and the Lords and received Royal Assent. There were 20 *Private Members' Bills* introduced under the *ballot*, of which 9 eventually received Royal Assent; 21 Private Members' Bills were introduced under *Standing Order No. 39*, of which two eventually received Royal Assent; and there were 66 Private Members Bills introduced under the *ten-minute rule*, of which none received Royal Assent. This gives us therefore a total of 107 Private Members' Bills introduced, of which 11 were eventually successful. (*HC Sessional Information Digest 1983–84*, p. 38)

THE ORIGINS OF A PRIVATE MEMBER'S BILL

David Tench of the Consumer's Association here explains the origins of Austin Mitchell's House Buyers' Bill of 1983:

'In June 1983 just after the General Election when the new session had started, we thought, "What shall we do this time?", and since we had over the years expressed a lot of dissatisfaction in *Which?* and elsewhere about the house transfer system as we call it, we thought, "let's have a go at that again". So we devised a proposal to remove the monopoly that solicitors have on conveyancing . . . and sent it to each of the MPs who drew a place in the ballot. Now one of the techniques we've found is that it pays to be quick off the mark so that I, for example, actually go to the ballot when it's drawn at 12.00 on the day in question and rush back the half mile from Parliament to my office immediately after the ballot and get the word processor moving. By an hour and a half after the ballot is drawn letters are actually going into the House of Commons post office and into the pigeon holes of the 20 MPs who have drawn a place in the ballot. That is intended to impress them that we know what we are doing and are quick off the mark. Mrs Whitehouse, of course, also knows this technique; she is inclined to grab people by the hand as soon as she can find them and say, "What about my issue?". That's one of the techniques of lobbying, to be quick off the mark. Then you just sit back and wait for any of the 20 to get in touch with you and say, "I'm mildly interested". In June 1983 nothing much happened and the last day for putting in the proposals came and I concluded that this was going to be one of our fallow years and nothing would happen. About 2.00 in the afternoon the telephone goes and it's Mr Austin Mitchell who says, "They tell me that I've got to get my proposal in by 5.00, I haven't really decided yet, didn't you send me something? What do you think I should do?" So I said, "I'll be with you in five minutes". [The House Buyers Bill duly received its First Reading in the House of Commons on 20 July 1983].'   (Malcolm Davis, *Politics of Pressure*, BBC 1985, p. 65; *HC Sessional Information Digest 1983–84*, p. 25)

RECENT EXAMINATION QUESTIONS	Spend ten minutes or so preparing outline answers to the following questions. Outline answers to questions **3**, **7**, and **12** and a fuller tutor's answer to question **1** are given in the following sections.
Question 1.	'A Member of Parliament is merely a piece of voting-fodder for his party machine.' How significant a part is played by the individual MP? (Cambridge, Pub. Aff., June 1983)
Question 2.	Should MPs rebel, abstain, and cross vote more than they do? Why don't they? (London, Govt and Pol. Stud., Paper 1, Jan. 1982)
Question 3.	Should back-benchers have more power than they have at present? (London, Govt and Pol. Stud., Paper 1, June 1984)
Question 4.	Evaluate the claim that parliamentary party committees are the most effective way for back-bench MPs to influence front-bench policy. (AEB, Govt and Pol., Paper 1, June 1985)

Question 5.

How may back-bench members of the Government's own party bring pressure to bear on a Prime Minister to change policy? Illustrate your answer with examples.

(AEB, Govt and Pol., Paper 1, June 1983)

Question 6.

What are the principles involved in whether an MP should be reselected by his constituency association before each General Election?

(London, Govt and Pol. Stud., Paper 1, Jan. 1981)

Question 7.

What is meant when it is said that an MP is a representative and not a delegate?

(London, Govt and Pol. Stud., Paper 1, short answer question, June 1983)

Question 8.

Why do some MPs oppose the select committees of the House of Commons?

(London, Govt and Pol. Stud., Paper 1, short answer question, June 1982)

Question 9.

How far and in what ways, can the Government control the proceedings of the House of Commons?

(Cambridge, Pub. Aff., Nov. 1984)

Question 10.

How is discipline exerted in British parliamentary parties? How effective are the methods of exerting discipline?

(JMB, Brit. Govt and Pol., June 1982)

Question 11.

What do you consider to be the most important aspects of the work of an MP and why?

(JMB, Brit. Govt and Pol., June 1982)

Question 12.

Whom should an MP obey? His parliamentary whips? His constituents? His party conference? His conscience?

(London, Govt and Pol. Stud., June 1981)

OUTLINE ANSWERS

Should back-benchers have more power than they have at present?

Question 3.

Answer

(a) Much depends on our definition of the purpose of elections and the associated role of the MP. If the object of elections is to produce a government *capable of ruling effectively*, then the present parliamentary system which is geared mainly towards expediting government business might be judged adequate. It could then be reasonably argued that MPs should probably not receive much more power than they have at present.

(b) Many would argue that the powers of the new wave of select committees formed in 1979 are sufficient to enable MPs *to check on the efficiency* of government departments and *to reveal any shortcomings* in administrative practice.

(c) It can be argued that the regular opportunities afforded to MPs for the debate of government legislation and policy are sufficiently extensive to ensure that the work of the Government is *well publicised and subjected to critical appraisal.* The implicit suggestion here being that it is *not* the function of MPs fundamentally to impede the work of the Government or the implementation of its policy.

(d) Others would argue that the primary role of MPs is to *represent constituency interests* and to act as *legislators* on *their own initiative.* In that case the amount of time and opportunity which they have to question ministers, or to raise issues of constituency concern in debates, or to bring forward Private Members' Bills, might be judged far too limited.

(e) Opponents of the view in (d) above would suggest that the Government already has enough difficulty getting its necessarily heavy legislative programmes through Parliament each session. Any further allocation of time to constituency matters or the personal interest of MPs would merely further prevent the exercise of good government.

(f) It may be useful to compare the UK with the USA. Some MPs wish to adopt American practices whereby members of Congress, particularly on the very powerful Congressional standing committees, can subject the administration to gruelling analysis and can and frequently do destroy the administration's legislative proposals. Many American commentators, on the other hand, feel that the powers of the Congressional committees are far too great and that they prevent much useful legislation from going through. These commentators compare the paltry legislative achievements of an average Congressional session with the much more effective implementation of the UK legislation. One is reminded of Hobbes's comment that the tyranny of the one (perhaps the Government) is to be preferred to the tyranny of the many!

SHORT ANSWER

Q.7.

What is meant when it is said that an MP is a representative and not a delegate?

Answer

A *delegate* is expected to transmit certain views expressed by those who have chosen him; he is therefore bound by their wishes. In strict constitutional theory a Member of Parliament is elected to *represent* his constituents, that is to say he is not expected to carry out a precise programme approved by them, but is instead selected on his personal merits and his integrity and may vote and act according to his conscience. Thus in the 1979–83 Parliament some members of the Labour Party and one member of the Conservative Party in Parliament changed their allegiance and went over to the newly formed Social Democratic Party (SDP) *without resigning* their seats and fighting by-elections. As a consequence they were taking advantage of their status as representatives rather than delegates.

| Q.12. | Whom should an MP obey? His parliamentary whips? His constituents? His party conference? His conscience? |

Answer

(a) We can interpret the word 'should' in the question in two quite different ways. Firstly to imply a *moral* or *ethical* obligation, and secondly to imply an obligation rooted in *political prudence*. These two interpretations in fact give rise to very differing answers.

(b) If we concentrate on the *moral* or *ethical* sense of 'should', we find the situation is complicated because there are several competing theories about the MP's representative role.

- the *Burkean theory* that the MP is chosen by his constituents, but once in Parliament must be guided by his conscience;
- the diametrically opposing theory that the MP is the *servant of his constituency in Parliament* and must therefore strive to reflect opinion among his constituents;
- the notion that he has probably been elected *as a result of membership of a party* rather than on the basis of his individual appeal and that he enters a Parliament which is historically and institutionally dominated by the party system. If his party has made him he should repay it with loyalty;
- in the case of a Labour MP, but not in the case of a Conservative, he has to reckon with his own party constitution which establishes conference as the supreme policy-making institution.

(c) If we interpret the question in terms of obligations based on *political prudence*, then the MP's object must be to conciliate as many powerful forces as possible. If he obeys his conscience in defiance of whips, constituents, and party conference then his parliamentary life is presumably likely to be a short one.

Refusal to obey the *whips* will certainly endanger his chances of promotion to ministerial status, and could ultimately lead to expulsion from the party which would make his re-election very difficult. But if he has taken the precaution of obtaining the support of his constituency party, then the whips may not wish to push matters to a crisis, although here a lot will depend on how frequent his disobedience to the whips turns out to be.

Obviously the MP will be unable to obey the dictates of all of his *constituents*, and on some matters he can probably fairly safely take an independent line which displeases most of them, but this cannot become a habit or else his chance of re-election will disappear. In the case of the Labour Party MPs must take care to conciliate their constituency party as they now have to face mandatory reselection as candidates before each election.

Obedience to the wishes of the *party conference* is less necessary unless the decisions of the conference have been taken up by the MP's front bench and are also supported by his constituency party. Annual party conferences may reflect a momentary mood among delegates, and MPs and parliamentary parties in general can always claim that circumstances have changed in such a way that conference resolutions no longer apply.

(d) Clearly, there is no simple answer to this question: part of the MP's task is to seek to reconcile, wherever possible, the various demands upon his loyalty. Where these turn out to be mutually exclusive then the MP will have to make difficult choices.

A TUTOR'S ANSWER

Q.1.

'A Member of Parliament is merely a piece of voting-fodder for his party machine. How significant a part is played by the individual MP?'

Answer

It is tempting to accept that MPs are little more than lobby-fodder: Party whips are powerful and governments are seldom defeated on major issues. In the same way it is almost unheard of for opposition MPs to vote with the Government or, indeed, to abstain if their whips put pressure on them to vote against the Government.

Back-bench rebellions are not, however, unknown, particularly on the Government side when the Government has a large parliamentary majority. This was the case in Febuary 1986 when Conservative MPs, particularly those from Midlands constituencies, voted against the Government on the issue of a prospective take-over of Austin Rover by Ford. Almost by definition these rebellions are a token show of resistance and do not seriously endanger the Government's legislative programme. We can argue that there is not a great deal of difference between a majority of, say, 100 and a majority of 90. Even when the MP *does* rebel he may be doing so not to please his own conscience but in order to placate a constituency party which is worried about some aspect of government policy or indeed official opposition policy. In that case it is just another part of the party machine which is pressurising the MP, as in the case of Conservatives under the Thatcher Government whose constituency associations are predominantly 'wet', or Labour MPs with 'Hard Left' constituency parties.

On the other hand it is open to some MPs to make a much more decisive impact on Parliament. Some are renowned for their investigative efforts and for their performances at Question Time, a good example being the Labour MP, Tam Dalyell, who played a major role in bringing to light many of the circumstances surrounding the sinking of the *General Belgrano* during the Falklands War. Members of Parliament do play an important part in extracting information from the Government which is of use to the public generally or to their constituents, or which can be used for more partisan purposes. Thousands of questions are asked annually, either for written answer, or for oral answer at Question Time, though the usefulness of parliamentary questions as a device for extracting really significant or sensitive information has been called into question. In fact MPs appear more formidable as investigators of government and administrative acts, when acting as members of back-bench committees rather than as individuals. The effectiveness of investigative select committees has been much increased in recent years, particularly since their reorganisation along 'departmental' lines in 1979. Members on select committees have succeeded in shedding considerable light on the processes of administration, but even in select committees party divisions are appearing, so that their all-party nature is being cast into doubt.

Members of Parliament do have other functions, in the exercise of which they are largely free from the pressures of the whips. Many of these are of somewhat doubtful effectiveness; for instance they may *introduce Private Members' legislation*, but the number of Private Members' Bills is small and the casualty rate among them is very high. They may *institute adjournment debates* in the last half-hour of Commons time on four days a week, but these debates receive relatively little publicity and are perhaps not long enough to be really probing. In addition, MPs act as a *channel* for constituents' complaints and grievances against administration. Each MP has been described as an Ombudsman to his constituents, but one former Parliamentary Commissioner for Administration (i.e. a genuine Ombudsman) has pointed out that MPs have neither the time nor the resources to investigate fully the complaints of constituents. It is becoming increasingly acknowledged that more complaints should be passed on by MPs to agencies such as the Parliamentary Commissioner. The MP acting alone has usually to be satisfied with a fairly standard departmental response to a constituent's complaint.

Obviously the role of an MP will vary from one individual to another. Some MPs are extremely voluble, others go for months at a time without even speaking in the House. Some MPs have a reputation as very good constituency representatives, i.e. those who work hard for the interests of their constituents, while others see themselves much more as Members of a national legislative body. Yet others make use of their position in Parliament and their contacts with their party hierarchy and other policy-makers to take on parliamentary consultancies. Clearly, their clients do not feel that the consultants are of no significance, for consultancy fees can be high.

A STEP FURTHER

A good many back-bench MPs produce volumes of memoirs, usually upon retirement, and these can generally be consulted quite profitably. In addition, of course, the activities of MPs are quite frequently the subject of articles and exposés in the press and on television. They are usually happy to visit schools and colleges in order to discuss their work with students, and are also able to arrange visits for groups of students and individuals to the House of Commons. Meetings and visits of this sort usually stick in the memory and provide fascinating insights, but nevertheless some specialist reading will also help. Among the useful studies may be mentioned S. A. Walkland and Michael Ryle, *The Commons Today*, (Fontana 1981) and Philip Norton, *The Commons in Perspective* (Martin Robertson 1981).

Once again students should refer for up-to-date comment to *Parliament in the 1980s*, ed. Philip Norton (Basil Blackwell 1985), particularly the chapters by Norton himself on back-bench independence, and by James W. Marsh on the constituency MP. There is also a very useful appendix in this book by Ken Batty and Bruce George, MP, on finance and facilities for MPs which is critical of the relatively low level of pay received by the ordinary back-benchers. It also relates the varying use made of research assistants to the age of MPs (with older MPs being rather less inclined to employ an assistant), and to the availability of party research findings (with the Conservatives being relatively well provided for in this respect). For an insight into the working of the Commons from the point of view of a recently retired Speaker, reference should be made to George Thomas, *Mr Speaker: the Memoirs of Viscount Tonypandy* (Century Press 1985).

Chapter 8

Whitehall and County hall: The balance of power

As we shall see in the following section, perhaps the greatest key to the tensions which currently exist between central and local government is the question of finance, and no discussion of local government finance can avoid the question of the *rates*. A word of explanation concerning the rates may therefore be helpful. Rates are paid as a separate tax to the local authority by private householders, industry and commerce.

A number of steps are invariably involved in the payment of rates:

• First, assessors attached to the Inland Revenue, and therefore independent of the local authority, give each property a rateable value of so many hundreds or thousands of pounds.

• Second, the local authority settles on a rate poundage, that is to say it decides to tax at the rate of so many pence per pound of rateable value: therefore if the authority decides on a rate of 150p in the £, the total which will be levied on a property with a rateable value of £1,000 will be £1,500.

• Third, the rate is levied annually and may be varied from one year to another by the local authority.

Rates as a tax have been criticised because they do not reflect the real level of wealth in a community. For instance some sections of the community are immune, and the payment of rates is not strictly related to services used. If a local authority raises its rate too high then it begins to have a decidedly adverse effect on commercial life within the area. In spite of earnest attempts by the political parties to find an alternative, the rates remain the only form of local taxation. They generally meet less than 50 per cent of a local authority's annual financial needs. It is this fact, that local government cannot support itself out of its own resources, that has led to many of the tensions which have marked the relationship between the local authority and Whitehall in recent years.

ESSENTIAL PRINCIPLES	Local government and its problems used to be regarded by many students as a somewhat tedious, perhaps rather arid, field of study. It is therefore one of the most significant, if unintentional, achievements of governments that in recent years they have transformed local government into a particularly interesting and important area of study.
PROBLEMS FACING LOCAL GOVERNMENT	

Degree of Independence from central government	We are bound to see local government as one of the principal political problems facing us in the later twentieth century. The issue centres on the question of how much *independence* local authorities should have from central government control. It is an issue which has proved so difficult to resolve because there are many different ways of approaching it.
The legal approach	If we adopt a rigidly *legalistic* approach to the problem then we shall have to argue that local government always owes its structure and its powers to the decisions of Parliament. A local authority exists because it has been brought into being by Act of Parliament. The nature of its obligations and responsibilities is defined by Parliament. It exercises powers of initiative only when Parliament has delegated such powers to it, and what Parliament has delegated Parliament can revoke. Seen from this point of view therefore, the situation is quite simple: if a government can persuade Parliament to legislate for the local authorities then the local authorities must obey.
The 'moral' or 'independent' approach	The trouble with this sort of argument is that it ignores the quite widespread feeling that a local government has a *moral* right to exist, based on tradition or on the needs of the locality, and independent of the wishes of the rulers in Westminster and Whitehall. Those who adhere to this 'moral' view may point out, for example, that many local communities in England have a tradition of self-government going back for nearly a thousand years. This is particularly the case with some of the ancient English boroughs. County councils are a little less than a century old, but even in their case there is a much longer tradition of county *communities* which in some sense enjoyed independence from control from London and which were in effect self-regulating.
The 'demographic' and 'social' approach	Even if we adopt a less historical approach, it is still possible to set up cogent *demographic* and *social* arguments in favour of considerable autonomy for local authorities. It can be argued that with increasing population and with increasingly complex social problems, often of a distinctly regional or subregional nature, central government cannot hope to be sensitive to the precise needs of any locality. It must

therefore rely very heavily on local authorities to prescribe their own remedies for particularly local problems. This, it is argued, will in turn involve the giving of power to the local authorities to manage resources effectively rather than to be simply the blind instruments of central government requirements.

CHANGES IN THE STRUCTURE AND POWER OF LOCAL GOVERNMENT

Such problems as these might have remained matters for academic debate had it not been for the fact that during the past generation successive central governments have acted dramatically to transform the structure and the powers of local authorities. Thus we have seen important developments in the London Government Act of 1963 which created the GLC and in the Local Government Act of 1972 which created the Metropolitan Counties and reformed the boundaries of local authorities throughout England and Wales. The latter involved abolishing some ancient authorities, including for example the historic county of Rutland, and creating others out of nothing, as for example in the case of the counties of Cleveland and of Avon. The 1972 Act also created the Metropolitan Counties of Greater Manchester, Merseyside, West Midlands, South Yorkshire, West Yorkshire, and Tyne and Wear. Since Margaret Thatcher's first Government came into power in 1979 we have been subjected to a veritable torrent of legislation and regulation which has substantially altered the picture of local government in the UK.

The modern debate centres on the contention by central government that local government must be rigidly organised *in the best interests of the nation as a whole*. In its present form the argument revolves round the issue of public expenditure. Any government which diagnoses excessive public expenditure as the cause of the nation's economic ills is bound to turn on the local authorities simply because they are responsible for much of the public spending. It is the local authorities, for example, who are responsible for most of our expenditure on education, on road-building and maintenance, on social services, on refuse collection and disposal, on the maintenance of emergency services, and on recreational provision.

LOCAL GOVERNMENT FINANCE

Traditionally there have been three principal sources of finance for such expenditure.
- Firstly, the *sale by local authorities of services* such as the renting of council houses or the charging of fares on council transport, or of admission fees to museums, parks, and so on.
- Secondly, there are the *rates*: a levy whose severity varies from authority to authority.
- Thirdly, because the first two sources of revenue come nowhere near meeting the financial needs of local authorities, the authorities have been forced to turn to *central government* for a grant-in-aid. On the principle that 'he who pays the piper calls the tune', it has been the existence of this grant which has given to central government much of its practical power over the local authorities.

It has been the area of finance, and especially central government control over local authority finance, that has led to the whole question of central/local relationships becoming so acute and troublesome in recent years. Margaret Thatcher's Government in particular has taken many steps to curb the capacity of local authorities to spend. New systems for allocating the central government grant to local authorities have been devised in an attempt to cut out the local authorities' bargaining powers.

One system is the *Grant Related Expenditure Assessment* (GREA). In the case of any one local authority this involves an initial calculation, which is exceedingly complex, of the amount of money which that authority will need to spend *if it is to maintain the national average level of service provision*. Secondly, a calculation is made of the amount of money which the authority can raise *if it charges the national average level of rates*. The *gap* between the two figures is the amount of money available in central grant.

A second system in use in the first half of the 1980s was known as the *target system*. Under this central government simply looked at the local authority's expenditure over the last few years, and then imposed a percentage cut in order to peg back the local authority's spending. The trimmed-down figure obtained from these calculations was known as the target.

The problem was that both GREA and target systems operated side by side and this produced the apparently absurd situation of local authorities being congratulated on the one hand for having kept within their GREA for the year, and a little later being told that they would be fined by the Department of the Environment because they had failed to meet their target.

Under the powers granted to him by the local government legislation of 1980 the Secretary of State for the Environment is indeed now able to fine a local authority which fails to keep its spending under control. The fine takes the form of 'holdback', a cut in the following year's central government grant. Try as they may, local authorities seem unable to escape the net being cast by central government. Some authorities, for example, attempted to escape from the restrictions on their spending power by increasing dramatically the level of rates charged, but this move was in turn met by the so-called rate-capping legislation of 1984. This enabled the Secretary of State to impose a ceiling on the rates levied by a number of specified local authorities. Rate-capping has in turn led to the politics of direct confrontation, with one major local authority, Liverpool City Council, insisting that it will neither cut its spending programme, nor even attempt to push its rates as high as possible. The result has been to create a massive financial crisis in the city, which may prove disastrous to its inhabitants and embarrassing to the Government.

It should be clear from this that by the mid-1980s the financial situation for local authorities had become extremely complex. The figure which the Government told them they needed to spend in order to maintain adequate provision of services was in some cases *higher* than the figure the Government told them they ought to spend in order to meet their expenditure reduction targets. Consequently, on 25 July 1985 the Environment Secretary told the House of Commons that the system of targets and penalties in operation since the early 1980s would *not apply* from 1986/87. This was on the grounds that the system had been criticised as operating unfairly towards low-spending councils, especially those which were spending below their GREA. In future overspending *relative to GREA* would produce much more severe grant reductions. It has been changes in tack of this nature, added to the general escalation of restrictive legislation in the 1980s, which have engendered the atmosphere of tension and uncertainty in local–central relations.

ABOLITION OF THE GLC AND METROPOLITAN COUNTIES

A final sign of the determination of central government to assert its control over the localities is to be found in the decision by Margaret Thatcher's Government to abolish both the GLC and the Metropolitan Counties, the alleged grounds for abolition being that they all involved a duplication of services already provided by lower-tier local authorities and were consequently simply not cost-effective bodies. The so-called Abolition Act was passed in 1985 to come into effect in 1986. None of the doomed bodies was exactly venerable: the GLC had been established for a little over twenty years and the Metropolitan County Councils for little more than twelve years, but in both cases the action of the Government brought loud complaints that the interests of local communities were being trampled underfoot. Particular unease was created by the transfer of some services previously administered by the GLC to non-elected bodies nominated by the Government, such as for example the London Regional Transport Authority, a move regarded by many as a suppression of local democracy.

However, it should be added that in the central–local government relationship the pressures have not been all one way. Many local authorities have taken to pursuing policies which might properly be described as appropriate to the national Government. For example, since Manchester declared itself a 'nuclear-free zone' in 1980, over 170 local authorities have adopted this title and have devoted considerable sums to the advancement of unilateralist policies. This process has been described as a distortion of the status and role of local government in our political system.

In the past generation, there have been suggestions that many of the functions of local government should be transferred *upwards* to elected regional governments. There already exist many examples of the regional deconcentration of non-elected administrative bodies though the regions involved are far from consistent; the Inland Revenue divides England and Wales into twenty-three regions, the National Health Service recognises fourteen hospital regions in England, and British Rail has carved Britain into five regions.

If the problem of identifying a region capable of meeting several governmental requirements could be solved, we might presumably expect greater co-ordination of services, within the region, than is possible within, say, an existing group of counties. On the other hand, citizens might well find a regional tier of government too remote, and too large. In the atmosphere of financial stringency in government which marks the 1980s, it is unlikely that potentially costly experiments in establishing a new tier of government will be attempted.

The central–local government tensions of that period have had two effects which, though totally contrasting, have both served to remove regional government from the political agenda. In the first place, central government has relied more and more on its regulatory powers; as the Kilbrandon Commission has noted, 'regional political power could still be practically useless unless it were to be accompanied . . . by a new style of thinking, positively favourable to devolution and based on co-operation rather than the exercise of central authority'. (*Royal Commission on the Constitution*, 1969–73, Cmnd 5460, Section 282) In the second place, the defensive reaction against central governmental regulation has often tended to take the form of stressing the need for the representatives of a locality, such as a town or city, who are fully conversant with that area's specific problems, to be in charge of its destiny. Thus regional government satisfies neither Whitehall's appetite for control, nor the localities' appetite for freedom: it is a casualty of the struggle between the two.

The issues raised by these tensions between central and local authority are crucial ones. If central government is to be capable of applying national remedies to national problems then it will need to sweep away the capacity of local authorities to interfere with and interrupt that process, whatever the harm to tradition and local sensitivity in the process. On the other hand, if local authorities are ever again to be genuine local governments, rather than simply administrative extensions of the central authorities, they will need to be put on a secure financial footing. This might be by means of a new system of local taxes (e.g. poll tax) to replace the inflexible and outmoded rates, or by means of the receipt of a fixed proportion of national taxation. It is clear, therefore, that we have been forced to face up to problems which, if they are to be solved, will require, almost inevitably, large-scale dislocations of our political structure.

USEFUL APPLIED MATERIALS

PURPOSE OF LOCAL GOVERNMENT

The Redcliffe–Maud Commission on Local Government which reported in 1969 made the following classic statement of the purpose of local government:

'Local government is not to be seen merely as a provider of services. If that were all it would be right to consider whether some of the services could not be more efficiently provided by other means. The importance of local government lies in the fact that it is the means by which people can provide services for themselves; can take an active and constructive part in the business of government; and can decide for themselves within the limits of what national policies and local resources allow, what kind of services they want and what kind of environment they prefer. More than this, through their local representatives people throughout the country can, and in practice do, build up the policies which national government adopts – by focusing attention on local problems, by their various ideas of what government should seek to do, by local initiatives and local reactions . . . Central government tends by its nature to be bureaucratic. It is only by the combination of local representative institutions with the central institutions of Parliament, Ministers and Departments that a genuine national democracy can be sustained.

'. . . We conclude then that the purpose of local government is to provide a democratic means both of focussing national attention on local problems affecting the safety, health and well-being of the people and of discharging in relation to these things all the responsibilities of government which can be discharged at a level below that of the national government. But in discharging these responsibilities local government must, of course, act in agreement with the national government when national interests are involved.' (*Redcliffe–Maud Commission on Local Government*, Vol. 1, Cmnd 4040, HMSO 1969)

PARTY PROGRAMMES FOR LOCAL GOVERNMENT IN 1983

Something of the wide disparity of attitudes towards local government in the main political parties can be seen from comparison of references to local government in the party manifestos compiled for the 1983 General Election.

The Conservative Party promised to legislate to curb excessive and irresponsible rate increases by high-spending councils and to provide a general scheme for limiting rate increases for all local authorities. They promised to require local authorities to consult local representatives of industry and commerce before setting rates, to give more businesses the right to pay by instalments, and to end the rating of empty industrial property. The Conservative manifesto went on to claim that the Metropolitan Councils and the GLC had been shown to be 'a wasteful and unnecessary tier of government'. They promised to abolish them and to return most of their functions to the boroughs and districts.

In the Labour manifesto was a statement of belief in 'active local democracy' and a consequent pledge to repeal the Conservative legislation allowing the Government to impose ceilings on local authority spending and to impose penalties on local authorities whose spending exceeds those ceilings (i.e. the Local Government Planning and Land Act of 1980). Labour also promised to repeal the ban on supplementary rates (the Local Government Finance Act 1982) and to restore the right of local authorities to spend additional amounts from revenue on capital expenditure in excess of loan sanction limits. Finally, Labour promised to recast the rate support grant system in order to give fairer treatment to areas in greatest need and the maximum freedom of action for local authorities to control their own budgets.

The Alliance proposals were to introduce proportional representation for elections to local government, and to simplify local government structure. The latter would ultimately be achieved by abolishing the Metropolitan Counties and the GLC, and by allowing a restoration of their powers to some of the former county boroughs abolished by the 1972 Local Government Act. There was to be provision for introducing a local income tax which would pave the way for the abolition of the domestic rates and would reduce the dependence of local government on central grant. Finally, the Alliance promised to extend the right of local communities to have statutory parish or neighbourhood councils.

RECENT EXAMINATION QUESTIONS

Spend ten minutes or so preparing an answer to each of the following questions. Outline answers for questions **5**, **7**, and **9**, and a tutor's answer to question **1** are provided in the following sections.

Question 1.

How much freedom of action is left to local government authorities in Britain?

(Cambridge, Pub. Aff., Nov. 1985)

Question 2.

Now that about one-third of all public expenditure arises from the activities of local government, can its continued existence be reconciled with the economic responsibilities of central government?

(London, Govt and Pol. Stud., Paper 1, June 1982)

Question 3.

'He who pays the piper calls the tune'. How well does this popular saying capture the relationship between local and central government?

(Cambridge, Pol. and Govt, June 1984)

Question 4.

Even more of local authority activities should be paid for directly by central government. What effect would such a development have upon local government?

(Cambridge, Pub. Aff., June 1984)

Question 5.

How would you account for the systematic and accelerating loss of local government powers to central government since 1945?

(Cambridge, Pol. and Govt, June 1983)

Question 6.

'The main trouble with local government is that it is neither democratic nor properly accountable.' Discuss in the light of recent problems.

(London, Govt and Pol. Stud., Paper 1, June 1985)

Question 7.

(a) By what methods may central government control the work of local authorities? (b) To what extent have there been significant changes in the use of these methods during the 1970s and 1980s?

(AEB, Govt and Pol., Paper 1, June 1983)

Question 8.

'Despite their dependence on local government grants, local authorities retain great independence in most areas of policy-making.' To what extent is this an accurate statement about central/local relations since 1970?

(AEB, Govt and Pol., Paper 1, June 1985)

Question 9.

What discretion do local authorities have?

(London, Govt and Pol. Stud., Paper 1, short answer question, June 1984)

Question 10.

Why should local government not be financed wholly from central government?

(London, Govt and Pol. Stud., Paper 1, short answer question, June 1983)

Question 11.

Why not abolish local government altogether?

(Cambridge, Pol. and Govt, Paper 1, June 1985)

Question 12.

Assess the means possessed by local authorities of exerting pressure on central government and resisting pressure by central government.

(JMB, Brit. Govt and Pol., June 1985)

OUTLINE ANSWERS

Q.5.

How would you account for the systematic and accelerating loss of local government powers to central government since 1945?

Answer

(a) Some powers have been lost by local government because the functions to which they relate have been defined by central or regional government as *national* rather than *local* ones. This has been the case, for example, with the responsibility for building and maintaining trunk roads which was transferred to central government in 1946; hospitals were transferred to regional hospital boards in 1946; local electricity and gas enterprises were transferred to public corporations in 1947 and 1948; valuation for rating purposes was transferred to the Inland Revenue in 1950. In some of these (and other) cases the transfer has been to regional bodies or to public corporations and not to central government proper. However, regional authorities and public corporations are, because of their smaller numbers, more amenable to central government control than are the mass of local authorities.

(b) Even where functions *have remained* with the local authorities, the way in which those functions are exercised has become increasingly subject to central government determination. In other words the discretionary element in local government powers has diminished considerably. This is partly because the public perception of the role of central government has changed. When things go wrong it is primarily regarded as central government's fault rather than the fault of individuals or local authorities. This has induced central government to be more active in managing the affairs of the localities.

The *capacity of central government to regulate and monitor* the work of local government has increased considerably as a result of the transport and communications revolution of the last half-century. In addition, as the pressures for uniform national development have increased, central government has become ever more sensitive to the *capacity of local authorities to defy central policy or to undermine it* (e.g. individual authorities' reluctance to implement comprehensive education in the 1970s or the refusal of some authorities to cut expenditure during the 1980s). This has led to central government moves to break the capacity of the local authorities for resistance.

(c) Another major factor has been the structure of local government finance. While the number of services to be provided has increased, particularly in the fields of education and social services, the basis of local authority finance has remained constant. In particular the principal element of revenue available to local government, i.e. the rates, has proved incapable of dramatic extension. The rates are not a flexible tax and do not reflect the true levels of wealth in a community. Consequently the element in local government revenue which most dramatically increased in the period from the mid-1940s to the late 1970s was that provided by central government grants, which moved from a little over 30 per cent of local government income in the period around 1945 to over 50 per cent by the late 1970s. Relatively greater financial burdens on central government naturally resulted in greater determination by central government to ensure how the money was being spent, i.e. the operation of the principle of 'he who pays the piper calls the tune'.

In recent years the financial situation has changed somewhat: the proportion of local government finance being met by central government has declined since the Thatcher Government came into power in 1979. This period has seen perhaps the greatest acceleration of central government restrictions on local authorities, e.g. in 1980 the introduction of GREA, a new system of setting levels of rate support grant designed to restrain overspending; in 1982 the ban on the levying of supplementary rates; in 1984 the introduction of rate-capping, i.e. the setting for selected local authorities of ceilings for their rate demands; in 1985 the abolition of the GLC and the Metropolitan County Councils and the transfer of their functions *downwards* to boroughs and districts and *upwards* to centrally appointed boards. The motive behind these moves has been the Conservative Government's general desire to hold down public expenditure as part of its programme for economic regeneration. Given that local authorities account for one-third of public expenditure, they have become prime targets for central control.

Q.7. (a) By what methods may central government control the work of local authorities? (b) To what extent have there been significant changes in the use of these methods during the 1970s and 1980s?

Answer (a)
- Central government may *construct legislation* which restricts or controls the work of local authorities. For example the Education Act of 1944 not only created a framework for education to be provided by local authorities, it also contained the provision that the minister might intervene if a local authority was deemed to be acting unreasonably in its provision of education.

  Note also the financial controls imposed by the 1980 Local Government Planning and Land Act, the 1982 Local Government Finance Act, and the rate-capping legislation of 1984. Central government departments frequently issue *circulars* to local authorities which, although they do not have coercive powers and are often the result of central and local negotiations, may be followed by legislation if they are ignored.
- Central government may *excercise default powers*. If a local authority defaults on its obligations under a piece of legislation, then central government may act coercively. This occurred in the Clay Cross case of 1972, when an urban district council refused to employ the provisions of the Housing Finance Act. The Government, therefore, ultimately appointed a Housing Commissioner who took over the running of the council's housing functions.
- Given that central government provides a large proportion of the revenue of local authorities it is able to control their activities by *threats to withhold grant*, by the *actual reduction of the grant*, or by the *reduction of a local authority's capacity to raise revenue* by means of the rates.

(b) There have been considerable shifts in the use of the machinery of central government control during the 1970s and 1980s. These have resulted from what has been termed the breakdown in the collectivist social-democratic consensus in British politics. Local authorities have seen themselves as having to provide the maximum service possible in order to satisfy their electorates. Central government, on the other hand, has seen itself as picking up the bill for service provision and has grown increasingly restive at what some governments have regarded as local authority overspending.

In the early and mid-1970s central government's policy was to make local authorities more efficient. This involved reallocating powers between different tiers of local authority and redrawing the local authority map in order to reduce the number of authorities. It was hoped that these measures would avoid undue duplication of provision and achieve a more efficient provision.

By the end of the 1970s and throughout the 1980s, however, the central government had come to see a sharp restriction on the financial freedom of local authorities as the only solution. This was the context for the introduction of a new means of allocating the rate support grant, the restrictions on setting supplementary rates, and the imposition of ceilings for rate levies.

One of the major changes has been the tendency of governments since 1979 to view the expenditure of each authority *separately*. Previously local government expenditure was seen as a *whole*, i.e. in global terms, and high spending by individual authorities was not penalised. It was argued that this was indicative of greater need on the part of high-spending authorities. This was no longer accepted, with spending levels now being fixed for individual authorities and penalties being introduced where those levels are exceeded.

There has been a very obvious politicisation of the powers of central government. This again relates to the breakdown of political consensus which is alleged to have existed before the 1970s. Since the early 1970s there has been a visible growth in the number of local authorities seeking to thwart the intentions of central government. This in turn has provoked central government into the use of default powers and into restrictive legislation. The use of *default powers* actually occurred in the Clay Cross case, and was *threatened* by the Environment Secretary against Norwich in 1981/82. In the latter case, the Labour City Council in Norwich allegedly dragged its feet in implementing the Housing Act of 1980 which established the right of council tenants to buy their council properties. For examples of *restrictive legislation*, see the Conservative Government's local authority finance legislation of the 1980s which has been aimed mainly at allegedly high-spending Labour authorities. See also the decision by the Conservative Government to abolish the Labour-controlled GLC and the Metropolitan County Councils.

Q.9.   What discretion do local authorities have?

Answer   Some local authority functions are discretionary rather than compulsory, e.g. the provision of museums, of recreational facilities, of transport services. Local authorities also have discretion as to the precise rate demands which they may make, though they have to operate within certain limits, i.e. the rates have to be high enough to cover projected expenditure, while some authorities are subject to rate-capping, i.e. the Secretary of State for the Environment may impose an upper limit on the rates which they may legally set. Local authorities also have discretion in fixing the fees for services which they provide, for example bus fares or museum admission charges. Again local authorities have discretion in the matter of planning decisions, subject to appeal to the Secretary of State.

A TUTOR'S ANSWER
Q.1.

How much freedom of action is left to local government authorities in Britain?

Answer

Over the past few years the freedom of action of local authorities has been progressively restricted. For many years local authorities have been under the statutory obligation to provide a satisfactory level of service in certain areas of administration, such as education. In addition, of course, local authorities have to obey the law: if Parliament legislates to the effect that local authorities should allow sitting tenants of council houses to buy their houses under specified conditions, then local government must accept this legislation and implement its provisions.

The main thrust of restrictions on local authorities' freedom of action has more recently been in the financial sphere. Local government is dependent on central government support if it is to maintain its services, and the existence of that central government support in the form of the rate support grant has always given the central authority a power to bargain with local government. More recently, however, the nature of the relationship has been tightened up. The 1980 Local Government Planning and Land Act published a new system for the allocation of central government grants known as GREA. This attempted to fix a standard level of service provision for the whole of the country. It introduced a system of financial penalties for authorities which were deemed to 'overspend', that is, deemed to exceed the necessary levels of service provision. It is *possible* to maintain a high level of spending, but only at the cost of progressive reductions in central government grant as the penalty system bites, with consequent financial crisis, as demonstrated in the celebrated case of Liverpool City Council in 1984/85.

Central government has also moved to block off one of the main methods by which local authorities under financial pressure from declining central government grant might increase their resources, namely that of pushing up the rates. The 1982 Local Government Finance Act banned the levying of *supplementary* rates; further, the 1984 rate-capping legislation introduced a procedure whereby the Secretary of State for the Environment may impose an upper limit on the rate to be levied in a number of specified authorities. Initial rate-capping legislation applied only to a handful of authorities but, of course, the principle is capable of extension if necessary.

There are areas where local authorities still retain initiative and some freedom of action. They are able to decide in very general terms on the areas on which they wish to spend, as long as, of course, they have the financial resources available. Some local authority functions are discretionary rather than mandatory, in other words they are not obliged to provide services but may do so if they wish. Into this category fall such things as the provision by district councils of museum facilities, parks, and recreational facilities. In areas such as planning, the local authorities, and in particular the district councils, are able to approve or reject planning applications and so determine the nature of development which takes place in their areas. Even here, however, local authority planning decisions are subject to appeal and possible reversal by the Secretary of State for the Environment. Finally, since the 1972 Local Government Act there seems to have been an increase in the politicisation of the local authorities. In other words the political parties have come to dominate local governments to an extent not visible before the 1970s. This in a sense is a further restriction on freedom of action in that local authorities are now much more likely to toe a general party line than to react perfectly flexibly to the requirements of their locality.

A STEP FURTHER

This is a field in which both legislative and local political developments have proceeded at such a rate in recent years that almost all of the published studies are out of date while they are still in the press. It is worth while looking out the excellent chapter by Geoffrey Lee, in Bill Jones's, *Political Issues in Britain Today* (Manchester University Press 1985). *Keesing's Contemporary Archives* contain excellent summaries of recent legislation and of some of the political controversies which it has occasioned. It cannot be assumed that local councillors will understand the complexities of the relationship between their authority and central government: in fact they are often as bemused as anyone else by the intricacies of the relationship, particularly in financial matters. Nevertheless, local councillors are still worth consulting if only to find out how far they *feel* themselves to be restricted in their functions by the constraints imposed by central government.

An excellent though highly critical account of the working of local government is provided by Alex Henney, *Inside Local Government: A Case for Radical Reform* (Sinclair Brown 1984). Having been a senior local government official Henney writes from recent, and, one suspects, bitter, experience. He is particularly good on many of the technicalities, particularly the financial ones, and provides a wealth of detailed statistical and financial information; he is also good on such basic issues as the accountability of local government and its efficiency. Interested students should also make the effort to track down a recent report by the Comptroller and Auditor-General, *The Operation of the Rate Support Grant System* (National Audit Office, HMSO 1985). The report highlights the confusion which changes in local government finance have produced among local officials and councillors. It also traces the development in the early 1980s of a new government policy aimed at increasing the local authority's accountability by cutting back on the proportion of local government spending met by central government.

Chapter 9

Representing the people

GETTING STARTED	In the course of this chapter we shall be looking at, among other things, the extent to which the electoral system produces an adequate reflection of the views of the electorate. It may therefore be helpful to run through some of the major voting systems which are in use.
(a) First past the post	This is the system currently in use in British parliamentary and local government elections. It operates in single-member constituencies, and to be elected a candidate simply has to obtain the *largest single block of votes*. This is known as obtaining a *plurality* of the vote. In over half of the constituencies in the 1983 General Election the successful candidate obtained a plurality, but not a majority (i.e. over 50 per cent) of the votes.
(b) The second vote system	This also operates in single-member constituencies, but makes provision for *two* ballots. If on the first ballot no candidate has a *majority* of the votes, then the weaker candidates are eliminated. A second ballot is then held to ensure that someone gains a majority.
(c) Additional member system	In this system *half* of the seats in an assembly are filled on the basis of first past the post voting in single-member constituencies. The total number of votes cast nationally for each party is then counted, with the remainder of the seats being divided up between the parties according to the proportion of the national vote which they obtained.
(d) Single transferable vote system	This generally operates in multi-member constituencies and voters cast their votes in order of preference. On the first counting of the votes only first choices are taken into consideration. To be elected a candidate must secure a certain quota figure. The quota is as follows:

$$\frac{\text{Total number of votes cast}}{\text{Total number of seats} + 1} + 1$$

After the first counting of the votes it is quite likely that some seats will remain unfilled in each constituency. There is therefore a redistribution of votes cast for the already successful candidates. For example, if the required quota figure is, say, 20,001, and a candidate has obtained 25,000 votes, he has a 'surplus' of 4,999. When his votes are redistributed *all* of his 25,000 votes are arranged according to the second choices expressed on their ballot papers. The elected candidate's *second-choice* votes are then allocated to the other candidates using the following formula:

$$\text{Total of second-choice votes cast for each candidate} \times \frac{\text{The elected candidate's surplus}}{\text{The elected candidate's total vote}}$$

If this redistribution fails to get a sufficient number of candidates up to the quota then weaker candidates are eliminated and their second-choice votes are redistributed. It will be evident that the single transferable vote system is considerably more complex than the first past the post system.

ESSENTIAL PRINCIPLES

PARLIAMENT AS A REPRESENTATIVE BODY

The concept of representation is one of the most complex in politics. What exactly do we mean, for example, when we say that Parliament is a representative body?

a)   'Representative' might imply that Parliament stands for, or acts in place of, the voters or the people. However, this sort of definition perhaps raises more problems than it solves.

b)   We quite commonly assume that a representative is an *elected* person. This may not necessarily be the case: for example, the Queen, who is of course *non-elected*, is the Head of State and in a sense represents the British people. Again, ambassadors represent their governments, but are *designated* by them rather than elected.

c)   If we mean by representative that the structure of the population is faithfully reflected within Parliament then even an elected body like the House of Commons may in many respects be remarkably unrepresentative of the electorate. To be representative in this sense, about half of the Members of the Commons should be women; there should also be a wide age and social class distribution corresponding to the age and social class sets within the population, and there should be many black and Asian MPs. In practice the British MP is typically male, middle-aged, middle-class and white. We may say that the British Parliament does *not* represent the people in terms of social composition, sex, age, social composition or race.

d)   'Representative' might be used in the sense of Parliament reflecting the views and ideas of the voters or people. Many critics argue that even in this respect Parliament can hardly be considered a representative body, especially in view of the use of the first past the post system.

One theory of the role of the representative can ultimately be traced back to the late eighteenth century political philosopher, Edmund Burke. Burke insists that the Member of Parliament should *not* be bound to reflect faithfully the ideas of his constituents, even assuming that these ideas could be accurately ascertained. He has instead simply been chosen by his constituents as a fit person to act in their name. He retains the right to act and vote according to his conscience, and to change his mind without necessarily seeking the opinions of those whom he represents.

Even if the Member of Parliament *does* attempt to reflect the ideas of his constituents, he is still beset by many problems. The ideas of the constituents themselves may change, in which case it is far from clear whether he should attempt to reflect the electors' ideas as they stood on the *day* of his election, or as they *progress* throughout the life of the Parliament. In practice, MPs and political parties perform a kind of delicate balancing act between these two notions. On the one hand, governments habitually set much store by the notion of the *mandate*. In other words the idea that they have been elected on the basis of their party manifesto or statement or proposed policies, and that they therefore have a mandate or command from the electorate to carry out those policies. On the other hand, acknowledging that public opinion moves along, and that issues change in emphasis, most MPs recognise that it is a matter of duty or perhaps simply common prudence to keep in touch with developments among their constituents. Then if circumstances demand it, an MP, or even an entire government, may feel it quite in order to abandon or modify a particular policy.

THE ELECTORAL SYSTEM AND REPRESENTATION

We have so far assumed that voting in British elections, whether local or parliamentary, is a reliable means of ascertaining the views of the electorate. Once again, a closer analysis would seem to suggest that this is not necessarily the case. The *vote* in the parliamentary or local council election is indeed the most clumsy instrument of representation. In truth, just because someone votes for a candidate, it does not mean that we have any *precise* idea of the *views* which the voter wishes the candidate to represent. The party manifesto normally contains dozens of policy proposals. A candidate may agree with all of those or may dissent from some of them. We do not know whether the voter is voting for the points in the manifesto, or voting for the candidate precisely because the latter dissents from some of those points. We may assume that in a good many cases, probably the majority, the voter is ignorant of most of the points in the manifesto. But, of course, the vote does not reveal this; nor does it reveal whether the voter is opposed to some of the points in the manifesto or to some of the opinions of the candidate for whom he is voting.

But if the individual vote is clumsy, then the *British electoral system* taken as a whole may be said to be even clumsier. The first past the post electoral system used in Britain can and often does seriously distort the patterns of opinion among the voters. The 1983 General

101

Election provides us with some extreme examples of this: the Conservative Party, which went on to provide the Government, was seriously over-represented in Parliament in relation to the number of votes cast for Conservative candidates throughout the country. In contrast, the Liberal/SDP Alliance was very seriously under-represented in relation to the votes cast for Alliance candidates.

REMEDIES TO PROBLEMS OF REPRESENTATION

Direct democracy

There are many suggested remedies to the kind of problems detailed above, though, as might be expected, none of the remedies commands anything like universal support. The impossibility of deciding just what opinions are being conveyed in an individual's vote for a representative has led some to suggest that we should make less use of the *representative* principle and more use of the principle of *direct democracy*. Direct democracy refers to a process by which the electorate is from time to time invited to vote on a single, quite specific, issue. We are not altogether without experience of referenda of this sort. In 1975 the electorate was required to vote on Britain's continuing membership of the EEC. A more frequent use of such a system would undoubtedly prove costly and time-consuming, and there is no doubt that much of the initiative in a referendum lies with whoever sets the question on which the electorate is invited to vote. The results would therefore not necessarily inspire great confidence. Nor do we have much evidence that the electorate would be enthusiastic about such a system. If we take the example of Switzerland, in which fairly frequent recourse is had to the referendum, we find that the level of voter participation is sometimes as low as 35 per cent.

Proportional representation

More serious, perhaps, are the frequent calls for the adoption of some form of *proportional representation* (PR), such as the single transferable vote (STV) system. Once again, of course, there are arguments on both sides. Indeed, it may be argued that STV is not a truly *proportional* system at all: it still permits a disparity between the proportion of seats gained by a party and the proportion of first-choice votes cast for it or its candidates. The impact of STV is not, therefore, to achieve proportionality, but to allow voters to express their preferences among candidates much more clearly than is possible under the first past the post system.

The principal advantage of such a system is that it would more faithfully mirror the distribution of votes for each party throughout the country. Voters might feel free to vote for a party which they generally preferred, rather than to adopt the sort of tactical voting which is discussed in the next chapter. Proportional representation holds out to minority groups the prospect of a share of representation and may consequently encourage them to become more actively involved in politics as voters and as candidates. It also allows a greater range of opinions and interests to be voiced through elected bodies, and so may improve the quality of decision-making within them.

These arguments are countered by the claims that PR tends to produce a number of smaller parties in an assembly, and hence contributes to political fragmentation and perhaps to instability. Because it is a more complex system it is more costly to operate. Again, because PR systems are generally more complex than a first past the post system, it is often claimed that they may not be fully understood by the electorate. A further criticism is that because a system such as STV normally operates in a multi-member constituency the personal link between an MP and those he represents would be broken.

The debate is muddled by the fact that some of the arguments deployed against PR in general, relate to some, but not all, of the PR systems in use or in prospect. Again, many points made on both sides relate to experiences of PR in *other* countries, and assume that British reactions would be similar to those observed elsewhere. For example, in West Germany, where the electoral structure combines a first past the post element with a regional list element, parliamentary life has been dominated by centrist policies and by a small number of parties. But West German political culture, its twentieth-century political experiences, and recent economic fortunes, are all very different from those of the UK. There is therefore no guarantee that the West German system provides a model for the operation and consequences of a similar structure in Britain. Nevertheless, increasing political contacts with Continental Europe, where PR systems are widely used, and occasional flirtations with such systems within the UK as, for example, in the use of STV in Ulster for European and local government elections, will ensure that the reform of the system of representation remains on the political agenda.

USEFUL APPLIED MATERIALS

HOUSE OF COMMONS: A REPRESENTATIVE BODY!

The following figures based on the General Election Results of 1983 make it clear that the House of Commons, allegedly a representative body, does not necessarily reflect either the views or the social composition of the population.

	Conservative	Labour	Alliance
Votes	13,012,315	8,456,934	7,780,949
% of total vote	42.4	27.6	25.4
Seats in the House of Commons	397	209	23

Women MPs
October 1974: 27 women out of 635 MPs
October 1979: 19 women out of 635 MPs
October 1983: 23 women out of 650 MPs

Black or coloured MPs
October 1974: 0 out of 635 MPs
October 1979: 0 out of 635 MPs
October 1983: 0 out of 650 MPs

The Social and Occupational Backgrounds of MPs

(a)   An analysis of MPs elected in the 1970, February 1974, and October 1974 General Elections reveals that 0.9 per cent of Conservative MPs, 53.4 per cent of Labour MPs, and 100 per cent of Liberal MPs were drawn from classes 1 and 2 on the Hall-Jones Scale of Occupational Prestige. In other words the background of MPs was equivalent to that of a professionally qualified and high administrative staff, or of a managerial and executive staff.

(b)   At the other end of the scale 0.5 per cent of Conservatives were drawn from the ranks of *skilled manual* workers; 6.4 per cent of Labour MPs had this background, with a further 4.5 per cent of Labour MPs being drawn from *semi-skilled* manual workers. No MPs of any description were drawn from the ranks of the *routine manual* workers.

(c)   Viewing the same MPs from a slightly different angle we find that 57 per cent of Conservatives were drawn from the *business community*, but that only 5.1 per cent of Labour MPs came from that source. 30.9 per cent of Conservatives emerged from the *professions* with 32.8 per cent of Labour MPs having such a background. Only 1 per cent of Conservatives could be classified broadly as *workers*, while 27.6 per cent of Labour MPs fell into this category.

(d)   56.7 per cent of Conservative MPs had attended *public school*, against 19.1 per cent of Labour MPs. 52.6 per cent of Conservatives had attended *Oxford* or *Cambridge* universities, while only 20.7 per cent of Labour MPs had done so. 30.4 per cent of the Conservatives and 46.3 per cent of the Labour MPs had not attended any university.

(e)   In terms of age distribution, members of the two major parties were fairly evenly matched. 13.4 per cent of Conservatives and 14.6 per cent of Labour MPs were under 40 when elected. A rather higher percentage of Conservatives than Labour MPs were aged between 40 and 60 when elected, and a rather higher percentage of Labour MPs than Conservative were aged over 60 when elected. In the case of both parties, well over 50 per cent of MPs fell into the 40–60 age range at the time of election.

Note: (Figures based on tables constructed by Michael Rush in S. A. Walkland and Michael Ryle, *The Commons Today*, Fontana 1981, pp. 45–50)

A DEFENCE OF THE ELECTORAL status quo

Here the Conservative MP and former Cabinet minister, Francis Pym, whose ideas mark him out as very much a traditionalist, defends the present electoral system:

'Advocates of PR indict the existing system on three counts: that the number of seats won by each party is out of all proportion to the votes cast, that a large body of moderate opinion is under-represented in Parliament, and that the system polarises politics and produces

Governments elected on a minority vote that lurch alternately from one side of the political spectrum to the other. I would say that these criticisms amount to only one real charge: that Parliament is not properly representative of the people.

'The first comment to make in response to this charge is that there is no such thing as an ideal electoral system. We may sometimes envy the systems of other countries; they equally envy ours. Some criticisms of our systems are self evidently true but if PR was to be introduced in any of its myriad forms it would produce its own imperfections. That is not an argument against it but it suggests a need for a more reasoned approach to the subject than the mere assertion of opposing principles. Sometimes the argument tends to remind me of Bertrand Russell's paradox that a fanatical belief in democracy makes democratic institutions impossible.

'In my view an electoral system should ideally satisfy two needs: an accurate reflection of the popular role and the capacity for firm and effective Government. No system of which I am aware permanently satisfies both needs equally. PR does not necessarily produce weak government but it can tend to do so. The present system does not necessarily produce unrepresentative government but it can tend to do so.

'The major defence of the present system is that over a very long period of time it has achieved a reasonable balance between the two needs. By its nature it has almost invariably produced firm government, but also by its nature it has helped to avoid extreme government. When one party strays beyond the accepted bounds of moderation the pressures of the system bring it back and offer extinction as the alternative. Within this process the centre parties act as a barometer to the two main parties: when Labour or Conservative drift too far from the centre ground the barometer rises; when they return, it falls. In this way, although the popular will may not always be reflected in the government at that particular moment, it tends to be reflected accurately over time.

'The advocates of PR would like to promote the barometer so that it controls the weather rather than reflects it. I do not believe that this would result in Governments with greater popular support than at present although it would moderate the extremes of opposition and would thus produce governments that conform more closely to the popular average. However, it would also tend to produce coalition Governments and in my opinion coalitions are often – though not invariably – weak. I also feel that a major constitutional change of this nature should only be made under extreme duress, especially when the present system has stood the test of time so well.' (*The Politics of Consent*, Sphere Books 1985, pp. 96–7)

SOME ANTICIPATED BENEFITS OF PR

Here the Liberal leader David Steele suggests some of the possible consequences of a PR system.

'. . . detractors (of proportional representations) claim that too much power would go to minorities like the Liberals. Yet at present the two big parties are private coalitions over whose actual policy directions the public has little say. Electoral reform would enlarge their choices and ensure an open coalition based on a public majority with authority to run our affairs.

'. . . Once we have electoral reform, we shall by definition have more broadly based majority government. This may take the form of a coalition between parties in which a common programme is agreed, even at the sacrifice of some ideological baggage. But it is often forgotten that under a PR system a party can conduct the government on its own if it meets one simple condition. It has to gain 50 per cent of the votes or more. Any party which gains 50 per cent will have to be a great deal wider and more popular in its appeal than anything we have seen in Britain for years. Either way we shall have governments which represent the majority and can genuinely speak for the people. . . .'   (David Steel, *A House Divided*, Weidenfeld and Nicholson 1980, pp. 161–62)

A CRITIQUE OF PR

Some excellent material is put forward by R. J. Johnstone and P. J. Taylor, 'People, places and Parliament', *The Geographical Journal*, Vol. 151, No. 3, Nov. 1985, pp. 327–46. Here two political geographers join in the PR debate and marshal some interesting arguments in defence of the current system. This justification is expressed in terms of some of the problems associated with the formation of governments following elections in a PR system. It is conceded that PR gives greater equality of representation but *not* of party power (Johnstone, p. 335). Put at its simplest, this means that once a number of small parties gain representation in an assembly as a result of the application of a PR system they are quite likely to make or break government coalitions, and this gives them a disproportionate amount of power; disproportionate, that is, in terms of the numbers of people who voted for them. Taylor (pp. 342–3) defines a new form of electoral bias, which he terms electoral bias II, which is the difference between the percentage *vote* for a party over a *series of elections* and the percentage of *government tenure* of the party over the period covered by the elections. That is to say, if a party gets about 45 per cent of the vote over a period of time and gets about 45 per cent of the share of government over the same period of time, then there is no lack of proportionality involved. Using this principle Taylor constructs a league table of electoral bias II consisting of seventeen countries (mainly European with the addition of Canada, New Zealand, and Australia). Britain is the third *least biased* system, whereas West Germany, using the additional member system, is the most biased. In the case of West Germany the huge bias, 40.2 per cent, is the product of the capacity of one small party, the Free Democrats, to maintain its membership of government coalitions.

These are very challenging points, most particularly because they seem to break out of the argument over PR by declaring that it is in a sense irrelevant: what we should be studying is *proportional tenure* or comparisons formed on the basis of the exercise of power. The work is still at a research stage and so final conclusions are not really possible. Eventually, Taylor will have to take into account the problem that while we are able quite easily to quantify shares in government, we are much less able to quantify shares in policy-making: power consists in the making of policy, not simply in the ability to sit around a Cabinet table. But the moral of this story is that politics students should be aware of what people in other disciplines are doing. Sociologists, historians, lawyers, and geographers all have something to add to the study of politics, and when trying to research a topic for an extended essay, for example, the politics student should cast his net widely.

RECENT EXAMINATION QUESTIONS

Spend ten minutes or so planning an answer to each of the following questions. Outline answers for questions **1**, **8**, and **10** and a tutor's answer to question **4** are provided in the following sections.

Question 1.

Assess the likely benefits and penalties that would follow PR in Britain.
(London, Govt and Pol. Stud., Paper 1, June 1983)

Question 2.

Does Britain's electoral system provide a fair balance between representing public opinion and securing strong government?
(Cambridge, Pol. and Govt, Paper 1, June 1984)

Question 3.

Why do some significant groups fail to secure effective representation through pressure groups and political parties in Britain?
(Cambridge, Pol. and Govt, Paper 1, June 1983)

Question 4.

Discuss the proposition that electoral systems are meant to shape political attitudes rather than reflect them.
(London, Govt and Pol. Stud., Paper 1, June 1985)

Question 5.

(a) What criteria would you adopt to assess the democratic nature of an electoral system? (b) How democratic is the British electoral system?
(AEB, Govt and Pol., Paper 1, Nov. 1984)

Question 6.

Assess the effectiveness of the electoral system in providing (a) representative, (b) stable governments.
(AEB, Govt and Pol., Paper 1, Nov. 1985)

Question 7.

To what extent is it accurate to describe the British political system as a 'representative democracy'?
(AEB, Govt and Pol., Paper 1, Nov. 1982)

Question 8.

Assess the (a) strengths, (b) weaknesses of the argument that victory in a General Election gives a government a mandate to implement its manifesto.
(AEB, Govt and Pol., Paper 1, June 1985)

Question 9.	To what extent do you agree that those MPs who left their original parties and joined the SDP without fighting by-elections can still claim to have represented their constituents properly?
	(AEB, Govt and Pol., Paper 1, Nov. 1983)
Question 10.	What is meant by representative government?
	(London, Govt and Pol. Stud., Paper 1, short answer question, June 1984)

OUTLINE ANSWERS

Q.1

Assess the likely benefits and penalties that would follow the introduction of PR in Britain.

Answer

(a) In a system of PR party strength in an elected assembly is exactly proportionate to the percentage of votes cast for that party. Most PR systems do not offer *perfect proportionality*, but simply offer a means for getting closer to it than is possible under our present first past the post system. The benefits and penalties will vary according to the exact type of PR adopted.

(b) A system offering greater proportionality would remove some of the more obvious statistical absurdities in the present system. In the 1983 General Election the Conservative Party, with around 42 per cent of the vote, obtained 397 out of 650 seats. One could argue that the credibility of the Government suffers when it has a majority, over all parties combined, of over 140 seats, even though 3 out of every 5 votes have been cast against it. By allowing governments to claim that they genuinely had the support of the majority of the people a PR system would probably strengthen them.

(c) The 1983 General Election also provided a spectacular example of *under-representation* in the present system: whereas the Labour Party, with under 28 per cent of the vote obtained 207 seats, the Alliance parties with some 25 per cent of the vote only obtained 23. This presumably leaves many citizens feeling that their vote has not counted and that their views cannot be represented forcefully enough in Parliament. The introduction of PR would almost certainly bring benefits to smaller parties and would in a sense penalise larger ones.

(d) Just as PR would allow a greater range of opinion to be expressed in Parliament, it would reduce the chances that any single party would have a majority of seats. No party since 1945 has gained more than 50 per cent of the vote in a British General Election, yet most governments have had fairly comfortable majorities under the present system. Proportional representation would therefore tend to lead to coalition government. Supporters of centrist or consensus government would argue that this would bring the benefit of ending the destructive swing of the pendulum in British parliamentary politics whereby right-wing policies are pursued for a few years and then replaced with left-wing policies. Coalitions implied by PR would on this analysis create greater stability.

(e) The above arguments can, of course, be countered: coalition governments do not necessarily produce a healthy stability.

- They are often produced as the result of elaborate deals between party leaders, and might cause the voters to believe that politicians care more about office than about principle.
- It can also be argued that coalitions are weak; policies of each constituent party have to be watered down in order to reach accommodation with coalition partners. It may therefore be claimed that the voters do not actually get what they voted for if their party is one of those which makes up the Government.
- Coalitions also give inordinate power to the smaller parties among the coalition partners, so that although in a PR-based Parliament *representation* would be proportionate, *power* would not.

(f) Again some PR systems tend to erode the link between the MP and his constituents and some remove it completely. A partial PR system like STV generally involves multi-member constituencies, and a wholly proportional national list system involves no constituencies at all. In the case of STV, a series of multi-member constituencies might, however, bring some benefits. It can be argued that, as in a doctors' practice, constituents might appreciate having a *choice* of MPs to whom they could bring complaints or problems.

(g) It can be argued that most PR systems are of much greater complexity than the present first past the post system. Some voters may not understand how to operate PR voting. Still others may feel bemused and alienated by the mathematical complexity of the processes by which successful candidates emerge from, say, an STV election.

Q.8. Assess the (a) strengths, (b) weaknesses of the argument that victory in a General Election gives a government a mandate to implement its manifesto.

Answer (a) *Strengths* lie mainly in the convenience of this doctrine:

- It provides a government with a clear programme to implement.
- Members of the government party clearly understand the task facing them.
- It helps to prevent the election of a government on a 'fraudulent prospectus'.

(b) A number of *weaknesses* can be identified:

- No government since the Second World War has obtained a majority of the votes cast at a General Election. Consequently, governments cannot on this record claim to have the backing of the bulk of the people.
- There is no guarantee at all that the manifesto reflects the opinions or the wishes of even the majority of those who have actually voted for the government party. A great majority of voters do not read manifestos, and the majority do not know what is in them. Some who vote for a party vote not for its policies but for its leadership or its image. Those who vote because of policy considerations may support some items in the manifesto but not others. Thus the notion that the manifesto represents the views of a party's voters looks very much like wishful thinking.
- A government which takes office, having been in opposition, may discover when it is briefed by civil servants, and when secret information is made available to it, that its pre-election promises are simply not an appropriate means of resolving the actual circumstances of government. It may find also, of course, that circumstances change during its tenure of office, so that it may become extremely unwise to attempt to fulfil pre-election pledges. If the doctrine of the mandate is interpreted to mean that the Government is authorised by the electorate to carry out its manifesto programme and nothing contrary to that programme, then in the changed practical circumstances of government the doctrine could actually become quite pernicious, e.g. U-turns are sometimes desirable and indeed necessary.

SHORT ANSWER

Q.10.

What is meant by representative government?

Answer

Representative government is that which in some sense stands for, or acts in the place of, those whom it governs. We may take the phrase to mean that the Government is elected by a majority or at least a plurality of the people. Another commonly held attribute of representative government is that it reflects broadly the views of the majority or at least those of the largest single group within the polity. It is, however, also possible to argue that the phrase implies a government which reflects the social composition of the governed.

A TUTOR'S ANSWER

Q.4.

Discuss the proposition that electoral systems are meant to shape political attitudes rather than reflect them.

Answer

The proposition is perhaps most obviously valid in the context of electoral systems which only permit *one candidate*, sanctioned by the regime, to stand for each seat in an assembly, or which only permit contests between candidates drawn from the *one political party* sanctioned by the regime.

The purpose of such a system is fairly clearly to inculcate in the electorate the notion that there is *no practical alternative* to the values which underpin the regime. Such a system does not of course operate in the UK, but we must remember that electoral systems are devised and maintained primarily by those actively engaged in politics. Those who maintain, adapt, or oppose electoral systems will doubtless claim that their preferred system is indeed intended to reflect political attitudes; to do otherwise would be to run the risk of an accusation of political manipulation of the people. Even in, say, the Soviet Union, where only one candidate, officially sanctioned, is presented in the elections for each seat in the Soviets, the system is staunchly defended by its adherents. The electoral system is alleged to reflect the fact that the Soviet Union is a state of the working people whose attitudes can, according to Marxist/Leninist theory, be represented only by the Communist Party. There is consequently no need for competitive elections or for rival dogmas to be presented to the electorate.

So it is in a sense in the UK. Supporters of the first past the post system currently in use for most elections assume that British political attitudes are essentially *bi-polar*. Therefore the fact that the system tends to under-represent *third* parties (except where they are regional parties) is in fact perfectly natural! In their view the electoral role of third parties in this system is to act as a kind of *barometer*, displaying how well the two major parties are reflecting the opinions and attitudes of the electorate. If one or both of them should *not* be doing a 'good' job, then the barometer rises; if they *are* doing a 'good' job, then the barometer falls.

Advocates of alternative, PR systems, claim that these are fairer in that they are intended to reflect much more accurately the diversity of political attitudes. Votes for minority parties stand a much greater chance of being translated into actual representation. On the other hand, it could be argued that no electoral system, however refined, can actually reflect the political attitudes of the voters. This is because political attitudes are almost inevitably more complex than can be expressed by merely casting a vote for a candidate or for a sequence of candidates.

The fact is that electoral systems *do* shape political attitudes, and that those who maintain or advocate them are hardly likely to be unaware of this fact. For example, a first past the post system does tend to produce an acceptance that a two-party structure represents the natural order of things. The Liberal/SDP Alliance leaders may claim to be breaking the mould of British politics; but they thereby acknowledge that there is a mould to be broken.

Many other basic attitudes are associated with the *bi-polarity* which is generally produced by first past the post systems: examples are the belief that political change takes the form of a swing of the pendulum process, with first one party and then another enjoying more or less unfettered power. Another attitude often associated with bi-polarity is the view that the enjoyment of unfettered power is the 'natural' state for a government. Bi-polarity might therefore engender an overall attitude that politics is essentially played out in adversarial terms.

Against this a PR system tends to produce a different set of attitudes, because the over-representation of two major parties is diminished and the minor parties secure a much greater representation. Clear single-party governments are much less frequently produced. Politics becomes less adversarial and more of a *search for agreement and common ground* among potential coalition partners. Politics is therefore seen as a bargaining process in which give and take are necessary, even desirable, qualities.

The case of Northern Ireland is particularly interesting: in local and European elections a form of PR (i.e. STV) is used. It could be argued that this is designed to reflect political attitudes in the sense that it is intended to enable the Catholic minority in the North to achieve a degree of representation which would otherwise be denied to them. On the other hand, it could also be argued that the use of the STV system is designed to shape political attitudes in Ulster. It accustoms the Protestant Loyalist community to the idea of adequate Catholic representation and generates in the Catholic community a commitment towards parliamentary forms of politics rather than towards the violent and anti-constitutional forms offered by, say, the IRA.

Perhaps the conclusion is that it would be unduly cynical to accept the proposition that 'electoral systems are meant to shape political attitudes rather than reflect them' in its entirety, but unduly naïve to deny it completely.

A STEP FURTHER

The student who wants to examine the many ramifications of the differing electoral systems in greater detail has some excellent resources to hand. In the first place the local representatives of those political parties, such as the Liberal/SDP Alliance which would stand to benefit most from the change in the system, will undoubtedly be happy to discuss the matter and to suggest alternative electoral structures. From the considerable literature available it would be worth looking at the report of the *Hansard Society Commission* on *Electoral Reform* (Hansard Society 1976). Also see Enid Lakeman, *Power to Elect: The Case for Proportional Representation* (Heinemann 1982) and, on the other side of the fence, Angus Maude and John Szemerey, *Why Electoral Change?: The Case for PR Examined* (Conservative Political Centre 1982). Excellent surveys of the field are in addition provided by: V. Bogdanor, *What is*

Proportional Representation? (Martin Robertson 1984); by Geoffrey Alderman's chapter 'The electoral system', in R. L. Borthwick and J. E. Spence, *British Politics in Perspective* (Leicester University Press 1984); and by Bill Jones in the chapter 'Reforming the electoral system', in *Political Issues in Britain Today*, ed. Bill Jones (Manchester University Press 1985).

Chapter 10

Voting

The problem of identifying the factors which determine how people vote is obviously an absorbing one for practical politicians; indeed it has spawned a whole industry of academic enquiry by experts, the so-called psephologists. It may help to consider one or two of the concepts currently in use.

1. *De-alignment*: the decline in the tendency for members of a given socio-economic class to vote for a single party, e.g. for the middle class to vote Conservative, and for the bulk of the working class to vote Labour.
2. *Party identifiers*: voters who think of themselves as Labour or Liberal or Conservative; i.e. who vote the same way from one election to the next. Most voters identify with a single party, but the percentage is falling; 81 per cent were Labour or Conservative identifiers in 1964; only 70 per cent were Labour or Conservative identifiers in 1983.
3. *Swing*: a measure of the electoral change in a two-party system, i.e. of the net movement of votes from one party to the other. Traditionally, it is calculated by working out the *average* of the percentage gain in the Conservative vote and the percentage fall in the Labour vote (or vice versa). The notion of swing has been made much more complex by the rise of the Alliance parties.

There are many factors which may help explain why people vote as they do, but as we shall see, none of these factors will provide either a complete or a consistent explanation.

Religion

If we were to take Continental Europe as our model we should perhaps expect *religion* to play an important part in determining political allegiance. In the UK this is the case only in Northern Ireland, where Protestants tend to vote for the Unionist Party and Catholics for Sinn Fein or for the Social Democratic and Labour Party (SDLP). As for the rest of the UK the time seems to have passed when the Church of England could be described as the Conservative Party at prayer and when Nonconformists and Catholics tended to vote for the Liberals or for Labour. There is still some tendency for Conservatives to be predominant among the ranks of Church of England stalwarts, but that may be because the latter contain rather more well-off, middle-class typical Conservative voters.

Parental political attitudes

Again it has been suggested, on the basis of studies done in the 1960s, that *parental political attitudes* play an important part in moulding the political outlook of individuals. There does indeed seem to be a considerable statistical correlation between voting preferences and parental allegiances. However, it is difficult to determine whether this is the product of family influence or of broader environmental pressures, such as those exerted by neighbourhood, school, or workplace. Several different elements in the process of political socialisation often combine together in a complex nexus and it is quite impossible to disentangle them.

Social class

At the heart of the problem lies the issue of *social class* as a determinant of party allegiance. It was still possible in 1975 for one leading authority to pronounce categorically that 'class is the basis of British party politics: all else is embellishment and detail'. Less than a decade later it seemed wise to be more cautious: after the 1983 General Election joyful Conservatives proclaimed the end of the class factor in British elections, with a majority of more than 140 seats over all other parties combined. The Conservative Party must surely have cut across class barriers and become a truly national party! Both of these opposing views need to be questioned. If it *had* been true that class, alone or even predominantly, determined voting behaviour, then the Labour Party, with its working-class base, would have been in a permanent electoral majority for the past two or three generations, which it has not. On the other hand, the Conservative victory in 1983 was by no means as sweeping as the parliamentary situation suggested. The Conservative share of the vote actually went down as compared with 1979, and the traditional Labour vote was deeply split by the emergence of a new radical grouping, the Liberal/SDP Alliance, many of whose leaders (i.e. from the SDP) were former Labour Party members. Some factors, such as *old age*, may cut across traditional class allegiances. For example, Gallop pollsters suggested in 1976 that pensioners are influenced to shift votes much more readily than other social groupings, because of their particular concern with only one issue – the value which the

Government gives to their old-age pension. Even if we exclude senior citizens from the analysis it is quite clear that class groupings as traditionally defined do not provide the complete explanation for voting behaviour.

Social class for these purposes is normally defined in terms of *occupation*. For example, on the Hall–Jones Scale of Occupational Prestige, group one consists of high administrators and professional people and, at the bottom end, group seven consists of unskilled manual workers. Another and perhaps more common form of categorisation is the A, B, C1, C2, D, E scale adopted by many opinion-poll organisations. In this scheme category A consists once again of the higher administrative and professional class and category D consists of semi- and unskilled workers, with category E acting as a kind of 'residual' category which includes pensioners. Adopting these sort of categorisations we find that there is *overwhelming support for the Conservatives* among the upper groups, *general support for the Conservatives* among the middle-class sector, and *predominant support for Labour* among the working class. The latter is by no means an overwhelming phenomenon, with something over a third of working-class voters consistently supporting the Conservative Party.

These breakdowns in what would otherwise be a most convenient pattern of alignment between social class and voting behaviour can be explained in many ways: among the upwardly mobile middle classes, de-aligned voting may be explained as the product of residual parental influences upon persons who have progressed up the occupational scale. Conservative voting among working-class groups may be the result of what is termed 'deference voting', in which working-class people vote for a party not because they think that it represents their class interests, but because they think that its leaders are born to provide government and are fitted to do so by virtue of their superior social status. The force of this explanation has perhaps somewhat diminished in recent years with the general lowering of the social status of Conservative leaders and activists, a process which one Labour politician has summarised rather tartly as taking the Conservative Party out of the hands of the landowners and giving it to the estate agents.

Another possible explanation for the phenomenon of working-class Conservatism is that which we know as *self-assigned class*. It is possible, for example, that some groups who may be defined as working class on the basis of objective criteria such as occupational status, may *think* of themselves as middle class. Thus, if such an objectively defined working-class voter wants to become middle class and to acquire middle-class characteristics, or if he genuinely thinks of himself as middle class, then he is likely to vote Conservative as a badge of status.

On the other hand, one recent study of voting suggests that the class structure outlined above, based upon *occupational status*, is misleading. Instead it is suggested that class, for the purposes of political analysis, should be discussed in terms of the *conditions under which people earn their living.* This produces a new set of five categories, that is to say: salary-earners, non-manual workers doing routine jobs, self-employed persons, foremen and technicians, and the rest of the working class. This new form of class analysis arguably produces more consistent results in terms of explaining voting performance. The self-employed group turns out to be the most thoroughly Conservative; the salary-earners are divided between the Conservative Party and the Liberal/SDP Alliance, and the shrinking of the working class as defined under the new system is an explanation for the shrinkage of the Labour vote.

Clearly the debate on the relationship of social class and voting behaviour still has a long way to go and will still provide researchers with projects for many years to come. It is perhaps worth bearing in mind that voting *behaviour* may be affected by wholly different factors from those which determine basic political outlook. The most fundamental aspect of voting behaviour is simply deciding *whether or not to vote*, whatever one's party preferences. Here the decision may be crucially affected by the efficiency of the political parties in canvassing voters and in following up their canvass with attempts to turn them out on election day and even with offers to ferry them to and from the polling stations. The Conservatives, with more money, and usually more helpers available at election times than the other parties, have traditionally been seen as better able to translate their support into actual votes. Again, effective advertising and party political broadcasts strengthen existing commitments rather than winning converts.

Opinion polls

There can be little doubt that opinion polls, one of the great boom industries of recent decades, can both *affect* voting behaviour as well as *reflect* the preferences of the public. This effect may, however, work in unpredictable ways. It may cause elation among the party's supporters and create a bandwagon effect; on the other hand it may create a fatal sense of complacency in the party which is found to be in the lead in the run-up to an election. This is one of the possible reasons for the Labour Party's defeat in the General Election of 1970, in which it was shown to be leading the opinion polls until the very eve of the election. Yet again the opinion polls held shortly before elections may provoke tactical voting, an increasingly prevalent phenomenon in recent years. In the typical tactical voting situation, voters inclined to support the party shown to be running third in the polls may abandon their natural allegiance on the grounds that their vote will be wasted and then they simply transfer their vote to another party in the hope of keeping out their *least favoured* candidate. Naturally enough the parties themselves play on this relatively new-found sophistication among the electorate, and quite deliberately apply the 'squeeze' upon the supporters of the third party in the contest.

Type of election

Nor should we forget that voting behaviour is likely to change with the type of election. Of course, at *local elections* the turn-out is generally low. Nevertheless, voters do tend to use such elections, particularly when they take place in the mid-term of a Parliament when the Government is likely to be pursuing its most unpopular policies, as a means of criticising the Government. They consequently vote *against* candidates drawn from the same party as the Government even though the local issues may be quite separate from those prevalent at Westminster. Protest voting of this kind is also seen at *by-elections* in which the voters take the opportunity to reprimand or ginger up the major parties by voting for minority parties. There is an old maxim that the quality of the candidate is worth no more than 500 votes either way. While this may be applicable in General Elections, it is certainly not the case in by- elections in which the candidates have the full weight of the media focused upon them, with their every strength, and more importantly their every weakness, being publicly conveyed to the electorate. The result is that there have been examples in recent years of support for a party at a by-election crumbling after some particularly weak performance by its candidate on television. Nor should we forget the importance which attaches to the successful projection of an image by the party leaders during a *General Election*. This is most spectacularly illustrated in the 1983 General Election in the case of the so called 'Thatcher factor'. This gave rise to Conservative voting on the part of some people, not because of any admiration for Conservative policies, nor because of a tradition of Conservative voting, but simply because Margaret Thatcher, the Conservative leader, had successfully acquired an image of decisiveness in pursuit of clearly defined goals. In contrast Michael Foot, perceived as her principal rival, had acquired an image of indecisiveness and an inability to control the warring factions within the Labour Party.

Crises

Another short-term determinant of voting behaviour is the impact of *crises*, such as the Falklands War which prompted a wave of national support for the Government. Again the bombing at the Conservative Conference in Brighton in 1984 produced a reaction of sympathy for the Government. On the other hand, the miners' strike and the three-day week of 1973–74 and the winter of discontent of 1978–79 led many to feel that the Government of the day had lost its grip.

Policies

Finally, there are of course government *policies*: some may have a deterrent effect on the voters, such as Labour's confused defence policies in 1983; others such as Ted Heath's promise to cut inflation 'at a stroke' made just before polling in 1970, seem to have immediate and advantageous effects.

Even this very cursory survey of some of the possible factors affecting voting behaviour makes it clear that voting is not a simple phenomenon. Instead it is the product of many complex and sometimes conflicting factors. The British voter is not an automaton obeying the dictates of any single factor or any obviously combined group of factors. That much at least has been shown by the considerable shifts in voting behaviour which have taken place in recent years, particularly the rise in the Liberal vote and the considerable advance made by the Liberal/SDP Alliance, largely at the expense of the Labour Party.

USEFUL APPLIED MATERIALS

SOME DETERMINANTS OF SHORT-TERM FLUCTUATIONS IN VOTING INTENTIONS

Evidence from the 1983 General Election revealed the possible impact of some of the following factors listed under the headings below.

Opinion polls

There were nearly fifty major nation-wide opinion polls published in the month before the 1983 General Election. The number of *sampling points* varied from 35 to over 200, and all revealed a considerable Conservative lead. If the results are averaged out they show remarkably little fluctuation in the projected Conservative vote, which was running in the upper end of the 40–50 per cent range. In the event the Conservatives obtained less than 43 per cent of the vote. There are two reasons which are the most likely cause of this discrepancy: first, it is conceivable that respondents to the polls were in some cases suggesting a party which they thought *would* win rather than that which they *wanted* to win; second, the results of the polls may have produced a degree of overconfidence in Tory ranks with the result that some Conservative voters stayed away on polling day. The pollsters themselves conducted surveys which suggested that between 60 and 70 per cent of the electors *had* taken note of the poll findings, though only some 5 per cent of respondents admitted that the polls had influenced the way in which they had voted.

Television

A survey conducted for the BBC and the IBA on 8 June 1983, i.e. one day before polling, revealed that among *new voters* 36 per cent claimed that television had helped them to decide how to vote during the campaign. Among those who *were changing from their 1979 allegiance*, 39 per cent said that television had helped them to make this decision. Among those who were *planning to maintain their 1979 allegiance*, only 15 per cent claimed to have been helped to have reached this decision by television. Since reinforcement is less obtrusive than conversion, this may be an unduly low figure. All told, 21 per cent of those surveyed said that television had helped them to decide how to vote.

The impact of newspapers

Butler and Kavanagh suggest that 'the conventional wisdom is that the role of the press is to reinforce rather than change partisanship . . . but this issue should at least be re-opened'. (David Butler and Dennis Kavanagh, *The British General Election of 1983*, Macmillan 1984, p.218) However, given the fact that the public seems to show a steadily increasing awareness of the political biases of the various newspapers it is difficult to establish whether voters are, shall we say, Conservative because they read the *Daily Mail*, or whether they read the *Daily Mail* because they are Conservative.

Crises during the campaign

One only has to recall the political destruction of President Jimmy Carter as a result of the Iranian hostages crisis during the year preceding the 1980 presidential elections to become aware of how easily fortuitous events may affect voting intentions. In the course of the 1983 General Election campaign, however, many potential 'scandals' about the political intentions of the Conservative Party were unearthed by that party's opponents or by branches of the media. Yet they had remarkably little apparent effect upon the ultimate pattern of voting. This seems to have been the result of a skilful handling of those issues which were raised, and of equally skilful attempts to gloss over other potential issues by the Conservative campaign managers. This is well brought out by Butler and Kavanagh who comment that 'it is possible that these leaks did not make their full impact partly because there were so many of them, partly because as "leaks" they were suspect and partly because the Conservatives acted quickly to counter them. The contrast between the handling and the impact of these leaks in 1983 and that of the "Figures figures" seven days before the February 1974 poll was notable'.   (Butler and Kavanagh, op cit., p. 98)

Perhaps underlying the Conservative victory was another form of fortuitous event, namely the Falklands conflict of 1982, which had rallied most of the country behind the Government and which provided the backdrop to the Conservatives' claim to be the party of resolution and determination.

SIGNS OF MEDIA IMPACT ON VOTING BEHAVIOUR AND INTENTIONS

Developments in September 1985 revealed in different ways the possible extent of media impact on voting. A Gallup poll taken in the middle of the month revealed that the Liberal/SDP Alliance had a lead over the other parties, with Alliance 39 per cent, Labour 29.5 per cent, Conservatives 29 per cent, and other parties 2.5 per cent. The significant point is that the poll was taken immediately after the end of the SDP's Annual Conference, and at the beginning of the Liberal Assembly. The SDP Conference was seen as a particularly successful one for the party leader Dr David Owen, and received considerable media coverage. This suggests that in a period when the other parties were getting little coverage and the Alliance was centre stage, many voters felt drawn to the Liberal and Social Democratic Parties.

Also reported in mid-September was a survey conducted at Plymouth Polytechnic by Colin Rawlings and Michael Thrasher of results in local council by-elections over the summer of 1985. These results showed considerable losses for the Conservatives, who gained 35 seats, held 202 and lost 167: a net loss of 132. Although this sort of result is to be expected for the party of government in mid-term, the Labour Party surprisingly showed only a net gain of 8 seats; the SDP showed a net gain of 38, and the Liberals a startling net gain of 115, having gained 137 seats, held 68 and lost 22. This performance, which was far better than would have been anticipated on the basis of the

Liberals' standing in the national opinion polls, may well be due to the fact that local council by-elections receive very little media publicity. They therefore tend to be decided by the diligence or otherwise of local party workers. Here we perhaps see the surprising impact upon the political scene of the *absence* of a high level of media coverage. (*The Times* (19.9.85), p. 1; (20.9.85), p. 2).

THE ELECTORAL IMPORTANCE OF LEADERSHIP

The 1983 General Election was seen by many to revolve largely around the contrasting leadership styles of Margaret Thatcher and Michael Foot. Mrs Thatcher dominated the Conservative Party's election campaign press conferences, presiding over all but two of them: she seemed to have her party well under control and to know exactly where she was going. In contrast the Labour Party under Michael Foot's leadership seemed chaotic and not so much lacking in purpose as suffering from an excess of sometimes contradictory purposes. The real impact upon the electorate of images such as these remains, however, difficult to measure precisely. In May of 1983 a MORI poll revealed that if Mr Healey replaced Michael Foot as leader of the Labour Party, the Conservative lead, which was then 9 per cent would be reduced to nil. While in late May an audience selection poll on TV-AM showed that if David Steel replaced Roy Jenkins as Alliance leader, the vote for the Alliance Parties would move from a projected 20 per cent to a projected 29 per cent. On the other hand, a Gallup poll for the BBC Election Day Survey asking voters which party had the best team of leaders, reported 55 per cent going for the Conservatives, 16 per cent going for Labour, and 23 per cent for the Alliance. While the figure for the Alliance corresponds very roughly with the ultimate percentage of the vote achieved by the Alliance Parties in the election itself, the figure for Labour is considerably lower than the ultimate percentage of the vote won by the Labour party, and the figure for the Conservatives is much higher than the ultimate percentage gained by them in the election. This suggests strongly that for many voters it was not so much 'leadership' as the party policies, or their own residual loyalties, or hostility to a party, which eventually became the principal determinants of actual voting behaviour. (See Butler and Kavanagh, op. cit., pp. 133 and 280)

RECENT EXAMINATION QUESTIONS

Spend ten minutes or so preparing an outline answer to each question. Outline answers are provided for questions 1, 3, and 7, and a tutor's answer to question 2 in the following sections.

Question 1.

What light does analysis of voting behaviour throw on the claim that electoral competition is a peaceful reflection of the class struggle?
(Cambridge, Pol. and Govt, Paper 1, June 1980)

Question 2.

Assess the effect of national party politics on local election campaigns and results.
(AEB, Govt and Pol., Paper 1, June 1984)

Question 3.   'Principles and policies however important to the life of politics do little to explain a voter's party preferences.' Assess the accuracy of this statement and indicate which factors best explain party preferences.

(AEB, Govt and Pol., Paper 1, June 1984)

Question 4.   What evidence is there to suggest that social class as an influence on voting behaviour is declining in importance?

(AEB, Govt and Pol., Paper 1, June 1983)

Question 5.   Outline the major influences on voting behaviour and relate them to the electoral performance of the major parties since 1970.

(AEB, Govt and Pol., Paper 1, Nov. 1983)

Question 6.   Assess the relative importance of (a) party manifesto, (b) party image, (c) image of the party leader as factors that influence voting behaviour in General Elections.

(AEB, Govt and Pols., Paper 1, June 1982)

Question 7.   What have been the main trends in Labour voting at General Elections since 1974?

(London, Govt and Pol. Stud., Paper 2, short answer question, Jan. 1983)

Question 8.   How important is social class in voting behaviour?

(London, Govt and Pol. Stud., Paper 2, June 1983)

Question 9.   'Social class is no longer an important variable in determining voting behaviour in Britain.' Do you agree?

(Cambridge, Pol. and Govt, Paper 1, June 1985)

Question 10.   'The way most British people vote is not determined to any considerable extent by the election campaign.' How true is this?

(JMB, Brit. Govt and Pol., June 1982)

Question 11.   How true is it to say that voting behaviour in Britain is becoming more volatile?

(JMB, Brit. Govt and Pol., June 1984)

What light does analysis of voting behaviour throw on the claim that electoral competition is a peaceful reflection of the class struggle?

Answer

(a) To establish whether or not there is class struggle we must define classes. In the most conventional description of social strata, groups A, B, C1 are regarded as middle class and groups C2, D, and E as working class. The criteria used in establishing social strata groups are objective ones relating to occupation.

(b) Voting significantly fails to correspond to these class divisions. Himmelweit showed that 68 per cent of the working class voted Labour in 1964 and only 55 per cent in 1974 (H. Himmelweit, P. Humphreys, A. Jaeger and M. Leaty, *How Voters Decide*, Academic Press, 1981). In 1983, 38 per cent of manual workers and 39 per cent of trade unionists voted Labour, and a surprising 32 per cent of trade unionists voted Conservative. The Liberals have traditionally polled fairly evenly across the whole spectrum of class. At the same time some supposedly middle-class voters vote Labour, as in the case of the 16 per cent of the A, B, C1 groups who voted Labour in 1983.

(c) It is interesting to look at the reasons for Conservative working-class voting. It may be the result of the deference vote: that is to say the feeling that Conservative candidates should be supported because they have better education and are of a higher 'class' than the voter. Of course in a sense this is class-based voting, but it does not relate to class struggle; rather it is a fatalistic acceptance of the inevitability of class divisions and even of their general 'correctness'.

On the other hand some working-class Conservatives may be assigned to the working class on *objective* criteria, but may in fact *assign themselves subjectively* to the middle class. This form of Conservative vote, reflecting an aspiration to the middle class or a belief that one *is* middle class, may indeed be interpreted in a framework of class struggle. Similarly, some apparently middle-class Labour voters may vote Labour because of a family tradition of Labour voting, i.e. they may assign themselves in spirit at least to the working class. Many analyses of voting behaviour may therefore obscure the underlying patterns of class struggle.

(d) There is a solid core of class sentiment in voting; for example the A/B group vote overwhelmingly Conservative, while there seems to be an irreducible nucleus of working-class votes for Labour.

(e) Heath, Jowell, and Curtice (*How Britain Votes*) have recently produced a new definition of class for political purposes, i.e. the self-employed, salary-earners, non-manual workers in routine jobs, foremen and technicians, and working class. According to this definition of class, voting behaviour much more nearly falls into a class mould, e.g. self-employed are Conservative, salary-earners divide between Conservative and Alliance, working class are Labour.

Q.3. 'Principles and policies however important to the life of politics do little to explain a voter's party preferences.' Assess the accuracy of this statement and indicate which factors best explain party preferences.

Answer

(a) Many people may *think* that they vote on the basis of principles and policies, whereas their actual voting performance may be conditioned by other factors. Indeed they may have a fundamental misapprehension of the principles and policies of their preferred party. Survey evidence reveals a high level of ignorance of the policies of parties for which people intend to vote or have voted. For instance when, after the 1983 General Election, Tony Benn claimed that for the first time in a General Election since 1945 over 8 million people had voted for an avowedly socialist set of policies, he gravely over-simplified the situation. A very high proportion of those who voted Labour in 1983 had also voted Labour in 1979 and remained loyal *because they identified with the party* rather than because they had absorbed, understood, and endorsed the policy shifts which had taken place between 1979 and 1983. In the case of the Labour Party, many of its voters are out of sympathy with some of its key policies. In the General Election of 1979 only one-third of Labour voters endorsed the party's proposals to increase nationalisation, to increase social service spending, and to defend the existing rights and immunities of the trade unions. In the General Election of 1983, only one-third of Labour voters seemed to have approved of the party's defence stance.

(b) Voters may understand the nature of divisions between parties on political issues, but they may not consider those issues to be particularly important. For instance the support given by the Liberal/SDP Alliance to PR, which is accepted as a desirable thing by a large proportion of the electorate, is not considered to be important enough by many of them to warrant a vote for the Alliance.

(c) Party preferences are, undoubtedly, sometimes made on the principles and policies of parties. Some defections from Labour in 1983 seemed to have been made on the basis of the party's defence policy. Some support for the Conservatives in 1970 seems to have accrued as a result of Ted Heath's promise to cut inflation 'at a stroke'.

(d) The factors which explain party preferences are complex. Party preference as a statement of class allegiance is beginning to look suspect. According to conventional definitions of class 'de-alignment' is taking place; but according to a new definition of class based not on occupation or on occupational prestige but on the 'style' by which income is gained (e.g. self-employment, salaried employment, etc.) class is still an important determinant of party preferences. Long-term factors, such as educational background, parental influences, peer group pressures, are all more or less closely related to the class issue.

(e) Voters who express a preference for a party which does not apparently represent their class interests, may be assigning themselves to a class other than their objective class. On the other hand they may be casting a deference vote, i.e. voting for a party which may not represent or promise to further their class interest, but which they believe is naturally fitted to govern by reason of its members' superior social status. Other determinants include the image of the party and its leadership: a poor image which suggests personal incompetence or division among the party leadership is likely to drive even traditional voters for that party into abstention or even into voting for another party. In contrast the so-called Thatcher factor in 1983 allegedly produced votes for the Conservatives, even on the part of those who did not approve of what they knew of the Conservative programme.

(f) Obviously it is difficult to generalise across over 30 million voters. The above discussion for example is largely irrelevant to politics in Ulster where class is of little significance as a factor in voting and sectarian divisions based on religion are paramount.

SHORT ANSWER

Q.7.

What have been the main trends in Labour voting at General Elections since 1964?

Answer

The Labour vote since 1964 has been generally falling. It is true that in the 1966 election it reached a high point of nearly 48 per cent of votes cast and over 13 million in all, but since then the trend has been generally downwards. At no time since the early 1970s has Labour achieved more than 40 per cent and more than 12 million votes. In 1983 its vote slumped to a post-war low of under 28 per cent and under 8.5 million votes. Underlying this movement is a decline in the willingness of the solidly working-class community to vote Labour. Nearly 70 per cent of the solidly working class voted Labour in 1964, whereas only 55 per cent did so in 1974, and under 40 per cent in 1983. Parallel with these developments has been a regionalisation of the Labour vote. It remains strong in the North, but in many areas of the South and the South East has almost disappeared as a significant factor in elections.

A TUTOR'S ANSWER

Q.2.

Assess the effect of national party politics on local election campaigns and results.

It is a perfectly reasonable view that local government elections should be dominated by the affairs of the locality and by the characters of the candidates for election to the local council. Increasingly, however, this is not the case. Recent years have seen the increasing influence of parties and party politics upon local government and local elections

A major step in this direction was taken in the 1972 Local Government Act which reduced the number of councils in England and Wales from 1,390 to 422. By thus increasing the size and significance of local councils, the Act made it more worth while for the major parties to contest council elections seriously. It broke up the old club-like atmosphere that had existed in some of the smaller councils, and national party allegiance became a more prominent feature in the description and promotion of councillors. As a result national party politics came to have a considerable impact on both local campaigns and their subsequent results.

There is a clearly visible tendency for local elections to be seen as an opportunity to comment on the performance of the Westminster Government. Indeed, this tendency was apparent even before the 1972 Local Government Act. Governments tend to introduce the more contentious and potentially unpopular measures in their manifestos during the early and middle years of their term in office, in order to clear the ground for more attractive measures later on. Therefore, when local elections fall within this early or mid-term period, they tend to be used by the electorate as an opportunity to protest the actions of central government. A good example is the 1968 local elections which were a disaster for the Labour Party, reflecting the difficulties of a government which had been elected in 1966 and forced in the following year to devalue the pound and to abandon a push for growth. Again, following the Conservative victory in the 1970 General Election, the local elections of the early 1970s produced a rich harvest of seats for the Labour Party as the Government was in considerable trouble over its industrial relations legislation and over its handling of economic issues. Further, the local elections in the period around 1976, 1977, and 1978 were beneficial to the Conservatives as the country reacted against the 1974–79 Labour administration at Westminster. A similar phenomenon could be observed more recently in the heavy Conservative losses in the 1985 local elections, reflecting widespread disenchantment at the Government's national record and particularly at its squeeze on public, especially local government, expenditure.

The very distinction between national and local policies has become more blurred in recent years, especially with the Thatcher administration's moves to impose financial restraints on local councils. This means that the dominant parties in many non-Conservative councils have made opposition to the *Government* a key element in their election campaigns.

The effects of the national political situation on local results may, however, have been exaggerated on occasions. For example the seats which had been at stake in the huge anti-Labour swing of 1968 were not fought again until 1971, when it was natural that many of them would return to their traditional Labour allegiance. This accentuated the swing against the Conservatives in 1971. It could be argued that in this case local elections affected national politics as much as national politics affected local elections.

Nevertheless, it is a feature of local election campaigns that the party which is out of office at Westminster usually attempts to draw attention to the all too visible defects of the Government. Whereas the government party, if it is feeling at all defensive about its national record, urges the voters to keep the local election strictly local. It should perhaps be added that even with their *dual* function of providing local councillors and of commenting upon the performance of the national Government, local elections are still unable to seize the imagination of the electorate. The turn-out is generally low, at well under 40 per cent of the voters.

Substantial advances in local elections have been made in recent years by the Liberal/SDP Alliance, but the reason for this is hard to analyse. On the one hand it may simply reflect the much greater media attention which is given nationally to the Alliance than was previously available to the Liberals alone. But in fact the Alliance Parties tend to perform much better in local elections, particularly local council by-elections, than their standing in the national opinion polls would predict. A survey of local government by-election results conducted in late 1985 showed that the Alliance had been by far the most successful of the party groupings, even though during the period covered by the survey the Alliance had been running third in most of the national opinion polls. This probably reflects the long-standing community politics approach attempted by the Liberals in particular, which may be beginning to bear electoral fruit. This approach stresses the local dimension of elections, with 'campaigning' being seen as consisting of continuous contacts with the local community rather than concentrated attention in the month or so before polling day. Such an approach would seem to be going some way towards emancipating local elections from national policies.

A STEP FURTHER

The student who wants to examine voting behaviour and the forces which produce it in more detail is referred to the major series of studies of British General Elections which have been produced by David Butler and others for the past twenty-five years. These are published by Macmillan, with the elections of February and October 1974, of 1979, and of 1983 being studied by Butler in conjunction with Dennis Kavanagh. Their joint volumes contain a mass of tables, and useful statistics as well as helpful anecdotes and reference to the conduct of the election campaigns. A very stimulating recent survey of voting behaviour, which offers a new definition of class for purposes of political analysis is Anthony Heath, Roger Jowell and John Curtice, *How Britain Votes* (Pergamon Press 1985). Those pursuing the topic of class and voting should also try to consult Richard Rose, *Class does not Equal Party* (Strathclyde Papers No. 74, 1980).

Chapter 11   **Participation in politics**

One of the principal problems in analysing political participation is that of being able to pinpoint where participation in politics begins. Clearly, *political party candidates* are participants in the political process, and so are *party activists*. But it is much less certain whether *all* members of political parties can be counted as particularly committed. We can assume that many of the Conservative Party's 1.1 million members are 'passive' in the sense they have joined their local association for social reasons or as a general gesture of support, without intending to do much more than pay membership fees. Precisely because of its small numbers and recent foundation, the 52,000 membership of the SDP is more likely to share a sense of commitment to the party's activities. In the field of *pressure-group activity* many members of say, trade unions, join simply because they are obliged to do so by closed shop agreements, and many take no active part in union proceedings. Many pressure groups are not overtly 'political', but may become so if their interests are threatened.

It helps therefore to establish various *categories* of political participation:

- *constant*, virtually professional, participation, as in the case of elected representatives or the leaders of major economic interest groups;
- *regular but totally voluntary* participation, as in the case of party activists;
- *sporadically intense* participation, as in the case of those occasionally moved to demonstrate, to petition, to write to the press, to complain to representatives, or to form *ad hoc* pressure groups;
- *regular but purely formal* participation, exemplified by regular voting in local government and parliamentary elections;
- *irregular and purely formal* participation, as in occasional voting in local government and parliamentary elections.

This subject should also be considered not simply from the

standpoint of *how much participation* actually takes place, but also from that of *how many opportunities for participation* exist. If we are dissatisfied about the level of participation in Britain we must enquire as to the cause. Is it because involvement by all the people, or by specific groups such as ethnic minorities, though quite possible, is not considered worth while, or important? Or alternatively, is it because there are institutional and social barriers to participation? Or is it some amalgam of the two?

ESSENTIAL PRINCIPLES

FORMS OF PARTICIPATION

One of the chief ways in which a political system achieves stability and a wide measure of support among the citizens is by affording them plentiful opportunities for involvement in the *process* by which decisions are ultimately made. Let us examine the various forms which such participation may take in Britain.

1. The vote

First, of course, there is the opportunity for *voting* in parliamentary and local council elections. We have already seen that this may leave much to be desired as a means of expressing any views other than the broadest preferences for one party or another. Moreover, the fact that MPs and councillors are *not bound* by the wishes of the electors, means that the latter may feel little sense of involvement through their representatives.

2. Party membership

Second, elections offer scope for participation by *party members*, i.e. the more committed supporters. There is usually a need for volunteers to deliver leaflets to the voters, to assist in canvassing, to act as tellers at polling stations and committee rooms, and to ferry voters to and from the polls. This commitment is, however, relatively rare: the numbers directly involved can be counted in thousands rather than millions. Membership of political parties only involves some 5 per cent of the adult population, and the activists most regularly occupied in party business constitute a much smaller number. Party membership alone can give a sense of involvement without the substance of it.

3. Pressure groups

A more widespread form of participation in the political process is provided by *pressure-group activity*. Pressure groups are in a sense more flexible and attractive because they do not involve the commitment to a wide range of policies which is implied by membership of a political party: they may range from the local amenity group to the great national campaigning organisations, and from the raucous protest group to the discreet operation of the professional body. They may be defensive or sectional in nature, protecting the interests, mainly occupational, of their members, as with trade unions. Alternatively, they may be promotional, advancing some particular cause which may not be to the direct benefit of their members: examples here are the NSPCC or the RSPCA.

It is difficult to be precise about the numbers of citizens actually involved in pressure-group politics. It has been suggested that 5,000 is a good membership for a cause or promotional group, while 10,000 is quite exceptional, and even then many of the members will be inactive sympathisers. Much larger of course are the great trade unions, but these can hardly be said to be the vehicles for mass participation. Many trade-union members are unconcerned about the activities of their union. They do not participate in branch meetings and do not vote for local or national officials. They assume that the leadership will strive to better their conditions. For their part most trade-union leaders are content that the direction of politics should be left largely in their hands. Not all unions are like the NUM with its long history of regular consultations with the membership.

The *means* by which pressure groups apply their leverage vary enormously. Some, such as CND involve their members intensively in marches, demonstrations or in the mounting of information points in their homes. Others use their members and supporters primarily as a source of financial contributions. Many pressure groups establish contacts with relevant central or local government departments to whom they act as sources of information and advice. For the most part this sort of activity involves only a relatively few people. It is clear, however, that pressure groups *do* constitute an important vehicle by means of which people may feel that they are making some impact on their political environment. They go some way towards overcoming the problems of lack of involvement inherent in indirect or representative democracy.

If we accept the evidence of numerous surveys of the political attitudes and involvement of the British public, we shall see that most people do not want to be involved deeply in political matters in any form. The small minority of people who do wish to become involved have plenty of opportunities to do so: by joining political parties, by standing as candidates, by joining pressure groups, even by simply writing to the newspapers. The British system may fulfil the basic requirements expressed in the minority report of the Kilbrandon Commission on the Constitution, that the ordinary citizen should be involved in the political system and should be able to participate in the decision-making process. But our political culture does not place much stress on the importance of such participation. It is not regarded as a paramount civic duty. Those people who do make the effort to involve themselves are likely to be drawn from occupations in which leadership and articulacy are normal functions of the job. Members of the professions, managers, trade-union officials are all commonly represented in actively involved groups: it is not for nothing that the Labour Party has been described as the party of polytechnic lecturers. Equally it is not for nothing that entrepreneurial, managerial, and professional interests are so strong within the Conservative Party.

Active participation thus seems to remain pretty well the preserve of a few predictable categories of citizens. Attempts to break that mould have had only indifferent success. In the period of its origin in the early 1980s the SDP claimed that it was attracting large-scale membership from people who had not previously been involved, or indeed interested, in politics. In the early heady days that may have been the case, but since then many of those political novices seem to have returned to their 'obscurity'. Whether this voluntary limitation of those actively engaged in some form of political life is a good thing remains a moot question. From one point of view mass participation might be said to validate the political system, to indicate general support for it. On the other hand what we sometimes take for political apathy may indicate a general level of satisfaction with the system and no consequent need for individuals to exert themselves to change it.

USEFUL APPLIED MATERIALS

THE KILBRANDON COMMISSION CONFRONTS THE PROBLEM OF INCREASING PARTICIPATION

'At the time of our appointment there had been much discussion of a desire for greater participation in government. There had not emerged any clear idea of the form which that participation should take, and one of our most difficult problems had been to determine what "participation" might mean in practice and how strong and widespread the desire for it is.

'Greater participation could be achieved by giving existing elected representatives more control over what government is doing, or by increasing the numbers of the elected representatives, or by providing for more involvement in government activities in particular fields by persons not necessarily elected but in some way representing the general public. It could also take the form of more prior consultation by people affected by government decisions, or by better communication generally between government and people, so that the electorate was made to feel less remote from government. Participation could be more effective still if there were greater opportunities for it to be exercised locally; many people would be able to play an effective part in government only in their own localities, and there they would be knowledgeable and understanding about local issues and readily accessible to those affected by their decisions. . . . [The Commission went on to explore some of the issues raised in the above paragraphs and then went on to discuss the issue of communication as a form of participation.]

'Finally there is the more elusive concept of general communication between government and people – a state of mutual trust and understanding which enables each to appreciate the position of the other so that the people on the one hand will recognise the difficulties of government and the limitations on what it can do, and government on the other hand will be fully and continuously aware of what the people think about it and expect of it. We believe that in this sense there is at present a wide gap in communication. This belief is explicitly supported by the attitude survey and there are echoes of it in our general evidence. Several witnesses suggested that the chief fault of government is its inability to communicate directly and simply with the people. One essential element which seems to be missing is a demonstrated willingness on the part of government to listen as well as to inform. Put simply, the contention is that government needs to do more to discover and understand the views and problems of ordinary people. It should reach out more to maintain contact with the individual'. (*The Royal Commission on the Constitution 1969–73*, Cmnd. 5460. 1973, Sections 310–11 and 317.)

(It is interesting to compare these observations with some of the material collected below on attempts by local authorities in the mid-1980s to stimulate participation on the part of their residents.)

ATTEMPTS TO ENCOURAGE PARTICIPATION

Periods of political crisis tend to stimulate interest in the processes of politics and to increase direct participation in them by way of marches, demonstrations, and so on. For example, as the Conservative Government's financial squeeze on local authorities gathered ferocity in the course of the 1980s local councils, particularly those which were Labour controlled, responded in several ways. Many began to issue free newspapers drawing attention to council services and helping to instruct residents in the ways in which councils work. Many such newspapers attempt to enlist direct public support in the local council's various struggles against central government. The *Cambridge City Herald* of December 1985 provides one example. It voiced the council's opposition to the Government's civil defence policy and to the Government's plans for a reduction in building and planning regulations, commenting that

'the government is intending to push back the threshold of local government ability to control the environment in the interests of encouraging businesses but at the expense of the interest and welfare of the public'.   (p. 7)

The same paper in the same issue contained advice to its readers to lobby Members of Parliament against the Government's plans to remove restrictions on Sunday trading and its plans to bring in legislation curbing local authorities' powers to issue publicity. The *Liverpool News*, the information paper of the embattled Liverpool City Council, contains plentiful evidence of the council's attempt to mobilise the population of the city in its fight over funding with central government. For example, the issue of March 1984 notes that

'through its campaign the City Council has been informing all sections of the community, public meetings have been held throughout the City, the Council's case has been explained and councillors have answered people's questions in well attended meetings. The choices facing a Labour council have been openly discussed. The meetings showed a very high level of public understanding, they also suggested increasing support for the council's stand. The council's case is also being explained to community groups.'   (p. 1)

The issue of February 1985 contained information about ten public meetings at which councillors would be present, to be held on 26–28 February to explain the council's case and answer questions, and also advertised a demonstration and rally for 7 March.

A PRESSURE GROUP'S PROGRAMME

To illustrate the way in which some pressure groups are able to involve members and sympathisers in a wide range of activities, let us look at the Cambridge CND programme of events for the two months from early December 1985 to early February 1986:

10 December	Cambridge CND newcomers' meeting
12 December	Cambridge CND market stall
14 December	A trip for women to Greenham Common, the airbase at which the Americans have deployed Cruise missiles.
19 December	Cambridge CND monthly meeting
31 December	Christian CND Watch Night for Penitence and Peace in 1986 at a central Cambridge church
9 January	Cambridge CND market stall
14 January	Cambridge CND monthly meeting featuring a talk by a representative of National CND on the new Emergency Powers Bill
16 January	Cambridge CND monthly meeting
21 January	Cambridge CND newcomers' meeting
31 January	Cambridge CND Ceilidh at a local community centre
4 February	Monthly meeting
6 February	Involvement in a national CND demonstration at Molesworth Airbase
11 February	Cambridge CND newcomers' meeting

In addition to the above events there were regular Saturday CND stalls at Cambridge market.

INDIVIDUALS AND ORGANISATIONS INVOLVED IN THE *SCARMAN REPORT* OF 1981

As we have seen above, at times of heightened political or social tension public participation in the political process tends to increase and quite frequently new vehicles for such participation emerge. An example of this is the Inquiry set up by the Home Secretary in 1981 following the severe disorders in Brixton, which took place in April of that year. The Inquiry was conducted by Lord Scarman, one of the Law Lords, and it attracted considerable publicity. The following is an analysis of the written evidence presented to the Inquiry:

(a) Pressure groups and voluntary bodies: 88.
(b) Police forces, local authorities, and government departments: 30.
(c) Individuals: 167; in addition 450 letters were received from members of the public offering views on issues before the Inquiry.
(*Note*: Figures derived from the *Scarman Report*, Penguin Books 1982, pp. 241–8.)

A LOCAL COUNCILLOR'S WORKLOAD

Hilary Richmond is a Liberal councillor for the West Chesterton Ward of Cambridge City Council.

- She is a member of two City Council committees, the General Purposes Committee and the Community Services Committte. These meet at least once every six weeks.

- She is a member of the City Finance Panel, of the Peace Forum and of one City Council working party. The working party and the Peace Forum involve meetings about once per quarter.

- She represents Cambridge City Council on the executive of the Local Council for Voluntary Services which meets once per month. Councillor Richmond is also a member of that organisation's subcommittee on equal opportunity policy. The subcommittee meets about once every two months.

- She is the Cambridge City Council representative to the Riverside Club for Teenagers who have attended special schools in Cambridge, which meets twice per term.

- She is council nominee as governor of two schools, one primary school involving meetings three times per term and one secondary school of which Councillor Richmond is Chair of Governors. This involves meetings twice per term, and in addition meetings of two subcommittees on staffing and disciplinary matters. As Chair of the Governors of the secondary school she is automatically a member of the Forum of the Chairs of Governors of *all* Cambridgeshire schools. This involves meetings once per term.

- She is Cambridge City Council representative on the Nuclear Free Zones Steering Committee, a body which meets approximately once every quarter.

- Resulting from her membership of the executive of the local Council for Voluntary Services, Councillor Richmond has become Eastern Region representative on the Executive Committee of the National Association of Councils for Voluntary Services and also serves on that body's conference planning committee which meets every two months.

Membership of all of the bodies and committees outlined above of course requires considerable background work. For example, serving on the Community Services Committee and on the Local Council for Voluntary Services involves her in frequent meetings with, and lobbying by, several voluntary sector groups such as the Co-operative Development Agency, Overstream House, an organisation running Save the Children projects, the Rape Crisis Centre, Cambridge Women's Resource Centre, Centre 33, a young people's counselling organisation, and the Marriage Guidance Centre. In addition some organisations attempt to lobby all councillors on matters of importance to them so that as a result of the City Council's attempt to restrict traffic in the city centre Councillor Richmond, like most of her colleagues, is lobbied by the local Taxi Drivers' Association and by the Cambridge Association for Disabled People.

At ward level residents' meetings take place perhaps six times per year while Councillor Richmond and her fellow ward councillors try to arrange occasional surgeries for residents. These take place perhaps one per month. For about half of the year she tries to go out about once per week simply knocking on doors making contact with residents in order to discover their feelings on ward issues. She also has to react to two or three letters per week from ward residents and perhaps a dozen telephone calls per week from residents. There are inevitable party and pressure-group meetings and duties which need attention. These include party ward meetings about once per month.

The party group on the council meets every three weeks and the executive of the Constituency Association meets monthly, although Councillor Richmond usually attends once every two months. The Liberal CND Group meets four times per year and Councillor Richmond's particular interest in this area of policy involves her in meetings arranged by CND and the Liberal groups in many parts of the country. These currently run at the rate of about one per month. She is also a member of the Association of Liberal Councillors and attends that organisation's annual conference.

One or two points need to be made about the above material. Firstly, it will be obvious that we cannot take one councillor's activities as typical of those of all councillors. Councillor Richmond is a city councillor, that is to say she works at district level rather than at county level. County councillors probably have generally a rather greater committee load than district councillors, although in many cases their load of casework, that is to say their need to deal with residents' problems, is less acute. Again, Councillor Richmond's particular interest in a number of causes has led to her becoming involved in them at national level and this is not the case with many district councillors. It should be remembered that Cambridge is a relatively wealthy and expanding urban environment. The nature of the workload of councils and councillors in, say, rural districts, or in deprived highly urbanised districts, will have a character completely different from that of Cambridge. But bearing all of these factors in mind, it should be clear that the high level of political participation involved in becoming a local councillor involves much sacrifice of time and social freedom.

The above material also raises a problem of definition: at what point does participation become political? Many of the organisations and indeed individuals with whom Councillor Richmond comes into contact would not perhaps regard themselves as being politically orientated. Nevertheless, when a voluntary organisation seeks a grant from the local authority, or when a commercial association such as the Taxi Drivers' Association wishes to change projected council policy, or when a ward resident wishes to object to some planning proposal, then they are forced in a sense to act politically, and to participate in the political process by lobbying.

RECENT EXAMINATION QUESTIONS

Spend ten minutes or so planning an answer to each of the following questions. Outline answers to questions **1** and **9**, and a tutor's answer to question **4** are given in the following sections.

Question 1.

Should direct participation by the British public in the political process be further encouraged?

(Cambridge, Econ. and Pub. Aff., June 1980)

Question 2.

What measures would you suggest to encourage greater political participation at all levels of government by *one* of the following groups: ethnic minorities, women, young people?

(Cambridge, Pol. and Govt, Paper 1, June 1984)

Question 3.

Why is there a predominance of people with middle-class backgrounds in politics and in the Civil Service? Does it matter?

(London, Govt and Pol. Stud., Paper 2, Jan. 1985)

Question 4.

(a) How do the Conservative and Labour Parties select their parliamentary candidates? (b) Why are so few candidates drawn from the minority ethnic groups?

(AEB, Govt and Pol., Paper 1, Nov. 1985)

Question 5.

(a) Describe the changes in the procedures for the selection of parliamentary candidates in the Labour Party since 1980.
(b) Why did these changes occur?

(AEB, Govt and Pol., Paper 1, Nov. 1984)

Question 6.

Make a case for the activities of pressure groups and a case against them.

(London, Govt and Pol. Stud., Paper 1, Jan. 1981)

Question 7.

What inequalities exist in the possession and distribution of political power in Britain? Can they be justified?

(London, Govt and Pol. Stud., Paper 1, Jan. 1982)

Question 8.

Can you justify inequalities in the possession of political power and influence?

(London, Govt and Pol. Stud., Paper 1, June 1982)

Question 9.

'The Government can govern only through the support of all those who are governed.' How can the views of the governed be ascertained?

(Cambridge, Econ. and Pub. Aff., June 1981)

Question 10.

Local government in Britain appears to be faced with a widespread public indifference towards its affairs. Discuss.

(JMB, Brit. Govt and Pol., June 1982)

Question 11.

In what sense can the average citizen be said to participate in government?

(JMB, Brit. Govt and Pol., June 1981)

OUTLINE ANSWERS

Q. 1.

Should direct participation by the British public in the political process be further encouraged?

Answer

(a) We need to define 'direct participation'. It presumably means active membership of political parties, involvement in pressure-group activity, involvement in local and national referenda, and more extensive consultation of the public in the course of the decision-making process.

(b) On the surface further direct participation by the public looks obviously desirable. Involvement in the political process probably generates greater commitment to it. Such involvement is likely to increase the general level of political knowledge in the community, which is an important attribute of a successful democracy.

(c) It is hard to see how *some* aspects of direct participation might be 'encouraged', such as those which are essentially voluntary, e.g. membership of pressure groups and active membership of political parties. There are better prospects with other aspects of direct participation. As a matter of policy more referenda might be held and more consultation might take place. Particularly in a local political context, more direct participation might take some of the load off already overburdened local councillors. If amenity groups, residents' associations, and individuals could learn to put their suggestions or grievances directly to the council, or to lobby the relevant councillors rather than simply going through their own ward councillors, then the quality of local decision-making may well improve. Councillors could then act more effectively as the facilitators of communication between the public and council officials and committees. It could indeed be argued that even on a national level political decisions could be made with more confidence, and would have more binding force, if interested sections of the population had been given the opportunity to participate more fully in policy formulation.

(d) There are, however, distinct drawbacks to a higher level of direct participation in the political process.
- The necessary machinery is often expensive to set up and maintain.
- Direct participation may very often slow down the decision-making process.
- There is no guarantee that direct participation would achieve greater clarity of inputs into the policy-making process. This perhaps reflects the notion that the best committee is a committee of one.

- There is the essentially *élitist* point that decisions should be made by those who are best qualified to make them and that this does not generally cover the bulk of the population.
- There is the *cynical* point that an extension of the opportunities for direct participation would simply hand over the capacity to achieve crucial inputs into the system to groups which were well organised. In other words the policy-formation process is so complex that the important inputs are almost certain to be monopolised by the technically competent or the politically well disciplined.

Q. 9.	'The Government can govern only through the support of all those who are governed'. How can the views of the governed be ascertained? (This is a difficult format: in that the initial quotation seems to bear little relation to the subsequent question.)
Answer	The statement at the head of the question is manifestly untrue. Since 1945 no government has enjoyed the support of more than 50 per cent of those who have voted at General Elections. The 1983 Thatcher Government achieved only just under 43 per cent of the vote. Elections legitimise the subsequent actions of the Government, which proceeds to govern with the tacit consent rather than the support of those who are governed. Governments often succeed in governing in the sense of pushing through legislation and creating and maintaining policy until a General Election, when they may be rejected by the electorate, presumably on the basis of their past performance. This brings us to the issue of ascertaining the views of the governed. Presumably governments sometimes fail to be sensitive to the views of the people or at least to the views of a sufficient number of the people to ensure their re-election. This suggests that the machinery for ascertaining the views of the governed may be in some ways defective. The main channels of communication are as given under the following headings.
1. Elections	We are concerned here with both General Elections and parliamentary by-elections and also local council elections which are often used as a kind of barometer of popular feeling about the way in which the national Government is performing. The problem here is that any vote is a clumsy instrument for the expression of views. It records at best a broad preference for one party over others, though in the case of the 'tactical vote' it may not even do that. It does not indicate the strength of feeling for or against any one item in the party's manifesto, or for or against any one element in a government's policies.
2. Individual and group representation	Determined individuals may press their views upon Members of Parliament or local councillors, or they may write to the newspapers. Groups of concerned individuals may form interest or pressure groups in order to publicise and promote their views. There is, however, an element of distortion about both. Individuals or groups which make a

lot of noise and achieve a lot of publicity, may appear to represent far more significant currents of opinion than is actually the case. It is one of the tasks of politicians not to be unduly swayed by the energetic expression of what may be minority interests.

3. Opinion polls

Much more reliable indicators are provided by opinion polls. There are, of course, some spectacular examples of opinion polls getting it wrong: e.g. the polls which preceded the 1948 American presidential elections, or those which preceded the 1985 Brecon and Radnor parliamentary by-election. There is also the problem that they may tend to distort the transmission of the views of the governed by producing a temporary bandwagon effect in favour of a particular party or policy. But in general, as sampling techniques improve, the polls provide the best means by which politicians may take the political temperature at regular intervals. In the 1983 General Election the Labour leader Michael Foot affected to disbelieve the opinion polls which showed the Labour Party trailing badly and claimed he was interested only in the result of the 'real election': but in the event the result of the real election showed that the opinion polls had been consistently on the right lines. Opinion polls also allow politicians to penetrate beyond mere expressions of party preference in order to gauge the likes and dislikes of the public for individual policy acts.

4. Referenda

Referenda are in a sense a form of officially sanctioned opinion poll. The problem here is that everything depends on the subtlety (or lack of it) of the question which is set in the referendum.

A TUTOR'S ANSWER

Q. 4.

(a) How do the Conservative and Labour Parties select their Parliamentary candidates? (b) Why are so few candidates drawn from the minority ethnic groups?

Answer

(a) In the case of both parties the candidate selection process involves co-operation between the central organisation of the party and the constituency organisation. In the case of the *Conservative Party* an advisory committee on candidates assists the Vice-Chairman to keep a list of approved candidates. Constituencies in search of a candidate generally consult the Vice-Chairman who passes on recommendations from the list. It is, however, possible to go forward as a candidate in a constituency even if one is not on the Vice-Chairman's list. In the case of the *Labour Party* the NEC maintains lists of approved candidates which are simply forwarded to any constituency seeking a candidate.

At the next stage of selection, however, practice varies between the two parties. Individuals are able to apply direct for consideration to a Conservative constituency association, whereas in the Labour Party would-be candidates must be nominated by an affiliated organisation such as a trade-union branch, or a socialist or Co-operative Society, or a branch of the Young Socialists. This means that affiliated organisations act as a kind of filter in the case of the Labour Party. This difference explains why the numbers going forward as candidates are far greater in the case of Conservative Associations where there are frequently more than 100 names for consideration, while in the Labour Party the list of candidates for selection is generally less than 20.

With the Conservatives the task of sifting through the large number of hopefuls is consigned to a subcommittee of the local association's executive. This subcommittee generally whittles the possibles down to a short list of five or six who go before the executive and are questioned. Following this a decision is made by the executive by ballot. The selection is then ratified in a general meeting of the constituency association. In the case of the Labour Party the General Management Committee (GMC), rather like the executive in the case of the Conservatives, appoints a subcommittee to produce a short list. The short-listed candidates go before the GMC which makes a choice which is final, subject only to NEC approval. It should be noted that in the Labour Party this selection process is now mandatory in all constituencies even where there is a sitting MP, before each General Election.

There is perhaps greater opportunity for the authentic participation of most local members in the selection process in the Conservative Party: in a celebrated incident before the 1983 General Election the Conservative MP, Sir Anthony Meyer, was defeated in the selection committee for the new seat of Clwyd North West by an MEP (a Euro-MP), Miss Beata Brookes. He then successfully insisted that his name should be brought before the general meeting of the Conservative Association where he was in fact selected as the candidate for Clwyd North West in preference to Miss Brookes.

(b) In 1983 only 18 candidates who were black or Asian were put forward as candidates by major parties, and of these 8 stood for the Alliance, 6 for Labour and 4 for the Conservatives. Perhaps only one of these was believed to have a reasonable chance of winning the seat; in the event he did not, so that no black or Asian candidate was elected.

It will not do simply to argue that ethnic minority candidates are not selected because members of ethnic minorities do not put themselves forward for selection. It is true that some minority groups tend to stand outside the main currents of national life. We have here something of a chicken and egg situation in that we could argue that ethnic minority participation in conventional politics would be greater if our society encouraged it. The fact is that most local party selection committees see their job as being to select a candidate who will maximise the vote rather than make a social breakthrough. This makes selectors generally cautious in their approach. Most are conscious that an ethnic minority candidate may drive away white voters and are unwilling to test whether this piece of conventional wisdom is in fact valid or not. There are very few constituencies in which a single ethnic minority group even comes close to providing 50 per cent of the electorate, so that in all cases the reactions of the white voters assume very considerable importance in the eyes of selectors.

Selectors will generally look for a number of qualities which are reassuring to voters. Foremost among these is a record of conventional involvement in the community. Charity work, school governorships, service on the local council, office-holding in a pressure group, are some of the factors which might render a candidate 'safe'. It has hitherto been difficult for members of ethnic minorities to break through the barriers of prejudice and tradition and assume positions which command respect from those beyond their own ethnic groups. Until there is an established tradition of councillors, council leaders, mayors, magistrates, members of the professions, etc. being drawn from the ranks of ethnic minorities, most selectors will probably prefer to seek the conventional authority figure of the middle-aged (frequently middle-class) white male.

A STEP FURTHER

There are many useful textbooks and chapters in textbooks on the subject of participation, but this is above all a subject which the interested student can explore for himself by doing some field-work. Most organisations which invite political participation are in the business of publicising themselves and are consequently more than happy to take enquiries and to discuss their role in the political process with students. National campaigning organisations like Shelter, the Child Poverty Action group, and so on are generally willing to dispense information, as are organisations such as CND, which maintain a local presence and which tend to organise a fairly full calendar of demonstrations, marches, and fund-raising events. Any student who has leanings towards one or other of the political parties will be able to make contact with that party quite easily (the local party headquarters are generally to be found in the telephone book) and will probably be eagerly pulled in to help in the business of distributing leaflets, or, if election time is nearing, putting election addresses into envelopes and other such menial tasks. A fair degree of inconvenience and drudgery is of course exactly what much political participation, certainly in its early stages, is all about. It is an experience not to be missed in that it will convey in particularly lively fashion to a student the atmosphere at ward or constituency meetings; it will also convey some of the excitements and frustrations of active participation in the political process. For some valuable studies of various aspects of political participation it is worth looking at P. Lowe and J. Goyder, *Environmental Groups in Politics* (Allen and Unwin 1983) and *The Directory of Pressure Groups and Representative Associations* (2nd edn), ed. P. Shipley (Bowker 1979).

Chapter 12   The redress of grievances

GETTING STARTED

We are concerned in this chapter with the remedies available for citizens who either individually or in groups have grievances against a public authority, such as a local authority or a government department. We are not concerned with the remedies available in disputes between citizens. It will be helpful to glance at some of the technical terms used to describe actions by public authorities against which complaint may legitimately be made.

(a) *Ultra vires*: an action which is *ultra vires* is one which goes beyond the statutory powers which have been given to a body or which exceeds the statutory limitations upon its actions. Thus in the case *Attorney-General* v *Fulham Corporation* (1921) it was held that a local authority which had been empowered to provide wash-houses, that is to say places where the public could bring their washing in order to do it themselves, had acted *ultra vires* by providing instead a fully-fledged commercial laundry service.

(b) *Maladministration*: the term covers inadequate or improper administrative process. This can include unreasonable administrative delay, failure to consider relevant facts when making administrative decisions, consideration of irrelevant facts when making administrative decisions, loss of correspondence, corruption, bias, and failure to provide the public with correct information.

(c) *Rights*: most grievances against public bodies arise from a feeling that a citizen's rights have been ignored or trampled upon. The situation in the UK with regard to rights is a complex one: there is no all-embracing Bill of Rights which sets out in detail the freedoms available to the citizen. Rights fall into two main categories. First, there are *civil rights* which are principally concerned with civil and political freedom, such as the right of freedom from arbitrary arrest and imprisonment, the right of free speech, the right of freedom of the press, the right of free assembly. These are principally what are known as 'residual' rights, that is, in order to exercise them we do not have to rely on their being formally granted to us. Actions are lawful or rightful unless they are prohibited by law. Second, there are *social rights*, such as the right to welfare benefits. These do not exist until they are prescribed by law. There is for example no general right to work, though the absence of a job may be regarded by many as a perfectly legitimate grievance against public authority, i.e. the Government.

ESSENTIAL PRINCIPLES

REDRESS OF GRIEVANCE

One of the major themes of English constitutional history has been the gradual accumulation by the citizens of the means of seeking and securing redress of grievance against the 'authorities'. The purpose of this section is to examine in outline the various categories of remedy which are available and then to consider briefly their effectiveness.

Courts

In the first place an aggrieved citizen may have recourse to the *courts*. Public bodies, such as local authorities, may for example be *sued* for breach of contract. If a government minister in the purported execution of his duties commits a civil wrong then the wronged person may sue the Crown as the minister's employer. Another form of approach to the courts is the seeking of a *writ or order* to remedy some unlawful administrative action or omission. A writ of *habeas corpus* may be sought to secure the release of a person unlawfully detained. The order of *mandamus* compels the public authority to discharge its public duty, that of *certiorari* will quash an unlawful order or decision of a public body, while that of *prohibition* will prevent a proposed or continued unlawful act or decision by a public body.

In recent years members of the judiciary have shown themselves to be very willing to protect the interests of the individual against the encroaching activities of the State and public bodies in general. Even so appeal to the courts remains problematic in many ways. In particular those who seek judicial redress may well have to face considerable delay and expense. Also, the courts cannot rule on the merits of a policy decision unless the decision is manifestly 'unreasonable', that is to say unless the official who made the decision has manifestly taken leave of his senses. It has been well said by S. A. de Smith that 'a successful challenge to an invalid order or decision may prove a Pyrrhic victory; the winner may find himself back in square one with a heavy bill of costs and no statutory entitlement to any form of compensation'. (*Constitutional and Administrative Law*, p. 624)

Secondly, there may be complaints against administrative actions which concern not the unlawfulness of the act but its *inefficiency* or *inappropriateness*. In such cases recourse may be had to one of the Ombudsmen or Commissioners for Administration.

There are three types of Ombudsmen: the *Parliamentary Commissioner for Administration*, the *Local Commissioner for Administration*, and the *Health Service Commissioner*. Basically, all three have authority to deal with cases involving injustice caused by maladministration, that is to say they are not concerned with the normal content of decision nor the question of whether it is good or sensible, but only with the question of whether this decision was arrived at expeditiously by means of the proper procedures.

There are differences between the Commissioners, particularly with respect to freedom of access by the public:

1. A complaint to the *Parliamentary Commissioner* has to be made formally by a Member of Parliament, that is to say an ordinary citizen acting as complainant cannot get the Commissioner to act, but has to place the matter in the hands of an MP. If the Parliamentary Commissioner is involved by the MP (and this is by no means obligatory) and if the Commissioner feels that the matter complained of falls within his jurisdiction, then he will investigate and make a report. That report is not coercive, but simply puts the Commissioner's findings at the disposal of Parliament.

2. In the case of the *Local Commissioners* the complaint, which must be against the local authority, should be notified in the first place to a councillor of the local authority. If the complainant is not satisfied with the councillor's action it may be referred direct to the Ombudsman. Once again, assuming that the Commissioner feels able to act, any report which he may make is not coercive but makes his findings available to the authority.

3. In the case of the *Health Service Commissioner* the complaint must normally come from the member of public who is aggrieved, and must relate solely to administrative matters, that is to say not to matters of clinical judgement of medical staff.

Limitations on jurisdiction are indeed one of the principal problems of the Ombudsman. The Local Commissioners, for example, may *not* deal with the contractual and commercial acts of those authorities; may *not* deal with curricular matters in local authority schools or discipline or internal management of such schools; may *not* deal with police matters or with matters which relate to legal proceedings or to matters of local authority personnel.

The various Commissioners have at times attempted to increase their powers, particularly by broadening as far as possible the terms of reference of their office. For example, since the first Parliamentary Commissioner for Administration was appointed in 1967, the successive Commissioners have widened the interpretation of maladministration in order to extend their scope for investigation. Initially this has gone some way towards giving the members of the public more direct access to the Commissioner. It is now an established practice that if a member of the public approaches the Parliamentary Commissioner with details of alleged maladministration, the Commissioner may indicate that, if such a complaint were referred to him by an MP, then he would be prepared to investigate the matter. This quite clearly puts a certain degree of pressure on any MP to whom referral is made.

Perhaps the principal problem associated with complaints to the Ombudsman is the *lack of publicity* which his officers receive. Many members of the public know nothing of their existence, and although the complaints procedures involved are basically simple, individuals may prove to be somewhat intimidated. The *fear of officialdom* is also a potent factor in limiting complaints against a group over which the Ombudsmen have no jurisdiction, that is to say the police force. All such complaints are recorded and must be investigated, and in 1984 a new and independent Police Complaints Authority was set up to deal with the more serious matters. But in the public mind the fact that complaints against the police must perforce be investigated by the police often serves to render the whole process suspect, in spite of the counter-argument that the police have a strong vested interest in maintaining the integrity of the force.

The legal and administrative channels by which the redress of grievances may be solved are numerous. In addition to the ones which we have already mentioned there are many more such as the Equal Opportunities Commission, the Commission for Racial Equality, the consumer councils of public corporations, and the European Court of Human Rights. But it remains true that in general the less formal procedures of complaints to a local councillor or to a constituency MP, or the drawing of attention to a case by involving the media, remain the most obvious and direct means of securing redress or at least of letting off steam.

Perhaps the problem with all procedures for complaint against public authority is one of perspective: do we believe that such procedures are likely to ensure more efficient and responsible government, or do we believe that they are ultimately subversive of government because they involve it in wasting time in defending itself against potentially trivial or malicious attacks?

USEFUL APPLIED MATERIALS

THE OMBUDSMEN SEEK MORE POWERS

During the mid-1980s both the Parliamentary Commissioner and the Local Commissioners for Administration pressed for more powers, particularly for wider access to their offices.

The follow extract is from the final report of Sir Cecil Clothier who was Parliamentary Commissioner for Administration between 1979 and 1984.

'It is often said that I am not sufficiently accessible to the public and that access to me should be direct instead of through Members of Parliament. To my knowledge the only other national Ombudsman to whom access is indirect is the Mediateur in France. I have often deployed the familiar arguments in defence of our system, chief of which is that every Member of Parliament is an ombudsman for his constituents and that the body of members makes a natural and valuable filter for discriminating between simple and complex cases, the worthy and the unworthy. But five years' experience has led me to doubt the validity of these arguments, at any rate in opposition to some modification of our arrangements. At present the Member may and often does ask the Minister for the appropriate Department to let him have in the familiar phrase "an answer which I can send to my constituent" about his grievance. But on receipt of that reply the Member has neither the time nor the resources nor the powers, to verify by examination of departmental papers or witnesses the explanations offered, which must of necessity be composed on the basis of facts and opinions advanced by those against whom the complaint is laid. When Members do send me their files it sometimes happens that the Minister's letter of response is the starting point of an investigation which shows that there is more to the case than the letter might be thought to suggest. It has occurred to me that without resorting to either extreme about access to this office, it would be possible to provide that the citizen must first invite his Member of Parliament to attend to his grievance and if he, the citizen, is dissatisfied with the ultimate response then he should have a right to invite me to examine the progress made upon his complaint. This would be unlikely I think to result in any great increase of acceptable complaints, but it seems to me that it would be an improvement on our present arrangements if the citizen had a right to have my personal judgement on the standing of his complaint before he was finally, and without appeal, dismissed.

So far as I know I am alone among the hundred or so national ombudsmen of the world in having no powers to investigate on my own initiative apparent maladministration which has come or been brought to my notice. Only occasionally have I felt a particular wish to investigate something of my own accord and the ability to do so would have added no more than three or four cases to my workload in the five years about which I write. Yet I have felt it a reflection on a parliamentary democracy which prides itself on its considerate attitude towards its citizens that this country alone should impose such a restriction on its Parliamentary Commissioner. If it were felt that my discretion were not to be trusted I would be glad to share the right to initiate an investigation with the Chairman of the Select Committee of the House of Commons on the Parliamentary Commissioner, or with the whole Committee, to whom I might on occasion suggest that an investigation without a specific complainant would be in the public interest.' (*The Annual Report for 1983 of the Parliamentary Commissioner for Administration*, Sections 7 and 8.)

Similar complaints were made by the Local Commissioners for Administration in their report for 1984–85.

'Most Ombudsmen outside the United Kingdom can investigate on their own initiative a matter coming to their attention where injustice seems possibly to have been caused by faulty administration. Available figures show that about 5% of their cases are initiated by those Ombudsmen. Their Annual Reports show they attach much value to this power. The case for being able to initiate investigations is that if the Ombudsman service exists to investigate possible injustice caused by maladministration it should not be hindered by the fact that the complainant is not readily forthcoming. Perhaps because he or she is dead. After a decade's experience it is clear that the number of cases brought to notice in the media seem more significant and serious than some complaints properly referred to the Ombudsmen by individuals. . . . In their 1980 Review the Commission recommended that there should be choice of access to the local Ombudsmen so that complaints could be made *either* through a member of the authority *or* direct. Experience since then has only reinforced the case for this change as argued in the previous review.' (*The Local Ombudsmen Report for the Year Ended 31st March 1985*, pp. 49–50).

AN OMBUDSMAN'S POWERS ARE EXTENDED

Following recommendations in October 1984 from the House of Commons Select Commitee on the Parliamentary Commissioner for Administration, Lord Gowrie, Chancellor of the Duchy of Lancaster, agreed in July 1985 that the Ombudsman's jurisdiction should in the future extend to some fifty so-called quangos (quasi non-governmental organisations). These quangos include such bodies as the Commission for Racial Equality, the Equal Opportunities Commission, the Countryside Commission, and the Industrial Training Boards, and Lord Gowrie said, 'I believe that anyone who claims to have suffered as a result of maladministration by such a body, should have recourse to the Ombudsman in the same way as if a Central Government Department had been involved.' (*The Times* (9.7.85), p. 2)

TYPICAL CASES DEALT WITH BY THE PARLIAMENTARY COMMISSIONER

Some idea of the work of the Parliamentary Commissioner, and of the remedies which he is able to secure, may be gained from the following selections of cases, from the Commissioner's 1984 Report.

Case No.	Dept Involved	Problem and action
C553/82	DE/DHSS	Inadequate advice about entitlement to benefit on retiring at the age of 64. £518 *ex gratia* payment
C598/82	IR	Errors and delay in making of tax assessment. Tax arrears reduced by £1,511.70
C647/82	DHSS	*Ex gratia* payment of £230.96 to compensate for delay in payment of special hardship allowance

C685/82	DHSS/DE	Delays and mistakes in handling claims to sickness and unemployment benefits. National Insurance record credited with contributions resulting in payment of arrears of benefit totalling £54.81
C690/82	DHSS	Mishandling of various benefit claims from disabled person. DHSS to review their instructions
C705/82	IR	Direction by Collector of Taxes under Regulation 26(3) of Income Tax (Employments) Regulations improperly made. £3,954.23 tax waived

DE = Department of Employment; DHSS = Department of Health and Social Security; IR = Inland Revenue.
(From *Annual Report for 1984 of the Parliamentary Commissioner for Administration*, p. 3.)

PUBLIC AWARENESS OF THE OMBUDSMAN

Public awareness and appreciation of the work of the Ombudsman seems to be increasing slightly. A MORI poll conducted in the spring of 1985 asked respondents to choose, from a list of sixteen persons or institutions, the two or three which best looked after individual rights. A similar enquiry in 1973 had produced a 9 per cent response for the Ombudsman, whereas the 1985 survey produced 13 per cent who said that the Ombudsman was among those who were best able to protect the citizen's rights. This was 1 per cent below newspapers and television and 4 per cent below Parliament, but significantly ahead of the political parties, which scored only 9 per cent as they had done in 1973. (*The Times*, 1.7.85, p. 12)

APPEALS TO THE EUROPEAN COURT OF HUMAN RIGHTS

Members of the public who feel that their civil rights have been violated may appeal to the European Court of Human Rights at Strasbourg. Two such appeals in the late summer of 1985 illustrate the process: in one a London woman appealed against the abolition of the GLC and against the cancellation of the final set of GLC elections which had been due to take place a year before abolition. The court, however, ruled that 'Parliament as the elected representative of the British people may vote to abolish the GLC if this course of action recommends itself'. In another decision of the court the ruling went against British immigration rules which the Home Secretary subsequently announced were to be altered in consequence. (*The Times*, 11.7.85, p. 4; 6.8.85, p. 2)

RECENT EXAMINATION QUESTIONS

Spend ten minutes or so planning an outline answer to each of the following questions. Outline answers to Questions **8**, **9** and **11**, and a tutor's answer to Question **10** are given in the following sections.

Question 1.

Should the powers of the Parliamentary Commissioner for Administration be further extended?
(Cambridge, Econ. and Pub. Aff., June 1980)

Question 2.

How easy is it for the average citizen to secure justice in the law courts?
(Cambridge, Pub. Aff., June 1984)

Question 3.

Examine critically the objectives behind the establishment in 1967 of the Office of Parliamentary Commissioner for Administration and assess the extent to which those objectives have been fulfilled.
(AEB, Govt and Pol., Paper 1, Nov. 1982)

Question 4.

Assess the effectiveness of Ombudsmen for local government and for the National Health Service in the redress of individual grievances.
(AEB, Govt and Pol., Paper 1, Nov. 1984)

Question 5.

What are the powers of local government Ombudsmen?
(London, Govt and Pol. Stud., Paper 4, short answer question, June 1982)

Question 6.

What remedies are available to consumers with complaints against public corporations?
(London, Govt and Pol. Stud., Paper 4, short answer question, Jan. 1983)

Question 7.

How might the position of the Parliamentary Commissioner for Administration be strengthened?
(London, Govt and Pol. Stud., Paper 4, June 1983)

Question 8.

Britain is one of the few countries of the West whose citizens are not protected by a Bill of Rights. Why do you think this is so?
(London, Govt and Pol. Stud., Paper 1, June 1984)

Question 9.

How adequate is the machinery that exists for dealing with the public's complaints against the police?
(London, Govt and Pol. Stud., Paper 4, June 1984)

Question 10.

Assess the argument that the powers of the Parliamentary Commissioner for Administration (Ombudsman) are too limited for him to have a significant impact on governmental injustice.
(JMB, Brit. Govt and Pol., June 1982)

Question 11.

Describe three institutions that the citizen can make use of if he has a dispute with public authorities.
(London, Govt and Pol. Stud., Paper 1, short answer question, Jan. 1982)

Britain is one of the few countries of the West whose citizens are not protected by a Bill of Rights. Why do you think this is so?

(a) In a historic sense there has been an absence in Britain since the seventeenth century of the sort of major political and constitutional upheavals which might have given rise to a Bill of Rights. Governmental threats to rights have, arguably, not emerged in a spectacular enough form to create a need for a Bill of Rights.

(b) It can be argued that in Britain the citizen's rights are already well enough defended by a variety of forces so that there is no pressing need for a Bill of Rights. These might include:

- A *well-established Parliament* at the heart of the British political tradition. Its members are able to investigate and criticise governmental policies and to publicise the grievances of their constituents.

- A tradition of a *free press* and of *powerful interest groups* capable of defending the rights of their members has been held to be a better safeguard against tyranny than a Bill of Rights.

- The prevalence of the notion of the *rule of law* and the willingness of an *independent judiciary* to uphold the rule of law against actions by the executive, have also been said to offer adequate protection to the individual.

- British political culture is against the exercise of arbitrary powers, by any body, and it can be argued that this is the most crucial factor which makes for secure citizens' rights. An interesting contrast is with, say, the Soviet Constitution with its elaborate guarantees of civil rights, or with a political culture in which individual rights are at a discount.

(c) In the British system rights are generally residual, or prescriptive, and exist until they are limited by statute or by the legitimate rights of others. It can be argued that this system in fact provides a wider set of guarantees of individual liberty than would a Bill of Rights.

(d) It may be argued that the need for a Bill of Rights has been somewhat lessened in recent years by the UK's ratification of the European Convention on Human Rights and its acceptance of the jurisdiction of the European Court of Human Rights. The UK Government has been called before the court as a defendant against its citizens more than any other government. Several judgments have gone against the UK, e.g. the judgment against the security forces' use of torture in Northern Ireland in 1976, and the judgment against the use of corporal punishment in schools in 1982.

(e) One could examine the contrary view that the above may not be particularly valid reasons for the absence of a Bill of Rights. It may be naïve to see Parliament as a particularly strong defender of civil rights against an active and aggressive executive. Again the notion that the common law, as upheld by the judges, acts as a guarantee, can be countered with the theory of parliamentary sovereignty, whereby an active executive prevails upon a Parliament to narrow the scope of rights which may be upheld at common law.

Q. 9   How adequate is the machinery that exists for dealing with the public's complaints against the police?

Answer   (a) There is obviously fertile ground for debate here. Governments which have legislated to create the machinery for facilitating complaint against the police, e.g. the 1984 Police and Criminal Evidence Act, will obviously deem that machinery to be more or less adequate. On the other hand groups such as the National Council for Civil Liberties constantly press for improvements and extensions of the machinery for complaint.

(b) Again, the adequacy of the machinery almost certainly depends very much on the identity of the complainant. Middle-aged, middle-class, white citizens who may fall into the category of 'pillars of society' who are not overawed by the courts, by the police themselves, or by the formalities of complaint processes, may feel that the machinery which exists is perfectly fair and accessible. Whereas the young, the inarticulate, in some cases members of ethnic minorities and the easily intimidated, may feel that the machinery is not really designed to help them.

(c) Perhaps the greatest problem about the machinery for complaints against the police is that such complaints must be made to the police themselves. This, it may be suspected, intimidates many possible complainants.

(d) Once the complaint has been made then the procedures set down by the 1984 Act look impressive: for *less serious* cases the new process of informal resolution does a lot to 'humanise' the complaints machinery. For *more serious* complaints a senior police officer would be appointed to make an investigation and it may be that the new and independent Police Complaints Authority will step in to supervise the investigation. Once the investigation is complete and a report made, the chief officer of the force decides upon action. This is checked by the Complaints Authority which has the power to enforce more severe action if it feels that this is necessary, e.g. it may insist that the details of the case should be sent to the Director of Public Prosecutions.

The Complaints Authority should act as an impartial supervisor of the whole system of complaint: it is stipulated in the 1984 Act that none of its members should ever have been a police officer. Perhaps the problem with all this is that as long as the investigation of complaints is in the hands of members of the police force there will always be the suspicion that the principle that 'dog does not eat dog' will apply. In other words the effectiveness of the machinery depends in the last resort upon the integrity and public-spiritedness of the police themselves, and that is in part a matter of recruitment policy and training.

SHORT ANSWER

Q. 11

Describe three institutions that the citizen can make use of if he has a dispute with public authorities.

Answer

He can appeal to the *High Court* if he believes that the authority in question has acted unlawfully, i.e. has not carried out statutory obligations or has exceeded its legal powers. He can appeal to an *Ombudsman* if he believes that he is the victim of injustice as a result of maladministration by the public authority; the Parliamentary Commissioner for Administration in the case of a government department, the Local Commissioner in the case of a local authority, and the Health Service Commissioner in the case of the Health Authority. A number of *tribunals* are available to hear claims that a public authority has made a wrong decision concerning a citizen, e.g. supplementary benefit tribunals hear claims that the DHSS has incorrectly assessed supplementary benefits due to citizens.

A TUTOR'S ANSWER

Q. 10

Assess the argument that the powers of the Parliamentary Commissioner for Administration (Ombudsman) are too limited for him to have a significant impact on governmental injustice.

Answer

In one cardinal respect the powers of the Parliamentary Commissioner are such as to prevent his having a significant impact on governmental injustice: his function as defined by statute is to investigate maladministration by government departments, that is to say some failure of established administrative procedures. His powers do not extend to the investigation of the justness or otherwise of policy. Any injustice caused by the moral deficiencies or carelessness of deliberate policy is quite beyond his scope, as in addition are contractual and personnel matters, and actions taken by a Secretary of State to defend the security of the State.

Even in the investigation of alleged maladministration, however, the Parliamentary Commissioner's powers are not perhaps as extensive as they might be. He has no power to investigate suspected maladministration on his initiative, and he has no power to begin an investigation following a direct approach from an aggrieved member of the public. Members of the public must first present their grievances to an MP and then leave it to the MP to decide whether to pass the case on to the Ombudsman. Many MPs take very seriously the doctrine that each MP is an Ombudsman to his constituents and consequently they make personal approaches to the government department complained of and seek replies from ministers which they can hand on to their constituents. But as Sir Cecil Clothier, a former Parliamentary Commissioner has pointed out, MPs have neither the time nor the resources and powers of investigation to get to the bottom of many complaints. Sir Cecil suggested in his final report as Parliamentary Commissioner that the Ombudsman should be given the power to investigate on his own initiative and should be made directly accessible to members of the public. This clearly reflects a feeling on his part that there were substantial shortcomings in the powers of his office. Sir Cecil also commented that he was disappointed that governments had not accepted the recommendations of successive House of Commons Select Committees on the Parliamentary Commissioner that he should have the right to investigate personnel, contractual, and commercial matters relating to government departments, and he suggested that Britain was the only country with a Parliamentary Commissioner which imposed such a restriction on his activities.

In fact once complaints against maladministration do find their way to the Parliamentary Commissioner and once he has established that they are within his jurisdiction and that they are valid, remedies are usually forthcoming from the departments in question. Although the Parliamentary Commissioner has no coercive powers but simply makes a report of his investigation, which is passed on to the House of Commons Select Committees on the Parliamentary Commissioner, the making of the report is usually enough to galvanise a department which has been found wanting. Financial settlements with an aggrieved person are frequently made and in many cases departmental procedures are reviewed and revised.

Perhaps one of the major problems faced by the Parliamentary Commissioner is not so much that his powers are too limited, but that there is insufficient knowledge of his office. As a result there is very little public pressure for MPs to pass material on to him and little public pressure for greater access to his services. His office issues useful explanatory leaflets, which are found in such places as Citizens' Advice Bureaux, and provides a video describing the work of the office, and the Commissioner's reports are generally models of incisiveness and lucidity: yet there is still little public awareness of his existence or of his functions. This as much as anything else limits his potential impact on governmental injustice.

A STEP FURTHER

This is one of those subjects in which politics students should not be afraid of stepping a little outside their discipline in order to follow up lines of enquiry. The constitutional lawyers have many interesting and useful things to say about the mechanisms by which redress of grievance against public authorities may be sought. A particularly clear discussion is to be found in S. A. de Smith, *Constitutional and Administrative Law*, 4th edn (Penguin 1981). On the question of whether sufficient means of redress exist, organisations such as the National Council for Civil Liberties have a good deal to say and can be relied upon to respond energetically to the student's enquiries. In addition Citizens' Advice Bureaux are a mine of information on this topic and are well worth a visit: for example they generally stock copies of pamphlets issued by all of the various types of Ombudsmen which describe the functions of those officers, the types of complaints which can and cannot be made to them, the methods of making complaint, and the likely consequences. The descriptions are clear and concise and a very useful supplement to the relevant sections in the textbooks. Available from the Citizens' Advice Bureau is the pamphlet 'Complaints Against the Police', detailing again with exemplary clarity, the procedures available under the Police and Criminal Evidence Act 1984.

Chapter 13

The expanding executive: statutory instruments and administrative justice

In 1929 the former Lord Chief Justice Hewart, published a now famous book entitled *The New Despotism*. According to Hewart the spectre of tyranny stalked the land and power was being drawn away from Parliament and, by extension, jurisdiction was being withdrawn from the courts. The main instruments of this new despotism were delegated legislation, particularly in the form known as statutory instruments, and administrative justice. Because these two subjects are often confused, or alternatively are often presented with undue technicality, it would be sensible here to attempt two simple definitions.

Delegated legislation takes place when Parliament, the sovereign body of the realm, delegates or gives power to some other body to issue rules and regulations which once issued have the force of law. The recipients of such delegated powers may be public corporations, local authorities, or government departments. In the last case an Act of Parliament may establish broad principles of future action, but may grant to the relevant government minister the authority to issue orders or regulations to secure the detailed implementation of the broad principles enshrined in the Act, which therefore becomes known as the parent statute. The regulations issued under the authority of such an Act are known generically as *statutory instruments*.

Administrative justice on the other hand, takes place following the grant of power to a public body other than a court of law, to decide a specific category of dispute between the citizen and the public authorities or between citizen and citizen.

ESSENTIAL PRINCIPLES

Over fifty years on, most commentators no longer share Hewart's suspicions although the volume of both delegated legislation and administrative justice has very largely increased since Hewart's time. This is not to say, however, that we can afford to ignore these developments. We can learn a great deal about British politics if we examine both the reasons for the continuing development of delegated legislation and administrative justice, and why they have both become accepted and acceptable facets of the British governmental scene.

FACTORS LEADING TO GROWTH OF STATUTORY INSTRUMENTS

There are many factors which explain the continued growth of *statutory instruments* and most of them reveal one aspect or another of the limitations of the conventional parliamentary legislative process:

1. Parliament, and the House of Commons in particular, often appears to be an overworked institution. The problem of an overcrowded timetable is certainly greatly diminished by its capacity to delegate to other bodies the formulation of detailed refinements, or explanations, of policies which it has already formally adopted.

2. Members of Parliament very often have their own special interests in selected areas of policy. Nevertheless, they are often compelled by the nature of the system to adopt a 'jack of all trades' role when legislating. It therefore makes sense to hand over much detailed and technical work to the government departments which are intimately and permanently involved in the relevant area of administration and which can call upon the sort of expertise which MPs do not usually possess.

3. There is also the important matter of speed and flexible response to changing circumstances. Should some rapid adjustment in administration be necessary to meet changing practical circumstances, this can often be achieved by a statutory instrument where a fresh Act of Parliament would prove far too laborious. Statutory instruments do *not* have to go through the several stages of debate and detailed consideration which are applicable to a parliamentary Bill. They *are* generally subject to either *negative* or *positive* procedure: in the first case they will have effect *unless* an MP 'puts down a prayer' against them, resulting in an adverse vote in the Commons or Lords. In the second case they will have effect *only* if a resolution in their favour is carried in the Commons and the Lords. In both cases, but especially in the case of negative procedure, which is also the more common, the procedure is quick and simple and involves minimal disruption of the parliamentary timetable.

FACTORS LEADING TO GROWTH OF ADMINISTRATIVE JUSTICE

We may divide administrative justice into two broad categories. Firstly, decisions given by a minister following an inquiry which the minister is either statutorily obliged to hold or which he has discretionary power to hold should he so wish. Secondly, decisions by administrative tribunals which are generally permanent in nature and whose chairman and members are appointed by the relevant minister. Somewhat similar factors explain the continuing growth of *administrative justice*.

1. It is obvious that inquiries and tribunals are able to take a great load off the conventional courts of law which are heavily enough burdened with cases as it is. The burden would be that much greater if the courts had to deal for example with planning appeals (the province of the Secretary of State for the Environment) or the tens of thousands of cases per year which are handled by tribunals such as supplementary benefit appeals, and problems involving National Insurance and industrial injuries.

2. There is again the matter of expertise. Tribunals are specialised bodies and consequently their members develop considerable familiarity with and expertise in the matters which they investigate and upon which they pronounce.

3. As in the case of delegated legislation, speed and flexibility are important. However, inquiries and tribunals have developed piecemeal, with the result that there is no single set of rules or principles which governs their operation. Despite this they do tend to be less formal in their procedures than the conventional courts, to be more flexible in adapting their judgments to specific circumstances, and to be generally quicker in dealing with cases.

4. This factor is perhaps a corollary of the third: namely that administrative justice tends to be cheaper to operate than the more conventional variety.

REASONS FOR ACCEPTANCE OF DELEGATED LEGISLATION AND ADMINISTRATIVE JUSTICE

This rapid examination of some of the reasons for the vitality of delegated legislation and administrative justice will provide an important part of the answer to the question of why they have both become accepted parts of the processes of legislating and dispensing justice. They are both so thoroughly useful that Parliament and the courts of law tend to see them not as rival systems, but as complementary ones.

We need to point out in addition that many of the potential constitutional dangers of these processes have been removed by the creation of the effective supervision systems. In the case of *statutory instruments* the period since the mid-1940s has seen the evolution of parliamentary select committees charged with the task of scrutinising statutory instruments and, should they fall into one of a number of suspicious categories, reporting them to the House. It may be objected that the select committees are liable to be swamped by the sheer volume of statutory instruments, but proposed instruments *are* printed and published and laid before the House so that MPs with a special interest in their content, or in the general area to which they relate, may examine them and, if necessary, raise the alarm. Relevant pressure groups are also able to perform the same function.

Turning now to *administrative justice* we should note the creation in the 1950s of the Council on Tribunals. This is an advisory body intended to keep tribunals under review, to advise on the regulations for the procedures of tribunals or statutory inquiries, and to suggest to the relevant ministers possible members of tribunals. The tribunal is not a well-publicised body and it has no coercive powers, but it has had some impact, at least in bringing order and regularity into the diverse procedural systems of scores of tribunals and inquiries. If the Council on Tribunals is somewhat lacking in teeth, it is still possible for an appeal against a tribunal's findings to be made to the Queen's Bench Division of the High Court. If, for example, a tribunal has not observed the rules of natural justice, such as the provision that no one should be judge and party in the same cause, or the provision that both sides should have a fair hearing, then the High Court will entertain the appeal. Similarly, the appeal would be heard if there is an error on the face of the record of the tribunal.

Neither delegated legislation, nor administrative justice therefore takes place without a degree of publicity and some form of supervision. This fact goes a long way to allay the sort of constitutional fears which were raised by Lord Hewart. Yet it should perhaps be pointed out that although Hewart almost certainly overstated his case, and although many control systems have been maintained and developed since he wrote, there is no justification for complacency. Statutory instruments may still on occasion be the means by which potentially contentious matters are rushed through Parliament. Ministerial inquiries still leave government ministers with the opportunity to make decisions irrespective of the merits of the cases which have been advanced. Again the Council on Tribunals often appears to be a relatively puny body, with an over worked, part-time, mostly unpaid membership, a limited budget, and a tiny back-up staff, seeking to monitor proceedings in hundreds of thousands of cases every year.

USEFUL APPLIED MATERIALS

MR SPEAKER'S COUNSEL GIVES REASONS FOR THE PERSISTENCE OF DELEGATED LEGISLATION

A classic statement of the reasons for *delegation* was made by Mr Speaker's Counsel in a memorandum presented to the Select Committee on Procedure, 1966–67.

'(a) The normal justification is its value in relieving Parliament of the minor details of law making. The province of Parliament is to decide material questions affecting the public interest; and the more procedural and subordinate matters can be withdrawn from their cognizance the greater will be the time afforded for the consideration of more serious questions involved in legislation.

'(b) Another advantage is speed of action. Action can be taken at once in a crisis without public notice which might prejudice the object of the exercise. For instance an increase in import duties would lose some of its effect if prior notice were given and importers were able to import large quantities of goods at the old lower rate of duty.

'(c) Another advantage is in dealing with technical subjects. Ministers and Members of Parliament are not experts in the variety of subjects on which legislation is passed, e.g. trade marks, patents, designs, diseases, poison, legal procedure and so on. The details of such technical legislation need the assistance of experts and can be regulated after a Bill passes into an Act by delegated legislation with greater care and minuteness and with better adaptation to local and other special circumstances than they can be in the passage of a Bill through Parliament.

'(d) Another is that it enables the department to deal with unforeseen circumstances that may arise during the introduction of large and complicated schemes of reform. It is not possible, when drafting legislation on a new subject, to forecast every eventuality. It is very convenient to have power to adjust matters of detail by statutory instrument without of course going beyond the general principles laid down in the Bill.

'(e) Another is that it provides flexibility. Circumstances change and it may be desirable to take power to deal with changing circumstances rather than wait for an amending Bill. This is particularly convenient in regard to economic controls, for instance, exchange control and hire purchase.

'(f) Finally there is the question of emergency; and in time of war it is essential to have wide powers of delegated legislation.'   (HC Paper 539, pp. 113–14, quoted in A. H. Hanson and Malcolm Walles, *Governing Britain*, 4th edn (Fontana 1984), pp. 280–1).

CONTINUING CONSTITUTIONAL CONCERN OVER STATUTORY INSTRUMENTS

The Joint Commons and Lords Select Committee on Statutory Instruments issued a special report for the parliamentary session of 1977–78 which revealed that it was worried about certain tendencies in the field of statutory instruments:

'Regrettably . . . the affirmative procedure is very rarely invoked; and on occasion the Committee are being critical of the choice of negative procedure which too frequently results in the avoidance of Parliamentary control, e.g. criticism levelled at the choice of negative procedure for an Instrument closely connected to the expenditure of some six million pounds and for another which made substantial amendments to an Act of Parliament. The Committee consider that the Government should make known the criteria that will govern the choice between affirmative and negative procedure and that the department should apply those criteria rather than follow the demands of departmental convenience.'

Again, criticising an import duties order which was retrospective for a period of seven months, the committee complained that 'on occasions both Government and the governed appeared to accept with complacency that an obligation to obey a Ministerial Order can arise without any knowledge on the part of the citizens on the terms of the Order.' (*First Special Report of the Joint Scrutiny Committee on Statutory Instruments*, quoted in Hanson and Walles, op cit., pp. 287–8)

RECENT EXAMINATION QUESTIONS

Spend ten minutes or so planning an answer to each of the following questions. Outline answers to questions **5**, **8** and the short answer to question **1**, and a tutor's answer are given in the following sections.

Question 1.

What are the powers of the Council on Tribunals?
(London, Govt and Pol. Stud., Paper 4, short answer question, June 1982)

Question 2.

Distinguish between government and administration.
(London, Govt and Pol. Stud., Paper 4, short answer question, June 1983)

Question 3.

(a) Examine the reasons for the growth of administrative tribunals since 1945 and give examples of such tribunals. (b) What are the strengths and weaknesses of such tribunals for redressing a citizen's grievance against the State?
(AEB, Govt and Pol., Paper 1, June 1982)

Question 4.

In sheer size and scope administrative justice now dwarfs the more conventional and familiar kind. Discuss.
(Cambridge, Pub. Aff., June 1983)

Question 5.

Has the liberty of the subject been affected by the growth of the Welfare State?
(Cambridge, Econ. and Pub. Aff., June 1980)

Question 6.

What part do administrative tribunals have in the dispensing of justice in Britain?
(Cambridge, Econ. and Pub. Aff., June 1980)

Question 7.

What do you understand by the separation of powers? To what extent does this characterise the British political system?
(Cambridge, Pol. and Govt, Paper 1, June 1980)

Question 8.

What are the principal safeguards against the excessive concentration of executive power in the UK?
(AEB, Govt and Pol., Nov. 1983)

Question 9.

Distinguish between a tribunal and an inquiry
(London, Govt and Pol. Stud., Paper 4, short answer question, Jan. 1983)

Question 10.	What we have under the British system of government is fusion of powers and not real separation of powers. How far is this true?
	(Cambridge, Pub. Aff., June 1983)
Question 11.	Why has delegated legislation become acceptable as a normal part of government?
	(Cambridge, Pub. Aff., Nov. 1984)
Question 12.	Does the continued expansion of delegated legislation threaten the survival of the rule of law in Britain?
	(Cambridge, Pol. and Govt, Paper 1, June 1985)
Question 13.	Assess the major criticisms of the principle and practice of delegated legislation.
	(JMB, Brit. Govt and Pol., June 1984)

OUTLINE ANSWERS

Q. 5.

Has the liberty of the subject been affected by the growth of the Welfare State?

Answer

(a) The Welfare State could be said to have augmented certain liberties. If we define liberty fairly broadly, e.g. the provision by the State of health care, of education in schools, colleges, and universities, etc. the attempts of the Welfare State to guarantee the subject against destitution have created for many people practical freedoms and opportunities which would have been denied to them in the absence of the Welfare State.

(b) On the other hand the Welfare State has in some senses encroached upon liberty. For example the development of the Welfare State has necessarily involved a high tax burden and so has restricted the liberty of the taxpayer to dispose of his or her money at will. It could also be argued that the Welfare State represents a restriction on freedom of choice, in that most of the beneficiaries are obliged to accept whatever type of service the State deems it appropriate to give them. Of course, as voters they do have some control over the nature of the services provided and there is a machinery of complaint: Ombudsmen, boards of governors of schools, and so on. Also, those with sufficient resources are not barred from opting for private medicine or education or private insurance schemes.

(c) Provision of services also entails regulation; those who wish to claim benefits must often disclose their assets and income. They may be subject to investigation, for example by officials of the DHSS, i.e. privacy is probably one of the liberties which suffers most from the development of the Welfare State.

(d) Some of the machinery established to facilitate the operation of the Welfare State, e.g. various types of administrative tribunals, is aimed mainly at expeditious decision-making and often involves a bewildering diversity of procedures. These may leave the subject confused and effectively weakened in the face of authority. Again, there are some safeguards: if, for example, tribunals fail to abide by the rules of natural justice then the aggrieved subject may appeal to the courts.

Q. 8.   What are the principal safeguards against the excessive concentration of executive power in the UK?

Answer

(a) It is conventional to cite institutions such as the *courts* and the *Ombudsmen* as effective lines of defence against the excesses of executive power. However, the fact is that both of these institutions do have their limitations.

- The courts have in recent years shown themselves quite willing to restrain the executive if it acts unlawfully. That is the limit of their powers. If the executive succeeds in pushing through Parliament legislation which confers upon it wide-ranging powers, then it is not for the courts to query the new law. The courts do not in other words occupy the same sort of constitutional position as is taken by the Supreme Court in the United States.

- In the same way the Parliamentary Commissioner for Administration is also somewhat limited, in that his jurisdiction extends only to injustice caused as a result of maladministration, that is, the improper functioning or the non-functioning of the normal administrative processes. Even if the Commissioner decides that maladministration *has* taken place, he has no coercive powers with which to remedy it, but has to report his findings to Parliament.

(b) In the case of both the courts and Commissioner therefore, *Parliament* appears as the key to a successful functioning of the limitations on the growth of executive power. Parliament as a sovereign body can indeed restrict the concentration of executive powers. It can *call back*, if necessary, the powers which it has delegated to government departments and ministers enabling them effectively to legislate (by way of statutory instruments). It can *monitor* through the statutory instruments scrutiny committees (i.e. the Joint committee and the House of Commons committee) the way in which those delegated powers are used. It can *investigate* through its select committees the functioning of government departments. It can *call ministers to account* at Question Time. It can *refuse to legitimate* a government's legislative proposals if it is thought that they would give the executive too much power.

(c) Of course, Parliament, and in particular the House of Commons, is subject to a generally effective whip system which means that a government can generally rely upon getting a majority for its legislative proposals and can generally avoid censure. We have to assume that if a government attempted a major transference of powers to the Executive in such a way as to endanger the whole balance of the Constitution, then this would be resisted even by its own back-benchers. Certainly pressure would be put upon them by their constituencies and by pressure groups.

(d) Looking at the problem more broadly, any moves to concentrate executive power to the point at which it became offensive to the political traditions of the country and to the political culture would provoke resistance on the part of interest groups, from the media and ultimately from the electors. Attempts, for example, by the Government to push legislation through Parliament by means of closure of debate tend to give it a tyrannical image, which may provoke unease among the voters.

Conclusion: the safeguards which will prove to be most effective will very much depend on the precise form that the concentration of executive power may take. If it is unlawful in form, then the courts will act; if it is an attempt to arrange a major shift in constitutional balances by legal means, i.e. by pushing through legislation, then Parliament would be the most effective line of resistance backed up by media and pressure-group activity.

SHORT ANSWER

Q. 1.

What are the powers of the Council on Tribunals?

Answer

It reviews and reports on the constitution and workings of tribunals; it may consider and report on holding of statutory inquiries by ministers or on their behalf; it must be consulted about the making of rules of procedure for inquiries and tribunals; it may make general recommendations about the membership of tribunals.

A TUTOR'S ANSWER

Q. 11.

Why has delegated legislation become acceptable as a normal part of government?

Answer

A major reason for the acceptance of delegated legislation as a normal part of government is its very wide range and extent. Government departments, public corporations, and local authorities all issue orders, regulations, and by-laws under powers delegated to them by Parliament. It would be totally impractical for Parliament to attempt to make such minute regulations directly. Workload in processing major pieces of legislation, in debating government policy and the great issues of the day, and in scrutinising the functioning of the Executive, is already immense. There is little time left to Parliament in which it might do the mass of detailed work which is carried out by means of delegated legislation. The existing full workload of Parliament therefore compels its Members to delegate legislative powers to others.

Another reason for the acceptance of delegated legislation is that Parliament may not necessarily have the technical competence to frame the sort of detailed regulations which are, for example, issued by way of statutory orders from government departments. Again, rules issued under delegated powers can usually be set out quickly and cheaply and can be adapted to changing circumstances. In comparison with the processess necessary for the issue of delegated legislation, the passage of a parliamentary statute looks extremely cumbersome.

It can therefore be argued that delegated legislation is made acceptable, both by the need for it and on its own intrinsic merits. But beyond this it is the more easily tolerated because it is capable of being controlled by Parliament in the last resort. The powers which Parliament has delegated it may revoke and that remains a powerful factor against abuse of delegated legislative powers.

As regards statutory instruments, Parliament has, since the 1940s, developed committees to act as watchdogs on its behalf. The most significant of those committees is the Joint Select Committee on Statutory Instruments. This scrutinises all of the statutory orders issued by government departments and reports to the Houses on any which are in its view suspect in some way. In the case of statutory orders which are subject to affirmative procedure, both Houses must vote for them in order to ensure that they come into force. Most statutory orders are, however, subject only to negative procedure, that is to say they come into force unless a member puts down a prayer against them and a resolution is carried rejecting them. It is with respect to these that the Joint Scrutiny Committee performs a particularly useful task in bringing dubious cases to the attention of Parliament. There is thus a powerful safeguard against the possibility that statutory instruments might be used by an unscrupulous government or minister for some unconstitutional purpose.

Finally, there is the safeguard that delegated legislation may be quashed in the courts. For instance, it might be shown that those who have issued it have acted *ultra vires* or beyond the powers delegated in the parent statute. The fact that any abuses in the exercise of delegated legislative powers can be detected and, if necessary, remedied by Parliament or the courts, helps to prevent delegated legislation from being seen simply as a potential evil, however necessary its use.

A STEP FURTHER

The best brief survey of this topic is provided by the chapter on 'Delegated legislation and administrative tribunals', in A. H. Hanson and Malcolm Walles, *Governing Britain*, 4th edn (Fontana 1985). For more detailed work students should go to the reports of the Parliamentary Joint Scrutiny Committee on Statutory Instruments, and for administrative justice to *Remedies in Administrative Law* (Law Commission Working Paper, No. 13, 1971). For some of the problems encountered by claimants appearing before supplementary benefit appeals tribunals, see Ruth Lister, *Justice for the Claimant*, Research Series 4 (Child Poverty Action Group 1974). It is, of course, worth keeping a close eye on the press for occasional instances of attempts by the House of Commons or House of Lords to resist the implementation of a statutory instrument. It is particularly worth looking at *The Times* law reports which occasionally contain instances of the judicial review of cases which have been heard by administrative tribunals. These usually concern the application of the rule that there should be no default of natural justice in a case before an administrative tribunal.

Chapter 14   Public enterprises in crisis

Public ownership of industries may take many forms. One possibility is that an enterprise may be *directly administered* by a government department, with the relevant minister in full control of the enterprise, and therefore fully accountable to Parliament for its progress. This was the case with the Post Office, until 1969. No major enterprise is now directly administered in this way; instead the *public corporation* (see below) prevailed and in 1969 the Post Office itself became such a corporation.

Municipal enterprises have similarly suffered a decline in prominence since their heyday in the early twentieth century. Many former municipal undertakings have been transferred to public corporations organised on a regional basis (e.g., gas supply, electricity supply) while, more recently, others have been privatised.

State shareholding continues to be an important form of public ownership. Under this system, a proportion of the shares in a limited company is publicly, or state owned. State shareholding was brought to a high point in the later 1970s, under the National Enterprise Board, but subsequently this was considerably wound down by the Thatcher Government, which disposed of many of its shareholdings, along with other state holdings in such companies as Cable and Wireless and the British Sugar Corporation. On the other hand, some public corporations have been converted in recent years into *limited companies*, following which a partial disposal of government shares leaves a situation of state shareholding (as in the case of British Aerospace in 1981).

Despite these changes, the most significant form of public ownership in the last generation has been the *public corporation*. It is only necessary to glance at the list of public corporations, which includes the National Coal Board, British Rail, the British Steel

Corporation, Post Office, British Gas, and the Central Electricity Generating Board, to realise that they represent a crucially important sector of the national economy. Over the past few decades the creation of public corporations, often by way of nationalisation, or their dismantling by way of privatisation, has been at the centre of many bitter political debates. Before considering the issues raised in these debates let us consider some of the main characteristics of a public corporation.

CHARACTERISTICS OF THE PUBLIC CORPORATION

1. It is founded by an Act of Parliament, and its activities are defined by that same Act, the provisions of which are quite specific to each corporation.
2. It has a corporate existence so it can sue and be sued.
3. It is in public ownership, not in the sense that the public can buy shares in it, but in the sense that it operates in the national or public interest.
4. It provides goods or services for which it charges in theory an economic rate; i.e. it seeks to cover all its own costs. It may, however, receive subsidies from the Government; in other words from public funds raised through taxation. Subsidies can be received if it cannot cover its costs or if it cannot raise enough money for investment from other sources.
5. It is managed by a board under the direction of a chairman. Chairman and board members are appointed by relevant government ministers. The sponsoring minister retains powers of dismissal. For example, the chairman of the National Coal Board is appointed by the Secretary of State for Energy. Theoretical division of responsibility between the chairman and the minister is that the chairman controls day-to-day management of the corporation, while the minister has the power to establish broad policies and objectives and to oversee investment programmes.
6. Staff of the public corporations are employees of the corporation itself, i.e. they are not civil servants.

ESSENTIAL PRINCIPLES

Now for some of the problems presented by public corporations. Firstly, what are public corporations for? In whose interests do they operate? Secondly, who controls the public corporations? Thirdly to what extent is the public corporation accountable to the public or its representatives in Parliament? Let us take these in order.

OBJECTIVE OF THE PUBLIC CORPORATION: THE PUBLIC INTEREST

At first sight the idea that the public corporations should function in the public interest seems simple enough. But does this mean that when it offers services to the general public they should be as cheap and plentiful as possible, even if this involves uneconomic corporations. Let us take the example of a branch line operated by British Rail. It may make a considerable operating loss and, in the aggregate, such lines may explain British Rail's financial instability. If the *rest of the rail network*, in the form of other customers of British Rail, has to shoulder the burden of loss imposed by such lines, then it may be argued that it would be in the public interest to abandon them. Again, if the *taxpayers* are burdened by additional tax demands in order to provide government subsidies for the rail network, then cuts in such uneconomic lines may be defended as being in the public interest. But the small community being served by an uneconomic branch line might well argue that it was a vital element in their lives, and that their own local perception of public interest would involve retention of the line. Here, therefore, we have three versions of the public interest: that of the mass of the consumers of the service, that of the public at large, and that of any one particular group of consumers or people affected by the service. All three versions are defensible and hence the confusion over the interpretation of the phrase 'in the public interest'.

But there are further problems: there may be differing *long- or short-term* definitions of the public interest. So in a period of relatively plentiful oil and gas reserves some coal-mines may be uneconomic to operate and it may appear that it would be to the general public's financial benefit to withdraw subsidies and close them. But, if other sources of power should run out at some future date, these closures might appear to have been somewhat short-sighted. These are among the issues raised, but not resolved, in the 1984–85 miners' strike. Another of the issues raised during that episode centred on the claim of the NUM that the closure of pits would have damaging effects that went beyond measurement in financial terms: the suggestion being that closure would entail disintegration of historical communities.

Clearly the concept of the public interest can be approached from many standpoints so that the purpose of a public enterprise is subject to many possible definitions and interpretations.

CONTROL OF THE PUBLIC CORPORATION

The issue of control is perhaps equally complex. It is, of course, always difficult to exercise effective control from the centre of a large organisation: as policies are translated from the centre down to the localities they tend to take on subtle nuances and alterations in emphasis. But even assuming that directions which were issued from the highest levels of a public corporation are substantially carried out in practice, we still have to ask whether it is, for example, the sponsoring minister or the chairman of the board of the corporation who is really in control.

The minister, as we have seen, appoints the chairman and the board but, as these are generally appointed with contracts for a fixed period, it is not unusual for an incoming minister to inherit a chairman appointed by a member of the previous Government. Should the chairman and the minister find themselves in disagreement it is by no means clear which of them should give way.

The distinction between the minister's control of overall

objectives and the chairman's control of management is often blurred. The minister does have power to issue a *general directive* which must be obeyed, but this has been used only very rarely. Like the power of dismissal it might well appear heavy-handed and tyrannical and could prove damaging to a minister's reputation. In recent years some notable and well-publicised clashes between ministers and chairmen have occurred. A more normal ministerial method of exerting control has been the so-called *lunch-table directive*. In this last case pressure is exercised by the minister in the course of informal meetings with the chairman, or by ministry civil servants during informal meetings with corporation staff.

The situation is made more complex by the fact that both sponsoring ministers and chairmen and board members often hold their posts for relatively short periods. Thus a minister may simply have to wait for a year or two until the end of a fixed-term contract rids him of an obstructive chairman. Alternatively the minister himself may be dropped or reshuffled, in which case his successor, struggling to master his new department, may be unable to maintain the ministerial grip on the public corporation's policy. Generally the longer a government stays in power the more it will be able to secure suitable appointments to public corporation boards.

ACCOUNTABILITY OF THE PUBLIC ENTERPRISE

Finally, the issue of accountability needs to be examined.

1. Ministers are, of course, accountable to *Parliament* for their actions or inactions. If a minister exercises one of his clearly defined powers, such as the dismissal of the chairman, then he can be called to account by Parliament in a debate or at Question Time. But the minister, when pressed on a certain policy adopted by a public corporation, can claim it is a matter of management and therefore not his responsibility, hence he is not to be held accountable.

2. Public corporations do issue *public reports and accounts* and these may be debated in the Commons, but their accounts are not subject to scrutiny by the Public Accounts Committee of the House. One attempt, in 1983, to establish this power by the Public Accounts Committee failed.

3. Various *Commons select committees*, however, do have powers to investigate the workings of public corporations. For example the Energy Committee can examine the actions of British Gas, the Central Electricity Generating Board, and the National Coal Board.

4. In a sense public corporations are also answerable to the *consumer*, but in reality the power the consumer can have over the corporation is often very limited. In many cases the public corporation has a monopoly, or near monopoly, on the service – for example British Gas, British Rail, the Post Office – and thus the consumer's capacity to shop around is limited. In the case of consumer complaints against defective service or lack of service

from public corporations no appeal is possible to the Ombudsman, whose jurisidiction does not extend to public corporations. There are consumer councils which are part of the structure of many corporations which may relay complaints and suggestions for improved service to the board, but these councils serve only to publicise problems (usually not very effectively) and to make recommendations which have no coercive force behind them. It is of little surprise, therefore, that the public corporation often looks like a powerful body ostensibly operating in the name of the public, but over which citizens have very little control.

USEFUL APPLIED MATERIAL

Public Corporation Chairmen in Revolt

At a time when the Government was attempting to pursue a vigorous policy of privatisation and also to clamp down upon public expenditure, it was to be expected that it would bear heavily upon the public corporation, attempting to direct them along paths which their Chairmen might not wish to follow. 1985 was such a period and produced some notable examples of public corporation Chairman showing signs of restiveness at what they regarded as untoward Government interference. In one newspaper interview Ian MacGregor, Chairman of the National Coal Board, revealed the extent of his differences with Mrs Thatcher and Energy Secretary Peter Walker. 'I'm used to getting my head beaten in' he remarked 'there's nothing new in that'. And again, 'People are not sure who is giving the orders . . . Why pay attention to MacGregor, they say, when Mrs Thatcher makes a speech saying something different.'

It was fairly clear that these differences of opinion had come to a head in the later stages and aftermath of the 1984–85 miners' strike. But the Government was also criticised by public corporation chiefs over its plan to force selective sell offs as part of its privatisation programme. Early in 1985 the Treasury produced proposals which would give Ministers power to sell off marketable portions of state-owned enterprises and to fix financial targets for public corporations. In giving evidence to the House of Commons Select Committee on Energy the Coal Board commented 'The Board believe it is a well proven principle of organisation that management will respond more actively in reaching the target which can be regarded as internally generated rather than one ultimately set from outside.' Sir Dennis Rooke, the Chairman of British Gas, was even more categoric in his statement to the Committee 'Not only the price of gas but the whole gamut of Corporate planning, capital expenditure and wage negotiations would become the implicit responsibility of Government. The Corporation's Board would be to all intents and purposes reduced to the role of a management committee acting at the ultimate behest of the Treasury.' By late 1985 there were signs that the energetic opposition of the public corporation Chairmen was beginning to take effect when Mr John MacGregor, Chief Secretary to the Treasury, announced that the Government would not pursue its proposals for the privatisation of viable sections of several public corporations during the life of the present Parliament.

The Times: 1.4.85, page 2; 29.7.85, page 1; and 16.11.85, page 40.

RECENT EXAMINATION QUESTIONS	Spend ten minutes or so planning an answer to each of the following questions. Outline answers to questions **6** and **7**, the short answer to question **4**, and a tutor's answer to question **9** are given in the following sections.
Question 1.	How effective is government control over nationalised industries? (Cambridge, Econ. and Pub. Aff., June 1980)
Question 2.	The problem is less one of public ownership than one of public control. What are the problems associated with the control of nationalised industries? (Cambridge, Econ. and Pub. Aff., June 1981)
Question 3.	'There is no point in having nationalised industries if they are to be run as commercial ventures.' Discuss. (Cambridge, Pub. Aff., June 1984)
Question 4.	What powers do departmental ministers exercise over public corporations? (London, Govt and Pol. Stud., Paper 4, short answer question, Jan. 1982)
Question 5.	Should (a) Ministers, and (b) MPs have more powers of control over public corporations? (London, Govt and Pol. Stud., Paper 4, Jan. 1983)
Question 6.	'Political control of public corporations is ultimately incompatible with the effective performance of their real tasks.' Discuss. (London, Govt and Pol. Stud., Paper 4, June 1985)
Question 7.	What are the advantages and disadvantages of administering nationalised industries through public corporations? (Cambridge, Pub. Aff., Nov. 1984)
Question 8.	Define privatisation and give two examples. (London, Govt and Pol. Stud., Paper 2, short answer questions, June 1984)
Question 9.	'The relations between the public corporations and Whitehall are unsatisfactory and in need of radical change.' Discuss. (JMB, Brit. Govt and Pol., June 1985)

'Political control of public corporations is ultimately incompatible with their performance of their real tasks.' Discuss.

Answer

(a) We obviously need to define what the *real* tasks of public corporations are. A report of the House of Commons Select Committee on Nationalised Industries in the late 1960s distinguished two tasks or obligations, of public corporations: (i) they should be responsive to the public interest; (ii) they should operate as efficient commercial bodies.

Much of the debate about the proper role of public corporations has centred on first the difficulty of *defining* the public interest, and secondly the proper *balance* between the two obligations or tasks pointed out by the Select Commitee. Indeed the same Select Committee report pointed out that the two categories of obligation on public corporations may not be reconcilable; in fact they had frequently proved to be in conflict with each other. The incompatibility, therefore, may lie between the two perceived tasks of the public corporations, each of which considered independently may be perfectly valid or 'real'.

(b) It could be argued that the public interest, however, defined, is best secured by means of political control; i.e. by a minister in an elected government accountable to Parliament.

(c) There is a strong and opposite case, namely that the commercial operation of a public corporation is best controlled by the board and its chairman, rather than by political appointees. It is the board and its chairman who are in charge of the day-to-day running of the organisation and whose concentration of expertise and attention to the commercial problems of the corporation arguably make them best fitted to determine its trading policies. It could further be argued that in order to facilitate this role of the board and the chairman, they should be largely emancipated from the political control which is represented by the ministerial power of appointment on short-term contracts. In other words, only a secure and reasonably long-term tenure for the board permits effective commercial planning to take place.

(d) A counter-argument to (c) is that there is little point in creating public corporations if they are to be expected to behave exactly like commercial organisations in the private sector. The suggestion here is that the public corporations are essentially different, and the difference lies in their obligation to be sensitive to the public interest which therefore becomes one of their real tasks.

Q. 7.

What are the advantages and disadvantages of administering nationalised industries through public corporations?

Answer

(a) The key to this question is the many roles both practical and theoretical, which nationalised industries fulfil, e.g. they trade, they provide employment, they provide a means by which the Government may manipulate the economy; they facilitate governmental control of strategic industry.

(b) In the light of these possible roles, the advantages of administration through public corporations include the following:

- They offer a reasonable balance between the various objectives of a nationalised industry. For example, the board can be expected to look after the commercial operation of the corporation, while the sponsoring minister can be expected to look after wider considerations such as the provision of employment and the role of the industry in relation to the whole economy.

- As public corporations are at present constituted, the sponsoring minister has an acknowledged role in setting their basic objectives and in monitoring their efficiency. This brings public corporations within the scope of ministerial accountability to Parliament. Parliament is therefore able to probe the conduct of public corporations in a way which it could not do if they were free of political control.

- Public corporations offer more scope for management independence and initiative than, say, the old departmental trading bodies.

(c) There are, however, many disadvantages to the administration of nationalised industries through public corporations:

- Parliamentary control is inadequate: if nationalised industries were run from within government departments then their finances would be subject to examination by the Public Accounts Committee of the House of Commons, which is not at present the case. In addition the division of control between minister and board makes it difficult for Parliament to establish the scope of a minister's accountability.

- It may be argued that in some respects public corporations suffer from undue financial restrictions. There are generally statutory limits to their borrowing powers, while governments since the 1950s have required loans to be raised from the Treasury. Since the mid-1970s, the Treasury net has closed more tightly on the public corporations with the imposition of cash limits, known as external financing limits, on borrowing. These restrictions may hamper investment programmes. In this area the public corporation may compare unfavourably with state shareholding as a means of public ownership.

- The present structure of public corporations, especially their relationship with government departments, means that there is often considerable confusion in corporation policy. In part this is caused by the often competing claims of Parliament, the minister, the department, and the board, to exercise control over the industry's development. The original hope that public corporations would be able to operate at arm's length from ministers has hardly been fulfilled. Ministers are almost inevitably unable to resist the pressures and the temptations to intervene in the running of corporations. This confusion would be to some extent removed if the running of nationalised industries were made a matter for government departments rather than public corporations. On the other hand, reform within the framework of the public corporation system may be possible (see for example the National Economic Development Office (NEDO) Report of 1976 suggesting the creation of policy councils which would be interposed between minister and board). If introduced these might reduce some of the tensions between minister and board, but on the other hand they might simply add yet one more element to those already competing for control.

SHORT ANSWER
Q. 4.

What powers do departmental ministers exercise over public corporations?

Answer

To ensure that public corporations operate in the public interest, ministers may issue general directives to their boards which must be obeyed. In practice this is done very infrequently. They may more frequently establish standards of performance and efficiency, appoint and dismiss board members, set up auditing procedures, determine the form of the accounts, and give or withhold approval for research, training, and education programmes. These powers are exercised by statute. In practice, however, the powers of ministers often extend much further. They use 'lunch-table directives' to interfere in matters such as price policy, plant closures, redundancies, and relations with unions.

A TUTOR'S ANSWER
Q. 9.

'The relations between the public corporations and Whitehall are unsatisfactory and in need of radical change.' Discuss.

Answer

Relationships between departmental ministers and public corporations may well be considered unsatisfactory, largely because the division of responsibilities between the minister and the board of a corporation have never been satisfactorily defined. Consequently, confusion persists over what should be the proper role of the public corporation.

Some elements at least are clearly defined in the relationship between minister and corporation. Ministers have certain technical powers over public corporations, such as the power to appoint auditors and to determine the form of the corporation's accounts. In addition ministers have the power to appoint or dismiss members of a corporation's board, so they do have the opportunity to appoint like-minded chairmen and board members. As most board members are on fairly short-term contracts this opportunity recurs frequently, but circumstances and hence relationships may change rapidly. This was evidenced by the change in the fortunes of Ian MacGregor, appointed as Chairman of the National Coal Board, after a period as Chairman of the British Steel Corporation, in March 1983. He was regarded very much as the Government's champion in its fight to slim down the coal industry. But over two years later, following the 1984–85 miners' strike, relations between MacGregor and the Energy Secretary, Peter Walker, and indeed with the Prime Minister, had reached an extremely low ebb. MacGregor was even talking in terms of 'getting my head beaten in' in meetings with government ministers.

The root of the problem in the relationship between Whitehall and the public corporation lies in the absence of a commonly accepted concept of the objectives of the public corporation. Should a corporation function in the public interest, providing services or employment even at the cost of subsidy from public funds? Alternatively, should it engage in trade, like any private organisation, with the same need to show financial viability? It is the departmental minister rather than the board's chairman who ultimately decides on objectives. Points on which he can and should intervene in the running of the corporation are unclear, and this fact can bring bitterness into the relationship. It is generally considered that the minister has to intervene in order to secure the wider public interest and that he should attempt to oversee the running of the corporation in order to ensure, if possible, its efficiency. Day-to-day management on the other hand should be left with the chairman and board. Different ministers will, of course, each have their own views on the limits of what constitutes 'management' and a minister's view will vary depending on political circumstances and the pressures upon him to intervene in the running of the industry. Consequently, public corporation boards complain that they are really unable to plan their management on a stable basis because they are subject to intermittent and haphazard intervention by ministers.

This problem has become much worse in recent years as a result of the differing attitudes of the major political parties to public corporations. Labour ministers have tended to place emphasis on the non-commercial aspects of a public corporation's operation. For example, when in 1975 the British Steel Corporation, under its Chairman, Sir Monty Finneston, planned to make 20,000 workers redundant in an attempt to reduce its very high losses, the Industry Minister, Tony Benn, resisted these plans. A sharp conflict between Benn and Finneston ensued. More recently the Conservative Government, with its far more 'commercial' outlook has appeared to have made most of the running. It has pressurised the public corporations into cutting unnecessary plant and staff.

A further confusing factor is added by the fact that the Treasury is able to impose external financing limits on the corporations. These often appear arbitrary to the boards and the procedure by which they are imposed gives the boards very little opportunity to discuss their detail with the Treasury. In the mid-1980s the threat that potentially profitable portions of public corporations might be privatised was added to all the other factors which promote uncertainty in public corporations. Arguably, this additional uncertainty acts to further limit the capacity of their boards to manage in the context of assured future policy.

A further unsatisfactory element in the relationship between ministers and public corporations is that although ministers are known to exercise very considerable practical control over the corporations that control is often 'informal', as in the case of lunch-table directives. The informal nature of that control makes it very difficult for Parliament to call ministers to account for policies and decisions which they have promoted. It is clear that the original hope that public corporations would be able to operate 'at arm's length' from sponsoring ministers has not been realised, and it is unlikely that any amount of tinkering with the system will bring substantial improvement.

Radical reform is possible: for example the precise powers of ministers might be much more clearly defined by statute. This would not, of course, solve the problem of extra-statutory intervention, or deflect the exercise of financial leverage over those corporations whose finances were not healthy. The NEDO Report of 1976 suggested the creation of a policy council for each corporation, comprising a president, a chairman of the board, some board members, civil servants, trade-union representatives, and user representatives, to establish the corporate objectives and to suggest the strategies necessary to achieve them. The board would then be left to execute those strategies. The recommendations were not taken up and were perhaps too radical: the temptation for ministers to intervene in public corporations on political grounds is perhaps too great to allow them to hand over control to a body such as a policy council.

A STEP FURTHER

The demise of the Nationalised Industries Select Committee of the House of Commons in 1979 is much to be regretted in that it has robbed us of a good source of reports on the public corporations and the nationalised industries generally. The investigation by the House of Commons of public corporations is now dispersed among the various 'departmental' select committees, such as those covering trade and industry, energy, and transport. This tends to make life a little harder for students. The various users' councils attached to public corporations continue to produce their annual reports, and even if we are sceptical about their impact,they remain valuable as an introduction to the perspective of at least one party in the political tangle. In recent literature there is a good general survey of the administrative and financial problems of public corporations, in John R. Greenwood and David J. Wilson, *Public Administration in Britain* (Allen and Unwin 1984). The chapter by Geoffrey Lee on 'Privatisation', in *Political Issues in Britain Today*, ed. Bill Jones (Manchester University Press 1985) gives a very competent survey of one aspect of the crisis facing the public corporations. Beyond this you can scan the newspapers and radio and television reports for references to government statements on the need for public corporation boards to adhere to strict financial discipline. The occasional rows which are made public in the relations between chairmen and relevant ministers are also a useful source of insight into the relations between Whitehall and the public corporations.

Chapter 15

Politics and the law

GETTING STARTED

In recent years the enforcement and interpretation of the law have become central political issues. The accusation has been made that both the police and the courts are politically biased. Local police authorities, dominated by local councillors, have attempted to extend their control over police forces; while the political opponents of governments have become much more willing to carry their opposition into the courts. The law, rather than some combination of self-interest, common sense, and industrial muscle has been made the chief regulator of one of the most contentious areas of modern politics, namely industrial relations.

ESSENTIAL PRINCIPLES

Perhaps the most important task in clarifying the discretion of the police and the judiciary, is first to define their constitutional status, and then to explain the sort of political disputes to which that status gives rise.

THE POLICE

The police are not government servants; they are enforcers of the law whoever enacted it and they are supposed to enforce it without reserve or favour.

With the exception of the Metropolitan Police, police forces are under the control of their own chief constables, at least as far as operational policing is concerned. This means that the *chief constable* of a force is responsible for the emphasis to be placed on different types of policing, such as crime prevention, investigation, and traffic, and on the broad allocation of his resources. It also means that the chief constable has to decide on the taking of pre-emptive action in order to avoid breaches of the law. This might involve rerouting or even preventing a proposed political march which he considers may provoke violent disturbances, or preventing would-be flying pickets from reaching the scene of a strike.

Many of these responsibilities bring chief constables almost inevitably into a political minefield in a period when violence seems to be an increasingly common aspect of political life. The banning of a march or demonstration easily attracts the suspicion of political censorship, while the interception of would-be flying pickets tends to brand the police as anti-union or anti-working class in the eyes of the frustrated activists. Heavy policing of areas frequented by unemployed youths, blacks, or other easily identifiable groups, often provokes the accusation of harassment. Equally, light policing of such areas runs the risk of being labelled as soft and slack, especially by the disciplinarian Right.

There are, however, other elements in the network of control over the police.

- The *local police authority*, usually identical geographically with a county, consists of two-thirds elected councillors and one-third lay magistrates, and is responsible for funding the force.
- The *Home Secretary* is ultimately responsible, through the Inspector of Constabulary, for ensuring its financial and operational efficiency.

There are, of course, possible areas of somewhat hazy or contentious jurisdiction which once again drag the police into the political arena. There have been a number of well-publicised clashes in recent years between chief constables and their police authority, as over whether the force should stock certain emotive items of riot-control equipment such as plastic bullets. Such clashes can easily be construed in party political terms, whether or not this is the correct interpretation.

Calls have been made for the police to become accountable to police authorities for the way in which they exercise their functions. It is argued that the possibility of being called to account would make them more cautious and fairer in their policing. Against this it is argued that the police are already accountable for their actions in courts where they, like anyone else, are subject to the criminal law. They are also accountable for their actions in the civil courts should they exceed or abuse their powers. It is suggested that the creation of a system of police accountability may lead to *political* control over the police, which in turn could be dangerous if exercised by a police authority in the hands of extremist councillors.

THE JUDICIARY

Members of the judiciary can hardly claim to be untouched by politics. In the first place they are appointed by, or on the recommendation of, politicians. Judges of the Court of Appeal, the Law Lords and the Lord Chief Justice, and the President of the Family Division, are appointed to their posts on the advice of the Prime Minister following consultation with the Lord Chancellor.

Other judicial appointments right down to the level of lay magistrates are made by, or on the advice of, the Lord Chancellor. The Prime Minister is, of course, a political figure, but so is the Lord Chancellor who has by convention a seat in the Cabinet. However, in the case of most judicial appointments, political considerations seem not to be important. A candidate's personal qualities and the degree of professional esteem which he or she can command, seem to be the most important factors. The Lord Chancellor will only make recommendations for appointment after extensive consultations among senior members of the judiciary.

In the case of *lay magistrates*, however, the circular from the Lord Chancellor in 1966 to the advisory committees which recommend appointment, established that the political leanings of candidates *should* be taken into consideration on the grounds that 'Justices should be drawn from all sections of the community and should represent all shades of opinion'. This could be construed as suggesting political even-handedness rather than political bias!

It is perhaps not so much in their appointment as in their implementation and interpretation of the law that judges are likely to fall foul of accusations that they engage in political rather than legal activity. They have, of course, the task of imposing sentences for breaches of the law. If the law in question is a politically contentious one, such as some of the laws of the early 1980s aimed at curbing what the Government saw as excessive trade-union powers, then the judges may well be seen by the opponents of such legislation as being in some way the collaborators of the Government. More fundamentally, whenever the phrasing or vocabulary of the law is unclear it will fall to the judge to interpret and clarify the statute so as to make it workable. In so doing the judges may run the risk that they seem to go beyond their proper role and begin effectively to create new law. If they do so in a politically contentious area then, of course, their interpretation will seem to indicate partisan activity. Some judges admittedly have done little to dispel the suspicion that they are more than ready to interpret the statute-book in a manner which they themselves regard as more rational.

Complaints of judicial bias perhaps arise more readily from the political Left than from the Right; partly because many on the Left are generally more prepared to view the judiciary as fundamentally conservative in both outlook and social background. Conservatives tend to be more respectful towards those established institutions which tend to maintain the existing fabric of society, such as the judiciary. Consequently they are usually more reluctant to denounce judicial decisions, even when these may run counter to their political interests, as indeed some do.

USEFUL APPLIED MATERIALS

PUBLIC ATTITUDES TO THE POLICE AND THE COURTS

In a period when we have heard accusations of degeneration into a police state and accusations of political bias in the work of the courts, it is perhaps interesting that public confidence in both institutions seems to be gaining ground. A MORI poll of early 1985 revealed that 47 per cent of respondents placed the *police* among the two or three institutions which best protected citizens' rights, whereas only 32 per cent of respondents had so placed them in a similar poll taken in 1973. Only 8 per cent of respondents listed the police as a significant threat to citizens' rights, compared with 32 per cent who named the trade unions, and 23 per cent who named the political parties as a significant threat. Again, 28 per cent of respondents in 1985 suggested that the *courts* are one of the two or three institutions which best protect rights, as opposed to 19 per cent who came into this category in 1973. Only 3 per cent of respondents suggested that the courts posed a significant threat to citizens' rights. The police, followed by the courts, were in fact seen as the best guarantors of citizens' rights in 1985. (*The Times*, 1.7.85, p. 12).

COMPLAINTS AGAINST THE POLICE

The Police and Criminal Evidence Act 1984 established a new procedure for dealing with complaints against the police. It set up a new Police Complaints Authority, composed of a chairman appointed by the Crown and at least eight other full- or part-time members who should be appointed by the Home Secretary. No member of the Complaints Authority should have been a constable in any part of the UK. Appointments would be for not more than three years at one time. The first Chairman of the Police Complaints Authority, significantly enough, was the recently retired Parliamentary Commissioner for Administration, Sir Cecil Clothier.

The new procedure for dealing with complaints was to be as follows: when a complaint is made against the conduct of a police officer, the chief officer of the force must decide whether the case is suitable for 'informal resolution'. If it is not, the chief officer must appoint a member of his own force or another force to investigate the complaint *formally*. The investigating officer must at least be of chief inspector rank and at least of the rank of the officer against whom the complaint has been made. The *informal* resolution procedure applies only if the complainant gives his consent and if the chief officer is satisfied that the conduct about which the complaint has been made would not, if proved to have taken place, justify a criminal or disciplinary charge. If the officer complained of is above the rank of chief superintendent, then the matter will be dealt with by the Commissioner of the Metropolitan Police, or, if outside the metropolitan area, by the police authority for the area, and not by the chief officer.

Complaints must be referred to the Police Complaints Authority if (a) there is allegation that misconduct resulted in death or serious injury, or (b) the complaint falls into a category specified by the

Home Secretary. In addition, any other complaint may be referred to the Complaints Authority. Indeed any conduct may be so referred which seems to the chief officer or to the police authority for the area to be possibly criminal or possibly to warrant disciplinary action, *even if such conduct has not been the subject of a complaint*. The Complaints Authority may itself require complaints to be forwarded to it.

Once a matter has been referred to the Complaints Authority it will supervise the investigation of the complaint and it will require a report from the investigating officer. In the case of officers of the rank of chief superintendent or below who have been the subject of complaint, the Complaints Authority may direct the chief officer to send a copy of the investigation report to the Director of Public Prosecutions; it may even direct the chief officer to institute disciplinary charges. In the event of disciplinary charges being brought they should be heard by a tribunal consisting of the chief officer of the relevant force, acting as chairman, together with two members of the Police Complaints Authority.

Some disquiet was expressed when it was announced, early in 1985, that the Police Complaints Authority was to appoint as an adviser a former Deputy Chief Constable of South Yorkshire. The Chairman of the Complaints Authority sought to make it clear that the appointment would not in any way jeopardise the Authority's impartiality. It was being made in order to increase the amount of technical advice available so that the Complaints Authority would not be taken by surprise or have the wool pulled over its eyes. Such an appointment would also help the Complaints Authority avoid making unreasonable, unobtainable demands on the police.

LORD DENNING ON JUDICIAL INTERPRETATION

The following is the opinion of Lord Denning, one of the most influential if sometimes controversial judges of the century, on the subject of the judicial interpretation of statutes. It should be borne in mind that Denning's views have been criticised in the House of Lords as 'a naked usurpation of the legislative function under the thin disguise of interpretation'.

'A judge believing himself to be fettered by the supposed rule that he must look to the language (of the statute) and nothing else laments that the draughtsmen have not provided for this or that or have been guilty of some or other ambiguity. It would certainly save the judges trouble if Acts of Parliament were drafted with divine prescience and perfect clarity. In the absence of it . . . the judge . . . must set to work on the constructive task of finding the intention of Parliament and he must do this not only from the language of the Statute but also from a consideration of the social conditions which gave rise to it and of the mischief which it was passed to remedy and then he must supplement the written word so as to give "force and life" to the intention of the legislature. . . . A judge should ask himself the question: if the makers of the Act had themselves come across this ruck in the texture of it how would they have straightened it out? He must then do as they would have done. A judge must not alter the material with which it is woven but he can and should iron out the creases.' (Geoffrey Marshall, *Constitutional Theory*, OUP 1971, p. 88, quoting (1949), 2 KB 481 at 499).

LORD DENNING ON THE CONSTITUTIONAL STATUS OF CHIEF CONSTABLES

In the following judgment Lord Denning describes the status of the Metropolitan Police Commissioner who is in charge of operational policing in the Metropolitan area to which the Home Secretary acts as police authority. He makes clear, however, that many of his remarks apply just as well to chief constables beyond the Metropolitan area, and indeed to the police generally.

'I have no hesitation . . . in holding that like every constable in the land he should be and is independent of the executive. He is not subject to the orders of the Secretary of State save that under the Police Act 1964 the Secretary of State can call on him to give a report or to retire in the interests of efficiency.

'I hold it to be the duty of the Commissioner of Police as it is of every Chief Constable to enforce the law of the land. He must take steps so as to post his men that crimes may be detected; and that honest citizens may go about their affairs in peace. He must decide whether or not suspected persons are to be prosecuted and if need be bring the prosecution or see that it is brought; but in all these things he is not the servant of anyone save the law itself. No Minister of the Crown can tell him that he must or must not keep observation on this place or that; or that he must or must not prosecute this man or that man; nor can any police authority tell him so. The responsibility for law enforcement lies on him: he is answerable to the law and to the law alone.' (*R.* v. *Metropolitan Police Commissioner ex parte Blackburn* (1968), 1 All ER 763, at 769).

A CHIEF CONSTABLE COMES INTO CONFLICT WITH THE POLICE AUTHORITY

Late in 1985 Mr James Anderton, Chief Constable of Greater Manchester, ordered some 500 rounds of plastic bullets (plastic baton rounds) together with 4 dischargers. He was condemned for this action by the Greater Manchester Police Authority dominated by Labour councillors, which ordered him to dispose of the bullets and dischargers. At this point Mr Douglas Hurd, Home Secretary in the Conservative Government, stepped in and announced in a reply to a parliamentary question that

'Where a Chief Officer concludes that he requires plastic baton rounds and this is endorsed by the independent professional advice of Her Majesty's Inspector of Constabulary I shall support him. In those circumstances I regard it as essential that plastic baton rounds should be available to the force concerned. My Department is consulting the Chief Officers of Police and the Police Authorities most immediately concerned to work out how such a requirement is best met.'

Mr Anderton's first step was to avoid the attempted ban by the

Greater Manchester Police Authority, by taking the plastic bullets and dischargers on loan from the Metropolitan Police Force and thereby depriving the Police Authority of its financial control over the acquisition of equipment. With the Conservative Home Secretary and the Labour-dominated Police Authority lining up on different sides, it was difficult for the actions of the Chief Constable to appear in anything but a political light. His own view that operational policing was being subjected to political interference was made clear in passages of a speech which he made to the Police Federation:

'I believe far too much time has been spent by the Committee on matters of no special local significance to the people of Greater Manchester. Much of what has passed for Police Committee business has been a total sham and of limited value either to the police force or the public we try to serve. I am quite sure that members of the Greater Manchester police and the majority of the public of this area would have made up their own minds a long time ago about the negative nature of the Police Committee and the disruptive influence it has on the normal daily work of the force.' (*The Times*, 27.11.85, p. 36; 30.11.85, p. 4).

THE POLITICAL AND SOCIAL BACKGROUNDS OF MAGISTRATES

Evidence collected by Peter Evans in a survey of British magistrates published in *The Times*, revealed the following:

(a) Sexual parity among magistrates is apparently being achieved: in 1973 33 per cent of magistrates were women, whereas in 1985 43 per cent were women.

(b) The political inclinations of English and Welsh magistrates in 1983 were as follows: 41 per cent Conservative, 28 per cent Labour, 11 per cent Liberal, 1 per cent SDP, 0.3 per cent Plaid Cymru, 18.7 per cent Independents/not known.

(c) There is evidence from some areas that the occupational distribution of magistrates does not reflect that of the community at large: a Midland Bench of nearly 400 magistrates contained in 1985 only 39 manual workers: a North-East Bench of 191 magistrates included 17 manual workers, 8 persons doing secretarial work, but 19 teachers and 15 company directors. On the other hand from another Bench came the comment of one magistrate that 'we reflect the local community pretty well, we have an electrician on the Bench and someone who works in a dry cleaning place, we have farmers and two teachers: our Chairman is a shopkeeper'. (*The Times*, (27.11.85), p. 12).

RECENT EXAMINATION QUESTIONS

Spend ten minutes or so planning an answer to each of the following questions. Outline answers to question **6**, **8**, and **12** and a tutor's answer to question **7** are given in the following sections.

Question 1.	Some people have claimed that Britain is becoming a police state. What are your reactions to this assertion? (London, Govt and Pol. Stud., Paper 1, June 1983)
Question 2.	Distinguish between the organisation of the police in London and in the rest of England and Wales. (London, Govt and Pol. Stud., Paper 4, short answer question, June 1983)
Question 3.	To what extent have judges been involved in making political decisions in recent years? How well equipped are they for this role? (JMB, Brit. Govt and Pol., June 1982)
Question 4.	What is the role of the police in maintaining public order? Are there legitimate criticisms of how they fulfil this role? (London, Govt and Pol. Stud., Paper 1, June 1981)
Question 5.	How can British courts review the activities of a government? (London, Govt and Pol. Stud., Paper 1, short answer question, June, 1980)
Question 6.	'The police should never be under the control of politicians be they national or local.' Are there any advantages in having a greater measure of political control over the actions of the police? (Cambridge, Pub. Aff., June 1984)
Question 7.	Is the judiciary above politics in Britain? (Cambridge, Pol. and Govt, Paper 1, June 1983)
Question 8.	Should the courts play a larger role in the control of government? (London, Govt and Pol. Stud., Paper 1, January 1983)
Question 9.	Can judges stay out of politics? (London, Govt and Pol Stud., Paper 1, June 1983)
Question 10.	What public controls are there over the police in England and Wales? (London, Govt and Pol. Stud., Paper 1, short answer question, June 1983)
Question 11.	To what extent have attitudes to the rule of law changed in recent years? (JMB, Brit. Govt and Pol., June 1985)
Question 12.	What are the main functions of local authorities in relation to the police? (London, Govt and Pol. Stud., Paper 1, short answer question, June 1982)

'The police should never be under the control of politicians be they national or local.' Are there any advantages in having a greater measure of political control over the actions of the police?

Answer

(a) Much depends on the nature of the control which may be exercised over the activities of the police. Such control may range from the power to hold the police accountable for their actions, to the power actually to direct those actions.

(b) If we assume that control signifies *the capacity to direct* we may well be more impressed by the potential disadvantages than by any possible advantages. The role of the police is to maintain public order and to uphold the law as sanctioned by Parliament. They are officers of the law and if they go beyond the law then they can be made to account for their actions in the courts. A greater degree of political control in this directive sense may blur the question of police accountability in that it may produce a possible confusion between the officers and the directing politicians.

   If we could trust the politicians to act always in conformity with the law then the issue might not arise, but we cannot necessarily do this. The 1980s have seen many instances of government ministers acting beyond their powers (e.g. in DHSS and Environment matters) as well as defiance of the law by many local authorities (e.g. Norwich City Council over the sale of council houses, Liverpool City Council over the setting of its rate). Because they are much more likely to be ideologically committed one way or another, it may be argued that there will be a stronger temptation for politicians to overstep the bounds of the law than for the police to do so.

(c) There are, however, some areas in which the police themselves might welcome more direction of their activities by political leaders. At present senior police officers have to exercise a good deal of discretion in politically sensitive circumstances, for example if the chief constable of a force believes that a proposed political march or rally is likely to lead to serious disturbances then it is his responsibility to decide whether or not to ban the meeting. This involves him in what may seem to be a politically biased act and many chief officers woud be glad to have this sort of burden shouldered by politicians.

(d) There are other possible advantages in greater political control. Greater political control *by the Home Secretary* might arguably lead to greater uniformity of policing methods and procedures over the whole of the country. This might encourage the more widespread adoption of policing methods in conformity with the wishes of those who elected the Government. Again , a greater measure of political control *by local police authorities* over their police forces might give the localities the distinct style of policing which their problems and their populations require.

Against this it may be argued that the style of policing which a local or national community may *want* is not necessarily the style of policing which it *needs*. If we are arguing along the lines of democratisation of policing we should remember that no *central government* since the Second World War has achieved power on more than 50 per cent of the vote. In fact, most *local authority* ruling groups are elected on the basis of the votes of only a very small percentage of the local electorate.

(e) Even if we interpret control of policing as meaning greater accountability of the police to political bodies, the possible advantages of such a situation scarcely seem to be overwhelming. The police are already accountable for their actions, such as to the courts, to their superiors, and now, since the 1984 Police and Criminal Evidence Act, to the independent Police Complaints Authority. It could be argued that a greater measure of accountability to *politicians* might render the police liable to political persecution and hence inhibit them from performing their task effectively. It might also prevent them from pursuing consistent policing policies if they had to change those policies every few years to accommodate their new political masters.

Q. 8.   Should the courts play a larger role in the control of government?

Answer   There are several possible forms which such a larger role may take.

(a) Firstly, the courts might expand their role within the already established framework of systems for the control of government. The courts share this work with other bodies, e.g. administrative tribunals, and the Ombudsmen. But the reason why these other forms of control have developed is that the courts (i) are insufficiently expert in some matters, (ii) do not have the time to deal with the mass of small matters which often come before Ombudsmen and tribunals, and (iii) are too expensive and too cumbersome for effective use by many who have complaints against the way in which government operates. From this it might be argued that it is impracticable for the present system of courts to extend its control over the administrative acts of government.

(b) Secondly, a new system of law and of associated courts might be created on the lines of the French system of administrative law. This would certainly bring greater uniformity and probably greater clarity into the process of control of government.

(c) Much the most controversial area for discussion is whether the courts should go beyond their current constitutional position. As currently constituted, the courts simply restrain Government from exceeding the powers which have been given to it by legislation, and compel it to carry out the obligations which have been laid upon it by legislation. If the judges feel that the legislation granting powers to the Government is 'bad' legislation then they are not at present in theory empowered to annul or amend it. That is to say the law is there to be upheld by the courts and not to be criticised or questioned by them.

Such a role for the courts is necessitated by the doctrine of the sovereignty of Parliament. Some commentators, however, including Lord Scarman, have argued that Parliament is so heavily under the control of the Government that it provides no effective check to the expansion of governmental powers and no effective controlling mechanism over those powers. This line of argument can lead to the conclusion that the courts should be empowered to extend their control over the Government, by imposing a test of reasonableness upon any of a government's actions. Of course, it could be argued that this would merely substitute the tyranny of the judiciary for the tyranny of a government. Alternatively, a Bill of Rights could be established on the lines of, say, the United States Constitution, so that the courts might measure a government's actions against this absolute standard rather than against the powers and capacities which the Government had effectively awarded to itself.

SHORT ANSWER Q. 12. What are the main functions of local authorities in relation to the police?

Answer The local authority for the area in which each police force operates appoints members of a police authority. This has the power to appoint chief constables and deputy and assistant chief constables for the force, subject to the Home Secretary's approval. The police authority is the disciplinary authority for those officers and can call upon them to retire in the interests of efficiency, with the Home Secretary's approval. The police authority (or committee) can require the chief constable to submit a report on any matter connected with the policing of the area. Subject to the Home Secretary's supervision the authority provides buildings, equipment, and uniforms for the police force. It determines the numbers of police at each rank in its area. The authority determines the police budget and provides part of the money from the rates, the remainder being made up by central government.

A TUTOR'S ANSWER Q. 7. Is the judiciary above politics in Britain?

Answer The judiciary is above politics in the sense that its members are not generally appointed to, or removed from, their office as a result of party political considerations. The partial exceptions to this rule are the lay magistrates who, since a Lord Chancellor's Circular of 1966, are appointed partly on the basis of their political views. But this hardly reflects an attempt by government to secure a monopoly or a preponderant interest among the lay magistracy. Rather it reflects an attempt to secure some sort of balanced spread of political opinion among magistrates who, as non-professional members of the judiciary, may perhaps be assumed not to have the degree of detachment which professional judges are expected to cultivate.

Above the level of the lay magistracy, judges are appointed by the Lord Chancellor or, in the case of Appeal Court judges and Law Lords, by the Prime Minister after consultation with the Lord Chancellor. In other words politicians do appoint throughout the entire judicial hierarchy, but they do so only after consultation with members of the legal profession and the judicial fraternity. The tradition of professional independence in these circles is so strong that it is difficult to imagine that appointments obviously designed to further party interests would be tolerated. This contrasts starkly with the situation in the United States, where the remodelling of federal courts by presidents is now almost an accepted custom. Once appointed, judges hold office during good behaviour and can be removed only by a resolution of both Houses of Parliament. In other words in practical terms they enjoy judicial independence.

Nevertheless, the claim that judges are involved in party politics is one which has been heard quite frequently in recent years. For example in the course of the 1984–85 miners' strike the President of the NUM, Arthur Scargill, alleged on several occasions that his union was suffering from the attentions of Tory judges. Most critics would contend that this is almost certainly to confuse the judges with the law which they must interpret and on which they must base their decisions.

In fact judges are frequently called upon to give rulings which are almost certain to be to the advantage of one side or another in a political dispute. This is the result of two principal factors.

Firstly, legislation which confers powers or duties upon the Government is often so complex that in attempting to implement policy the Executive may break its own rules. Attempts by ministers to attach conditions to the provision of social security benefits, or to withhold part of the central government grant to local authorities on the grounds of the latters' overspending, brought ministers before the courts in 1985. The results have been mixed, but in all cases the supporters of the successful party in the case have interpreted the ruling as a political victory.

Secondly, an increasing volume of legislation, particulary that of Conservative Governments directed against some of the activities of trade unionists, was intended to *prevent* individuals or organisations from committing acts or from engaging in procedures which they may honestly consider to be perfectly legitimate and justified. It is not, for example, a matter for serious dispute that theft, murder, or arson are morally wrong and obvious criminal acts. But it *is* a matter of earnest political debate whether mass picketing or secondary picketing is to be considered an unlawful act. A judge who has to consider whether the activities of trade unionists involved in an industrial dispute (activities which they may consider to be historically and morally justified) in fact contravene a government's legislation, is forced to make decisions which will be politically contentious. The decisions will inevitably provide the various parties with political ammunition and will appear to make political as well as, or even instead of, legal judgments.

There are, however, other, and perhaps more subtle, ways in which members of the judiciary are currently involved in politics. Precisely because of their qualities of fairness and probity, their opinions are valued both by the legislature and by the Executive. For example, following serious riots in Brixton in 1981, the then Home Secretary, William Whitelaw, set up an inquiry to investigate and report on the background to the riots, on the activities of the police in dealing with them, and on the relations between the police and the community in Brixton. His choice to conduct that inquiry was one of the Law Lords, Lord Scarman. The report involved Lord Scarman in making recommendations for future policing policy which went far beyond his normal role of judicial interpretation. In a somewhat similar fashion, when, in 1984, the House of Commons was considering a matrimonial proceedings Bill, it established a committee which heard evidence from several members of the judiciary. They were, of course, expert and helpful witnesses, but they were helping to *make* law rather than to interpret it. Indeed in the two years before June 1984 a total of twenty-eight High Court judges were engaged in non-judicial activities, that is to say they were members of inquiries or commissions of various sorts. These activities may not necessarily involve the judges in great controversy, though this could hardly be said to be true in the case of the *Scarman Report*. What is perhaps more important is that they blur the distinction between judicial activity and legislative work. Legislation is the function of politicians, and if judges begin to take part in it they become enmeshed in politics.

A STEP FURTHER

The miners' strike of 1984–85 provides a happy hunting ground for those seeking allegations of 'political' action by police and politically motivated judgments in the courts. The National Council for Civil Liberties has published an interim report by its own inquiry panel entitled *Civil Liberties and the Miners Dispute 1984* which is worth looking at. Another useful source is Bob Fine and Robert Millar, *Policing the Miners Strike*, (Lawrence and Wishart/Cobden Trust 1985). For a strictly objective blow-by-blow account of the miners' strike, police activity, and the relevant judgments, the interested student should turn to *Keesing's Contemporary Archives*, Vols 30 and 31 Longman (1984, 1985, pp. 33228–35 and 33550–5). More generally it is worth referring to Sarah Spencer, *Called to Account: The Case for Police Accountability in England and Wales* (National Council for Civil Liberties 1985).

An interesting survey of several aspects of this topic is *Law and Order in British Politics*, ed. Philip Norton (Gower 1984). It is also still worth looking at J. Griffith, *The Politics of the Judiciary* (Fontana 1977), and G. Drewry and J. Morgan, 'Law Lords as legislators', *Parliamentary Affairs* Vol. 22 (1969).

Chapter 16

The UK and the EEC

The European Economic Community (EEC) was inaugurated in March 1957 when ministers of France, West Germany, Italy, Luxembourg, Belgium, and the Netherlands signed the Treaty of Rome. It provided for the merging of the economies of the member states into a single area of common *economic* policy. It also provided for eventual *political* union. Four major institutions of the EEC were established:

1. A *Commission*, to be independent of member governments, would provide the Secretariat for the EEC, and would have the task of prompting and suggesting policies to the EEC's principal legislative organ, the Council of Ministers.
2. The *Council of Ministers* was to be composed of representatives of the member governments. These would make EEC policy, generally along the lines suggested by the Commission.
3. A *European Parliament* was created in order to monitor the workings of the Council of Ministers and the Commission.
4. A *Court of Justice* was created in order to adjudicate on problems arising from the application of a common Community Law.

In 1961 the UK tried to join the EEC, but in 1963 this application failed following a veto exercised by President de Gaulle of France. In 1967 the UK again formally applied for EEC membership, but once again the application was brought to nothing by the actions of President de Gaulle. The Edward Heath Government elected in 1970 began a determined attempt to gain membership, and in 1971 the House of Commons voted for entry. The Treaty of Accession to the EEC was signed by the Prime Minister in January 1972. In the course of the same year Parliament passed the European Communities Act, by which UK became a full member of the EEC with effect from 1 January 1973.

In 1974 Harold Wilson's Labour Government was elected with a commitment to renegotiate the terms of the UK's membership. Following that renegotiation the Government recommended that the UK should remain a member of the EEC and submitted that recommendation to a referendum in 1975. In that referendum 65 per cent of the electorate voted, with the recommendation of the Government being accepted by a majority of approximately two to one.

ESSENTIAL PRINCIPLES

IMPACT OF EEC MEMBERSHIP

Ever since the UK joined the EEC in the early 1970s there has been continuous debate as to the impact of the EEC membership. This has centred on two major issues: (1) the economic implications and (2) the constitutional and political implications.

CONSTITUTIONAL AND POLITICAL IMPLICATIONS

Although the two issues frequently overlap, the major concern for the student of politics is the constitutional and political implications. Let us take the constitutional issue first. Opponents of UK entry, and since 1973 of the UK's membership, have often suggested that it has involved *a loss of sovereignty*. In a strict sense this is quite true. Before entry into the EEC Parliament was technically a sovereign body, that is to say it enjoyed the unfettered right to legislate for the UK on any matter at a time. It had, in a technical sense at least, complete control over the raising of taxation and over the expenditure of public money within the UK. Membership of the EEC changed this situation. Membership involved the UK in accepting that the legislation of the European Community, in the form of EEC Regulations, would be directly applicable within the UK. The UK had also to accept that its Government might be *directed* by the relevant institution of the EEC to carry through specified legislation in the UK Parliament. Parliament had also lost its previously total control over taxation, since it was now possible for the EEC to appropriate a certain amount of UK taxation without the consent of Parliament. Thus at the Fontainebleau EEC Summit of June 1984 it was agreed that the UK should contribute to the EEC Budget a sum amounting to 1.4 per cent of VAT revenue in any one year. Again, with the UK now subject to EEC law, it follows that any infractions of that law by British individuals or companies, should be dealt with in the European Court, the judicial organ of the Community.

It may be pointed out, however, that this loss of sovereignty is somewhat notional. On the one hand there were already many organisations which in practice restricted the capacity of the UK Parliament to legislate freely. These have included the international financial organisations to which the UK has been indebted, military allies of the UK, and others for whom common prudence and diplomatic caution have dictated special consideration. In any case, no one seriously doubts that if Parliament should really wish it, it could withdraw the UK from EEC membership. Thus it appears that the surrender of sovereignty is a *de jure* rather than a *de facto* one.

It needs to be stressed that in joining the EEC, the UK did not simply put itself at the mercy of Continental Europe. Rather, it joined an association in which its voice counts. The UK, like all of the other EEC members, elects representatives to the European Parliament and these have an increasingly strong voice in Community affairs, including for example, the capacity to veto the EEC Budget. There is also the Economic and Social Committee which is consulted on proposed legislation with socio-economic applications. This committee, which consists of 189 members, is made up of representatives of employers associations, trade unions, and similar bodies from each of the member states of the Community. Again, the UK like every other EEC Member, is represented on the Council of Ministers, the principal political decision-making body of the Community. Although it was originally envisaged that the Council of Ministers should proceed by *majority decisions*, the Luxembourg agreements of 1966 instituted the system by which the Council in practice proceeds by *consensus*. Any member state which feels that a decision threatens its vital national interests, is entitled under the Luxembourg agreements to attempt to veto the proposed decision. The Luxembourg agreements, however, are *not* part of the EEC's formal Constitution, and there have been some recent signs that a return to majority voting may be under way. This is perhaps the logical outcome of the enlargement of the Community to a group of twelve rather than the original group of six.

The discussion of the EEC's impact should go far beyond the question of sovereignty. The UK's membership has prompted developments in the domestic *political* scene. For example, the question of whether the UK should remain a member of the Community provoked, in 1975, the first and still the only national referendum. As a part of the campaign leading up to that referendum we had the spectacle of the so-called 'agreement to differ' within the Labour Government's Cabinet. Under this 'agreement' Cabinet ministers were, very unusually, given the licence to disagree with the Government's announced policy of remaining within the Community, so long as that disagreement was expressed *outside* rather than inside Parliament.

Elections to the European Assembly have also given the British public *another occasion* for participation in the political process, though it cannot be claimed that they have so far taken to this with wild enthusiasm. In the European Parliament elections of late 1984, the British turn-out was a derisory 32 per cent, compared with nearly 60 per cent for the Community as a whole. But the 1984 election did underline the fact that the UK was alone among member states in using the first past the post system of election, though an exception to this was made in Northern Ireland where STV was employed. The fact that the UK was seen to be out of step in this respect with the rest of the Community has undoubtedly placed additional ammunition in the hands of those who advocate a system of PR for all UK elections. It has to be admitted, however, that up to the present time there seems to be little reason to disagree with the verdict of General de Gaulle.

His opposition to UK membership was well known, namely that the UK, in its traditions, in its institutions, and in its general outlook was not well fitted to understand and to be a member of the Community.

USEFUL APPLIED MATERIALS

A LAW LORD ASSESSES THE IMPACT OF THE EEC

In October 1974 Lord Scarman, one of the most distinguished of the Law Lords, made an important assessment of the impact on UK law and government of EEC membership. It included the following passages:

'The system works in this way. The European Treaties are part of the law of the land; for Parliament has so enacted. Each Treaty – and I will take the Economic Treaty, the Treaty of Rome, as my example – empowers the Community to legislate to give effect to the Treaties. The legislative power belongs to the Council of Ministers who act upon the initiative of the European Commission and sometimes, but not invariably, after consultation with the European Parliament. From the deliberations of these Bodies there emerge various sorts of Community enactments – Regulations, Directives, Decisions. Regulations have direct effect within Member States: that is to say they are part of the law of the land to be applied and enforced by our Courts . . . Directives are not necessarily part of the law when made – though they may be if they are so interpreted by the European Court of Justice.

'By these various types of instruments Community institutions make legal rules which bind us and must be enforced by our courts. Their drafting – indeed all the work of their preparation – is the task of the Commission, the appointed body of high-powered European officials who work full time for the Community in Brussels. The British Parliament plays no part in the preparation of Community legislation. Parliament completed its job when it enacted in 1972 that the Treaties and Community legislation deriving from them were to be part of English law and that the Courts were to accept the European Court of Justice as their authoritative interpreter. No doubt Parliament will create some means of scrutiny and consultation before the Community issues new legislation; but this will not alter the legal position. We now have a new source of law.

The Common Market Treaties leave a lot to the judges to do; an English Act of Parliament leaves as little as possible. The Treaty of Rome imposes upon the European Court of Justice the duty of ensuring the effectual implementation of the Treaty. Of all questions as to the meaning of the Treaties and their derivative legislation this is a Supreme Court. It is continental in style, outlook and procedure: its attitude to the Treaties is – absolutely properly I think – activist. It will interpret them and the Regulations made under them in a way that helps to achieve their purpose. If there is an omission the Court is prepared to remedy it. If words are capable of more than one meaning they will assign to them the meaning most consistent with the overall purpose of the Treaties – even if the meaning be a strange one. . . .

Lord Denning put it mildly when he said that we lawyers have to learn a new system. The Common Market presents us not only with a new style legislation but with a new and challenging role for the Courts.' (Lord Scarman, 'Common law or Common Market?' *The Listener*, 31.10.74)

THE LIMITATION OF SOVEREIGNTY AND THE CREATION OF SUPRANATIONAL AUTHORITY IN THE TREATY OF ROME AND THE EUROPEAN COMMUNITIES ACT

'In order to carry out their tasks the Council and the Commission shall in accordance with the provisions of the Treaty make regulations, issue directives, take decisions, make recommendations or deliver opinions. A regulation shall have general application, it shall be binding in its entirety and directly applicable in all Member States. A directive shall be binding as to the result to be achieved upon each member state to which it is addressed, but shall leave to the national authorities the choice of form and method. A decision shall be binding in its entirety upon those to whom it is addressed. Recommendations and opinions shall have no binding force.' (Treaty of Rome, Article 189)

'All such rights, powers, liabilities, obligations, and restrictions from time to time created or arising by or under the Treaties and all such remedies and procedures from time to time provided for by or under the Treaties as in accordance with the Treaties are without further enactment to be given legal effect or used in the United Kingdom shall be recognised and available in law, and be enforced, allowed and followed accordingly . . .' (Section 2(1) European Communities Act 1972)

RECENT EXAMINATION QUESTIONS

Spend ten minutes or so planning an answer to each of the following questions. Outline answers to questions **7** and **8** and a tutor's answer to question **1** are given in the following sections.

Question 1.

Evaluate the impact on Parliament of membership of the EEC.
(JMB Brit. Govt and Pol., June 1980)

Question 2.

Why has British membership of the EEC proved to be so divisive an issue within both the main political parties?
(London, Govt and Pol. Stud., Paper 2, June 1982)

Question 3.

What effect do you think the development of European institutions will have upon those of Westminster?
(Cambridge, Pub. Aff., June 1984)

Question 4.

What are the principal political advantages and disadvantages of British membership of the European Community?
(Cambridge, Pol. and Govt, Paper 1, June 1983)

Question 5. The growth of European institutions will make those of Westminster largely irrelevant. Do you agree?

(Cambridge, Pub. Aff., June 1983)

Question 6. Were the 1979 direct elections to the European Parliament a successful experiment?

(London, Govt and Pol. Stud., Paper 2, Jan. 1981)

Question 7. Consider the extent to which Britain as a member of European organisations may be said to have a written Constitution.

(JMB, Brit. Govt. and Pol., June 1984)

Question 8. Why worry that Britain has lost sovereignty to the European Community?

(London, Govt. and Pol. Stud., Paper 1, June 1984)

Question 9. To what extent and in what ways is it possible to pursue national interests in the political framework of the European Community?

(Cambridge, Pol. and Govt, June 1985)

Question 10. 'The rise of an EEC Assembly will render national parliamentary institutions as ineffective tomorrow as town councils became yesterday.' Do you agree with this assessment of the impact upon the British Parliament of representative European institutions?

(Cambridge, Econ. and Pub. Aff., June 1981)

OUTLINE ANSWERS

Q. 7.

Consider the extent to which Britain as a member of European organisations may be said to have a written Constitution.

Answer

(a) By a written Constitution we imply the following:

- A single document, or related set of documents, which constitutes a comprehensive but not necessarily exhaustive constitutional framework, defining basic political structure, the relationship between different elements in that structure, and the rights and duties of citizens.
- The Constitution thus established is *binding*, in the sense that it is difficult to change, and *limits* the activities of all branches of the political system, including the executive and the legislature.
- At least potentially, Britain's membership of the European organisations could be said to have given the UK a written Constitution. For example the UK now subscribes to the European Convention on Human Rights and consequently recognises the jurisdiction of the European Court of Human Rights. Although British governments have on occasion

modified their policies to fall into line with judgments of that court, Britain has *not* made the Convention part of its domestic law and there are no effective sanctions which could be taken against a British government which refused to abide by judgments of the European Court.

(b) More importantly, as a member of the EEC, Britain has accepted the Treaty of Rome of 1957, which establishes a political machinery for the Community and defines the relationship between that machinery and the domestic political institutions of member countries. In a technical legal sense, therefore, the sovereignty of the UK Parliament has been surrendered. This follows from the fact that Parliament can technically no longer legislate in ways that are contrary to the provisions of the Treaty of Rome or which are contrary to legislation which has been made by institutions set up under the terms of that Treaty. However, several points need to be made in qualification of this.

- The loss of sovereignty is legal rather than political: there is no coercive machinery available to the Community to bring a recalcitrant member into line.
- Member governments may, and sometimes do, ignore Community regulations and directives and member governments may withdraw altogether from the Community. To that extent the 'Constitution' represented by the articles of the Treaty of Rome is not binding.
- The Constitution is not comprehensive, it is only *potentially* so. It would presumably be open to the legislative machinery of the Community to establish a uniformity of political structure among member nations. In practice any such attempt would seem quite out of the question.
- A wide variety of political practices and institutions are able to exist within the framework of the Community. For instance, although it is now part of the political system of the Community that direct elections take place for the European Parliament, the electoral system to be used by each member country is *not* prescribed. The result is that while the Continental states use various PR systems, the UK (with the exception of Northern Ireland) uses its traditional first past the post system for EEC Parliament elections.
- We need to remember that the EEC itself often operates not according to rigid constitutional rules, but according to conventions and pro tem agreements. An example is the 1966 Luxembourg agreement, by which it was decided that no member state would be obliged to fall in with proposed legislation of the Community if its vital national interests were thereby threatened.

   The overall picture is that the EEC's written Constitution is supplemented, and even to some extent supplanted, by more flexible arrangements.

(c) Some major constitutional issues have yet to be faced: we do not know for example how British courts would respond if they were faced with the need to judge on a case brought under an Act of Parliament which plainly contravened the legislation of the European Community.

(d) Conclusion: membership of European organisations has clearly taken the UK a step towards a written Constitution, but there is obviously still a long way to go.

Q. 8.
Why worry that Britain has lost sovereignty to the European Community?

Answer

(a) Technically by acceding to the terms of the Treaty of Rome Britain has lost sovereignty and the UK Parliament is no longer a sovereign body. But there are those who would argue that there really is no need to worry about this situation in that the loss of sovereignty is simply legal, or *de jure*. Of course, it may be argued in return that a legal loss of sovereignty is simply the thin end of the political wedge and that a more substantial erosion of practical sovereignty will follow. If it does then there are some grounds for concern.

(b) There will almost inevitably be pressures to bring the domestic political and constitutional structures of member states into line, e.g. uniform methods of election; uniform structures of civil and social rights. It is unlikely that the British system will serve as a model for any such uniform procedures, and it could be argued that any procedures which differ significantly from the British system may not be appropriate in terms of British traditions and political culture. Indeed some would point to the much shorter and much more precarious history of democracy in some EEC member states e.g. Greece, Spain, Portugal, and even in West Germany and Italy.

(c) There is obviously a fear that a loss of sovereignty may mean that important national, social, economic, or cultural interests may not be preserved. It should be borne in mind that the 1966 Luxembourg agreements, whereby each member state is able to veto legislative proposals if these run counter to its vital national interests, are *not* part of the fundamental structure of the community. Rather, they are accepted as a temporary measure to facilitate the establishment of the Community in what are, historically, its early stages of development. Already there are important movements towards making majority voting on the Council of Ministers the normal means of decision-making.

If, as seems inevitable, the Luxembourg agreements are ultimately modified, then some British observers may be disturbed by the political structure of the Community itself. Power within the Community structure is weighted very heavily on the side of the supranational EEC Commission and the Council of Ministers. The EEC Parliament has no legislative powers and its powers of veto over legislation and of investigation of the executive are as yet only rudimentary. The element of democratic control of Community institutions and processes by representatives elected directly by citizens of the Community is therefore, as yet, rather weak.

A TUTOR'S ANSWER

Q. 1.

Evaluate the impact on Parliament of Membership of the EEC.

Answer

One of the impacts of UK membership of the EEC could be said to be the loss, by Parliament, of its *de jure* sovereignty. This is because the Accession Act of 1972 gives to present and future European Community law the force of law within the United Kingdom. The EEC regulations which are made by the Council of Ministers, are of general application; they are binding on member states in their entirety and they are directly applicable in all member states, that is to say they do *not* require the sanction of the Parliaments of those states. Therefore because the UK Parliament is subject to EEC regulations, it has in a technical sense lost the capacity to legislate on any matter it chooses. In this sense Parliament can indeed be said to have lost its sovereignty.

We must stress that this is the situation in theory and that the practice is rather different. In 1975 the Wilson Government pushed through Parliament legislation creating a consultative referendum on Britain's continued membership. In the event the vote was overwhelming to stay in the EEC, but had it gone the other way then presumably Parliament might have been required to legislate its way out. There might then have been an *economic* price to be paid for withdrawal. However, the EEC has no *political* machinery to coerce states to retain their membership against their will, so that it could be said that ultimately Parliament retains a *de facto* sovereignty. In addition Parliament could presumably, *in extremis*, press the UK's representatives on the EEC Council of Ministers to resist EEC proposals coming up from the Commission which would have a damaging effect upon the UK if implemented and issued as regulations or directives.

A second impact on Parliament of EEC membership has been to add to the range of parliamentary committees, namely the Select Committee on European Community Secondary Legislation (since 1976 the Select Committee on European Legislation). This was set up in 1974 with the task of considering draft proposals submitted by the Commission to the EEC for secondary legislation. It reports to the Commons on whether the members of the committee believe that such proposals raise questions which are of major legal or political importance for the UK. The Commons' reaction to the committee's reports was initially lukewarm. However, as the committee has become a more recognised part of the parliamentary scene and as interest in, and awareness of, the EEC and its processes has developed, then the Select Committee on European Legislation has been seen to be a more valuable part of the apparatus of the Commons. The Lords have developed a similar committee, the European Communities' Committee, whose terms of reference are virtually identical to those of their counterpart in the Commons.

A third, if somewhat indirect impact of EEC membership was the referendum of 1975, which has already been mentioned. This was not without its significance for Parliament: in particular, it served to damage the already somewhat dented Burkean notion of the role of the MP. According to this notion, the MP is not delegated by his constituents to express their views, but is rather chosen on the basis of his general worthiness and is simply required to act in Parliament and to vote according to his conscience. By referring the question to a direct vote by the electorate, Parliament was in effect admitting that the consciences of its Members was an inadequate basis for action in this very important constitutional matter.

A fourth impact of membership of the EEC has been in terms of party alignments within Parliament. Support for, or opposition to, membership has tended to cut somewhat across traditional party lines, except for the Liberals who have generally been solidly pro-Europe. Both pro- and anti-marketeers have been found in Conservative and Labour ranks, and this has tended to produce some unusual Parliamentary alliances during debates. Labour pro-marketeers were particularly prominent in the formation of the SDP in the early 1980s. It might even be argued that EEC membership has had, as one of its by-products, an influence on the formation of Britain's newest parliamentary grouping.

Finally, the development of the European Parliament has perhaps itself begun to have repercussions for the UK Parliament. In 1979 the practice of nominating Euro MPs from Members of national Parliaments was ended and direct elections took place. In the 1979 and 1984 Euro Elections, turn-out in the UK, with the exception of Northern Ireland, was very low. It cannot therefore be claimed that the European Assembly is as yet seen as a real rival to the UK Parliament by most UK voters. But citizens who wish to complain about EEC institutions or policies will now probably go to their Euro MP rather than to their Westminster representative. It would seem that after a period from 1972 to 1979, when some of its Members were overburdened by the addition of European and to an already heavy UK parliamentary work, the Westminster Parliament is now in the position of having lost one of its functions to the European Assembly.

A STEP FURTHER

An excellent survey of some of the implications both for constitutional structure and for policy of British membership of the EEC is provided by Michael Shackleton's chapter in *British Politics and Perspective* ed. R. L. Borthwick and J. E. Spence (Leicester

University Press 1984). A good survey is also to be found in the chapter by D. Coombes, on 'Parliament and the European Community', in *The Commons Today*, ed. S. A. Walkland and M. Ryle (Fontana 1984). Further investigation of this topic will almost certainly lead students into a closer analysis of the political structure of the EEC and they should look at S. Henig, *Power and Decision in Europe, the Political Institutions of the European Community* (Europotentials Press 1980) and *Policy Making in the European Communities*, edited by W. Wallace, H. Wallace, and C. Webb 2nd ed. (Wiley 1983). The institutional balances within the community change rapidly and the EEC Parliament in particular has been becoming more assertive in the 1980s. These developments must simply be followed in the press and in publications such as *Keesing's Contemporary Archives* (Longman).

Chapter 17

Characterisation and concepts in politics

This chapter seeks to develop some of the techniques for describing and analysing governments or political processes which we have encountered in previous chapters. We have, for example, discussed how far we can characterise government as Cabinet or Prime Ministerial or as representative. We have encountered concepts such as participation or class/party de-alignment. Nevertheless, it is worth emphasising at the start of this chapter that the way in which we understand political concepts, and the extent to which we believe any characterisation or classification of a specific political system to be at all accurate, will depend very much on the precise value system or systems which we adopt.

Liberal democrats and Marxists will clearly have very different understandings of the concept of *freedom*. The liberal democrat will place particular emphasis upon such factors as the capacity of citizens to oppose the Government or to criticise the political system by way of publication, marches, demonstrations, candidacy in elections, and so on. In establishing the existence of political freedom he will look for the independence of the judiciary from politicians, for the existence of a political culture, and for constitutional rules or conventions which limit the possibility of arbitrary action by government. He will also look for evidence that the citizens may call their government to account and that in practice they are able to replace one government by another if it should, in their collective view, prove unsatisfactory. Judged by these criteria the British system may give occasional cause for concern but is fundamentally marked by freedom.

The Marxist approach, on the other hand, sees politics and political life as inextricably bound up with the economic structure of a society. It is the economic system which constitutes the base of society, or its infrastructure, and this determines the form of the political superstructure. For the Marxist the key element in the development of society is class struggle, expressed as conflict between a series of ruling classes, such as slave-masters, feudal lords, and capitalists, and the lower, oppressed classes. The rules of the political game, that is to say those aspects of political culture which are imposed by the ruling class, are simply designed to perpetuate the dominance of that class. In Marxist eyes, therefore, liberal democracy is a sham which simply permits the people to believe that they are free while they remain in a state of economic exploitation and hence unfreedom at the hands of the capitalists (i.e. the bourgeoisie). The Marxist contrasts bourgeois democracy of this type with socialist democracy which places emphasis on economic equality and in particular on the removal of domination or exploitation of one social class by another. This is achieved by the elimination of exploiting classes. In such a society the need for emphasis on civil and political rights tends to disappear, given the assumption that politics is itself a product of the economic and class structure of the society. If exploitation and oppression have been removed from the infrastructure, then they will not show up in the superstructure of political activity.

The point of this discussion of liberal democratic and Marxist views of freedom is not to argue that one or the other is correct, but simply to reinforce the point that different approaches to the analysis of the British system will produce widely differing results. In fact the knowledge that there are radically different approaches which may be made to the study of the system will make some otherwise puzzling examination questions become intelligible. Whichever value system we prefer, and it is always wise in examinations to acknowledge the existence of more than one, we have to recognise that British politics and the British political system represents a complex case. It will not do, for example, simply to refer to the British system as an oppressive one, because that ignores the necessary distinctions between different types of oppressive systems; nor will it do to claim that the British system is marked by freedom and by nothing else. That would be to ignore much of the work of the National Council for Civil Liberties as well as to fly in the face of common sense. We must remember, and this is a point we must move on to examine in greater detail, that the British system will provide only a partial illustration of some basic concepts, and that any attempt to characterise or categorise the system must face the fact that, in many cases, diametrically opposing characterisations may *both* fit to some extent.

ESSENTIAL PRINCIPLES

POLITICAL CONCEPTS

Examiners very frequently invite students either explicitly or implicitly to define and discuss political concepts. Put simply, political concepts represent the ideas which lie behind the machinery of the governmental system, i.e. the ideas on which a political system is based. They are the means by which we classify structures and processes in politics, as when we talk about bureaucracy, democracy, corporatism, pluralism, and so on. It is indeed very difficult to write a politics essay without making use of concepts. The important thing to remember is that concepts, because they are broad generalisations, do not usually serve as exact descriptions of a system or a structure in practice.

Perhaps the first thing that needs to be stressed about the British political and governmental system is that it is not at all systematic. It is a notorious fact that Britain lacks a written Constitution. While such Constitutions are generally inadequate as precise descriptions of the day-to-day operation of politics, they do at least provide a series of 'ideal' *standards* for governmental and political activity, and in some cases a set of 'ideal' *structures* through which that activity should take place.

British constitutional *practice* is, on the other hand, based on a curious mixture of sources.

1. There are *statutes*, some of them of considerable antiquity and often the product of the policies of governments with very varied ideological objectives.
2. There are *constitutional conventions*, that is to say rules which are generally regarded as binding but which do not have the authority of statute behind them. The reason why conventions are binding is not the respect for their antiquity or their inherent dignity, but that they reflect important political realities. As soon as they fail to do this then they lose their status as conventions.
3. There are *judicial pronouncements*, by which judges have attempted to clarify or explain ambiguous or unclear sections of statutes, such as the phrase 'the interests of the State' employed in Section 2 of the Official Secrets Act.

It is very difficult to reduce to clear systematic formulae the structures and practices which emerge from such a diverse background. Let us look at the accuracy of two of the formulae which are sometimes applied.

Constitutional monarchy

Britain is a *constitutional monarchy*. This is true to the extent that the Head of State is indeed a monarch with certain (theoretical) wide-ranging prerogatives, such as the power to make war, to make peace, to exercise mercy, to award honours, to appoint a government, to dissolve a Parliament, and so on. But the monarchy is constitutional, in the sense that by convention the great majority of the prerogative powers are not exercised, while other former prerogative powers have been limited or eradicated by statute. Consequently, both in theory and practice the monarch is subject to strict constitutional limitations as to the exercise of powers.

Parliamentary government

Britain enjoys *parliamentary government*. This can hardly mean that Parliament actually governs, because it patently does not. Instead it suggests that the Government is habitually drawn from Parliament, that it is answerable for its actions to Parliament, and that its continued existence as the Government and its capacity to implement policy by way of legislation will depend upon the approval of Parliament. All of this is true up to a point, but there are important reservations. It is clear for example that governments are often less than enthusiastic about being answerable to Parliament. Sometimes this is for the very good reason that national security would be imperilled if Government were to give a full parliamentary account of its actions or plans. This has led, for example, to the convention that parliamentary select committees will not inquire into matters in which their investigations may endanger national security. A more fundamental reservation lies in the fact that as well as parliamentary government we have, to some extent, Cabinet government, Prime Ministerial government, and bureaucratic government. A good examination candidate invited to discuss one of these rather simple formulae will always take good care to set out not only the arguments which reveal it as a useful characterisation of the processes or structures of British government, but also the arguments which can reveal its limitations.

This is an appropriate place to glance briefly at some of the other key concepts which recur in discussions of British government and politics and which have not been dealt with in the previous chapters.

Bureaucracy

This is a political system in which government is in practice exercised by non-elected officials. The bureaucratic machine is highly structured, with precise duties and powers being allocated to the officials forming a given stratum. Officials are accountable not to the governed but to their superiors.

Responsible government

This is a system in which those who exercise government answer for their actions to the people or to the representatives of the people. In terms of British practice, responsibility of this sort takes two forms: *collective* (Cabinet) *responsibiltiy*, for which see above p. 11, and individual *ministerial responsibility*. This latter form centres on the idea that the minister in charge of a department is responsible primarily to Parliament for his own political and administrative conduct and for that of his department. In accordance with this doctrine therefore, a minister does not blame his civil servants when things go wrong and should there be a particularly conspicuous failure on the part of his deparment he may feel it is necessary to resign. Classic cases of this have been the resignation of the Minister of Agriculture, Sir Thomas Dugdale, in 1954 over the Crichel Down affair, and the resignation of the Foreign Secretary, Lord Carrington, and two junior ministers over the apparent failure of the Foreign Office to draw attention to the possibility of an Argentinian invasion of the Falklands in 1982. (There is a good brief discussion of ministerial responsibility in Dennis Kavanagh, *British Politics: Continuities and Change*, Oxford 1985, pp. 32–4.)

Sovereignty	This involves the capacity of a body to make and unmake legislation on any topic, generally within a specified territory. To be sovereign, the body in question should be the supreme legislator for that territory, and must not be bound by anything that it or its predecessor has done in the past. We may subdivide sovereignty into two categories: *de facto* or political sovereignty by which we mean the *practical* capacity to make and unmake law, and *de jure* or legal sovereignty, that is, the *authority* or *right* to make and unmake law. Thus during the earlier stages of the Falklands crisis of 1982 Britain claimed *de jure* sovereignty over the islands, even though there was an Argentinian garrison in place which effectively prevented the exercise of *de facto* sovereignty.
The rule of law	This implies a system in which all are equal before the law. Arbitrary action by the Government is strictly limited by the law, and citizens may be punished only as a consequence of breaking the law. Suppose we introduce the notion that for the rule of law to be effective the *spirit* of the law, as interpreted by the judges, must prevail in all matters. We then set the scene for a clash between Parliament and the courts as the sovereign body; that is to say, is the law simply what Parliament has legislated upon, or, in order to conform to the rule of law, must the law meet certain minimum standards of justice or fairness? The problem is an old one: it goes back at least to the early seventeenth century when the Lord Chief Justice Coke pronounced that 'Magna Carta is such a fellow that he will have no sovereign.'
A constitution	This is a set of rules which govern political activity so as to limit the exercise of arbitrary power by government against the governed, or to limit the capacity of citizens to act arbitrarily against each other. We normally recognise several types of constitutions, e.g. (a) the written Constitution, in which constitutional rules derive from a single document which establishes basic principles for the conduct of government, (b) the flexible Constitution, in which there is no central documentary source of reference: instead the constitutional framework is created solely by legislation, political conventions, and judicial interpretations.
Political culture	The various definitions of political culture run well into double figures, but basically it is the way in which people are orientated towards politics. It embraces the expectations which a people have of their political system and of politicians, providing the framework within which political actions might, or might not, be regarded as justified, and determining those beliefs and values which lead a people to act in certain ways politically. It is therefore the political culture of a society which establishes some actions as acceptable and others as unacceptable. The political culture is generally the product of a complex mixture of factors, such as history, social structure, regime

propaganda, and in some cases religion. It is worth remembering that there is no reason why we should assume that the UK is characterised by a single political culture: we have only to look at the contrast between politics in Northern Ireland and politics in the mainland of the UK to realise that there is a diversity of political culture. In addition to regional differences, various age-groups may be subject to quite different political cultural influences, as may be different social classes or ethnic groups.

Political consensus

Once again this is a term with many possible meanings. It has entered into the rhetoric of party politics, but even there it is not used consistently. For the Liberals of the late 1970s and early 1980s 'consensus politics' was virtually a synonym for the politics of moderation, the search for the middle road; but the same period saw the development of a Thatcherite disdain for consensus, which was equated by the Conservative leader with an absence of principle or conviction. In more neutral terms political consensus may be taken to indicate a general acceptance of certain ways of conducting politics and political debate, together with a widely shared support for certain basic tenets of policy, such as the desirability of a Welfare State, of a mixed economy, and so on. The phrase 'consensus politics' generally relates to a particular style of politics based on a search by the politicians for the policies most likely to unite the nation, rather than to please or advance the interests of any one section of it.

Élite

This is another word which is sometimes used loosely: for example it may be used to signify what is properly termed a *ruling class*, that is, a socio-economic group from which those who occupy positions of power are drawn, but all of whose members do not necessarily occupy such positions. It may be used to signify what is sometimes loosely called the *Establishment*, a network of people who are prominent in many spheres – artistic, academic, political, industrial, and so on – and whose social background and social contacts keep them in touch with each other. More precisely we may refer to a power élite. That is a group, not always necessarily in agreement with each other, who monopolise the senior positions in all of the important decision-making or power-broking structures.

Conspiracy theorists of British government, particularly on the Left, once suggested that leading entrepreneurs, the financial establishment (i.e. the City of London), those who control the media, and the 'mandarin' class of the Civil Service, together with the leaders of the Conservative Party, all constitute a power élite, though in terms of social background and indeed political outlook this claim bears less and less investigation as time goes on. We may perhaps distinguish several élites which frequently find themselves in competition or in conflict; but even then it may be argued that they are in a sense fused together by what is known as a system of élite consensus. That is, they may disagree, and disagree profoundly, but they will generally accept that the disagreement must be expressed, debated, and resolved principally among and between *the different élite groups* rather than by reference to their trade-union members, or their party members, or their shareholders, or the public at large.

USEFUL APPLIED MATERIALS

BERNARD CRICK ON DEMOCRACY

Some political concepts are so general as to be of very little analytical use. In the following extract, Professor Bernard Crick discusses some of the many and often contradictory uses to which the concept of democracy has been put.

'Democracy is perhaps the most promiscuous word in the world of public affairs. She is everybody's mistress and yet somehow retains her magic even when a lover sees her favours are being in his light illicitly shared by many another. Indeed, even amid our pain of being denied her exclusive fidelity we are proud of her adaptability to all sorts of circumstances to all sorts of company . . . so while democracy has most often been used to mean majority rule (which in a sizeable state can only mean majority consent) all kinds of special meanings have arisen (many to refute rather than to refine this common view). Perhaps its primary meaning to most people at the moment is no more than "all things bright and beautiful" or some such rather general sentiment. Then others hold that surprisingly enough democracy "really means" liberty even liberalism or even individualism even to defend the (democratic) individual against the (democratic) majority, – this is certainly an amiable view. The late Ernest Bevin once told the Trade Union Conference that it was not democratic for a minority to continue to question the decisions of a majority and he received the equally sincere and astonishing reply that democracy meant that he – an offending Brother – could say what he liked, when he liked, how he liked against whom he liked even against a majority of the TGWU. The word can be used as Tocqueville used it as a synonym for equality or, as Herbert Spencer used it, to mean a highly mobile free enterprise society with great . . . differences in station and wealth or it may be seen as the political system which places constitutional limitations even upon a freely elected (democratic) government (the most sought-after use but the most historically implausible and rhetorical).' (Crick, *In Defence of Politics*, pp. 56–7)

RECENT EXAMINATION QUESTIONS

Spend ten minutes or so planning an answer to each question. Outline answers for questions **3**, **6**, and **11** and a tutor's answer to question **8**, are given in the following sections.

Question 1.

How accurate is it to describe the UK as a liberal democracy?
(AEB, Govt and Pol., Paper 1, June 1985)

Question 2.

To what extent is it to describe the British political system as a representative democracy?
(AEB, Govt and Pol., Paper 1, Nov. 1982)

Question 3.	To what extent is a broad political consensus a feature of British political culture today?
	(AEB, Govt and Pol., Paper 1, June 1983)
Question 4.	What is meant by the term individual liberty and how far does it exist in Britain today?
	(AEB, Govt and Pol., Nov. 1985)
Question 5.	To what extent are toleration and consensus features of British political culture?
	(AEB, Govt and Pol., Paper 1, Nov. 1984)
Question 6.	Define the concept of government by consent.
	(London, Govt and Pol. Stud., Paper 1, short answer question, June 1985)
Question 7.	Does Britain have a balanced Constitution? Does it matter?
	(Cambridge, Pol. and Govt, Paper 1, June 1984)
Question 8.	'The State is not an obstacle to freedom: it makes freedom possible.' Discuss.
	(Cambridge, Pol. and Govt, Paper 1, June 1985)
Question 9.	Explain why you think Britain is or is not a democracy.
	(Cambridge, Pub. Aff., Nov. 1984)
Question 10.	'In recent years real doubts have grown about the adequacy of the British political system to adapt itself to social and economic change.' Discuss.
	(JMB, Brit. Govt and Pol., June 1984)
Question 11.	Distinguish between the concept of power and that of authority.
	(London, Gov't and Pol. Stud. Paper 1, short answer question, June 1982)
Question 12.	To what extent is Britain still a homogeneous, consensual, and deferential society?
	(JMB, Brit. Govt and Pol., June 1983)

OUTLIINE ANSWERS

Q. 3.

To what extent is a broad political consensus a feature of British political culture today?

Answer

    (a)   Broad agreement exists on the validity of basic political processes: parties in Parliament accept conventions of behaviour; the public accepts that change should be parliamentary rather than revolutionary; there is general respect for the law, for example Labour Party embarrassment that the Labour-controlled Liverpool City Council should propose to break the law by setting an illegal budget.

Avowedly extremist parties, e.g. the National Front, the Workers' Revolutionary Party do exist, but make little impact on the conventional political pattern.

(b) First, there is a breakdown of broad consensus on *policy*: the major parties have moved a long way from the 'Butskellism' of the later 1950s and early 1960s, when politics focused on a struggle for the middle ground, i.e. the Labour Party has moved to the left, the Conservative Party to the right.

Second, the Thatcher Governments since 1979 have worked for a revolution in attitudes: they have *sought* to end the post-war collectivist social democratic consensus, and to state in bold terms the choice between the 'enterprise culture' and a state-socialist programme. But it is difficult to establish how far movements in party programmes reflect the collapse of broad consensus over policy among the population. Not all Conservatives are Thatcherites (e.g. 'wets' and the Centre Forward group), while there is much evidence that many Labour voters do not share the perspectives of a more radical Labour programme (e.g. over defence in 1983).

(c) The problem is that the major parties, particularly the Conservatives, are seeking to *impose* elements of political culture from above, e.g. the greater spirit of economic individualism, suspicion of the State, etc. and this may take a very long time to filter down. Perhaps Tory 'wets', Alliance supporters and Labour moderates illustrate that a potentially broad consensus on policies may still exist.

SHORT ANSWERS

Q. 6.

Define the concept of government by consent.

Answer

Consent here does not mean that the governed necessarily agree to all of the policies of the Government. This would be most unlikely. Instead it means that the citizens accept the way in which the Government has been chosen. They did not necessarily participate in the choosing of the Government or in its emergence, but they feel that it has legitimacy and authority. Further, the concept implies that even if the citizens, or substantial sections of them, do not approve of the current Government or of the Government's current policies, they agree to be governed through the use of structures and processes of which they approve.

Q. 1.

Distinguish between the concept of power and that of authority.

Answer

Power involves the capacity to affect other people's behaviour using the sanction of force. Authority involves the capacity to affect other people's behaviour without the necessary sanction of force or resort to inducement. The two concepts may be connected: patterns of obedience to authority may be taught by the use of inducements or the sanction of force. But once it has been learned and becomes a social factor such obedience no longer requires the sanction of force, and so the two concepts in fact diverge.

A TUTOR'S ANSWER

Q. 8.

The State is not an obstacle to freedom: it makes freedom possible. Discuss.

Answer

We may define the State very succinctly as an instrument for the management of society, comprising all of the public machinery for the organisation and, if necessary, the coercion of the citizens. Beyond this simple definition, perspectives on the State diverge very rapidly as we cross the spectrum of political theory.

For the Marxist the State is always the instrument whereby the ruling class in a society secures its domination. That is to say, imposes its will and its interests on society as a whole. Following the socialist revolution, during the period, say, of the dictatorship of the proletariat, the State becomes the instrument of the domination of the working class. It is used to wrest privileges from the exploiting minority and eventually to abolish privileges, in order to shape the new system which ensures the freedom from oppression of the great majority of the people. In the case of a fundamentally capitalist and liberal democratic society like that of the UK, however, the Marxist will see the State as an instrument of bourgeois capitalist exploitation, therefore severely restrictive of the socio-economic freedom of the workers.

Non-Marxist approaches of course vary, but they generally see the State as being capable of exercising repressive or liberating functions. Reformist socialists, for example, seek to use the apparatus of the State in order to achieve piecemeal improvements in social welfare, reductions in the power of privilege, and progressive extensions of the public ownership of the means of production. In contrast, liberals will normally be highly suspicious of the State, seeing it as a possible restricting force on individualism. Liberals will thus seek to keep to an absolute minimum its coercive powers, which are to be used only when it has been clearly shown that individuals, or groups of individuals, are tyrannising others. For the Conservative the State is a necessary guarantor of law, order, and property, thus allowing individuals to go about ther legitimate business. On this view the State should create a freedom to prosper and should not interfere with that freedom in the name of egalitarianism or socialism.

It will be seen that with the exception of Marxism, which makes it clear that the State always has a single, clearly defined use, other perspectives involve the view that the State may be put to several possible uses. The disagreement lies in the quarrel over the nature and emphasis of that use. For instance, for many conservatives, particulary of the Thatcherite persuasion, the extension under Labour Governments of the Welfare State and of the state ownership of industry, involves a diminution of economic freedom. This follows from the resulting high taxation and the inevitable increase in the petty tyrannies of the army of bureaucrats, as well as from an erosion of the spirit of enterprise on which (Thatcherites would say) freedom is founded. Conservative administrations tend to develop those sections of the state machinery which are congenial to them and which are able to buttress the traditional order of society, in particular the police. For liberals and libertarian socialists this represents an unjustifiable threat to personal, political and social freedom, hence the bitterness of debates over the 1984 Police and Criminal Evidence Act for example.

Perhaps the fairest conclusion is that the State from almost any viewpoint may be both an obstacle to freedom and the means by which freedom is made possible. It all depends on who controls the State, the nature of the freedom, and the particular beneficiaries of that freedom.

A STEP FURTHER

The book by Bernard Crick, *In Defence of Politics* (Pelican Books 1964), from which one of the extracts in this chapter was taken, is essential reading for all students who want to consider political concepts a little further. It should perhaps be read in the middle of a course rather than at the beginning. Also of considerable use is Alan R. Ball, *Modern Politics and Government*, 2nd edn, (Macmillan) and Barbara Goodwin, *Using Political Ideas* (Wiley 1982).

The task of characterising and conceptualising political activity and structures can often lead to confusion, and it is extremely useful to have some works of ready reference to hand. Mention should be made of Jozef Wilczynski, *An Encyclopaedic Dictionary of Marxism, Socialism and Communism* (Macmillan 1981), which covers in fact far more topics than its title may suggest. Just as useful is Roger Scruton, *A Dictionary of Political Thought* (Pan Books in association with the Macmillan Press 1983). No dictionary of politics is to be regarded as giving the whole truth about any of the numerous topics which it attempts to cover. Articles are necessarily selective and brief. This applies particularly to Scruton's work which is always entertaining and stimulating but sometimes idiosyncratic. Many of his definitions reflect the kind of political thought which is indulged in by political philosophers rather than by practising politicians. Like all good dictionaries it is a stimulus to further work and comparison with other material rather than a substitute for such exercises.

Index